Delia Smith's Cookery Course Part One

Delia Smith's Cookery Course

Part One

BRITISH BROADCASTING CORPORATION

This book accompanies the BBC Television series
Delia Smith's Cookery Course. Part one of this series first
broadcast on BBC-2 from November 1978.
Executive Producer: Tony Matthews.
Producer: Jenny Rogers.

Published to accompany a series of programmes prepared in
consultation with the BBC Continuing Education Advisory Council.

First published 1978. Reprinted 1979 (four times).
Published by the British Broadcasting Corporation,
35 Marylebone High Street, London W1M 4AA.
ISBN 0 563 16261 9

This book is set in 12/13 pt Monophoto Baskerville 169.
Printed in England by Butler & Tanner Ltd, Frome and London

Contents

Edited by Jenny Rogers

Photographs by Bob Komar
Drawings by Ray and Corrine Burrows

Grateful thanks to Elaine Bastable, Linda Blakemore, Susan Goodman, Elisabeth Ingham, Caroline Liddell and Gwyneth Phillips for their help in the preparation of this book.

The BBC would also like to thank the following for the loan of equipment and accessories for the photographs:

Debenhams Limited, Oxford Street, London W1, for spice and storage jars on pages 169 and 217; pepper mills on the cover and pages 34 and 169; bread basket, page 67; oval plate, page 68; oval gratin dish, page 200.

Divertimenti, Marylebone Lane, London W1, for all equipment on pages 2, 3 and 41; bread board, page 67; oblong dish, page 68; pie dish, page 165.

John Lewis Limited, Oxford Street, London W1 for cutlery on pages 34, 71, 199, 200 and 235; plates, pages 34, 67 and 71; oval gratin dish, pages 68 and 199; sauce boat and dish, page 143; dinner plate and bowl, page 200.

Conversion tables

All these are *approximate* conversions, which have either been rounded up or down. In a few recipes it has been necessary to modify them very slightly. Never mix metric and imperial measures in one recipe, stick to one system or the other.

Oven temperatures		
Mark 1	275°F	140°C
2	300	150
3	325	170
4	350	180
5	375	190
6	400	200
7	425	220
8	450	230
9	475	240

Volume	
2 fl oz	55 ml
3	75
5 ($\frac{1}{4}$ pt)	150
$\frac{1}{2}$ pt	275
$\frac{3}{4}$	425
1	570
$1\frac{3}{4}$	1 litre

Measurements	
$\frac{1}{8}$ inch	3 mm
$\frac{1}{4}$	$\frac{1}{2}$ cm
$\frac{1}{2}$	1
$\frac{3}{4}$	2
1	2·5
$1\frac{1}{4}$	3
$1\frac{1}{2}$	4
$1\frac{3}{4}$	4·5
2	5
3	7·5
4	10
5	13
6	15
7	18
8	20
9	23
10	25·5
11	28
12	30

Weights	
$\frac{1}{2}$ oz	10 g
1	25
$1\frac{1}{2}$	40
2	50
$2\frac{1}{2}$	60
3	75
4	110
$4\frac{1}{2}$	125
5	150
6	175
7	200
8	225
9	250
10	275
12	350
1 lb	450
$1\frac{1}{2}$	700
2	900
3	1 kg 350 g

Introduction

The world is full of recipes—they spill out of shelves in bookshops, magazines devote pages to them, they turn up on the back of packaged foods, even on bottle labels. In the following pages there are a few more recipes—but I hope a lot more than that as well. We all need recipes, but very often the problem is that it's assumed automatically that whoever is going to use them knows at least the basics of cookery: in other words, that they have been *taught* to cook at some stage in their lives.

Traditionally cooking has been a skill handed down within families, from mother to daughter. And indeed what better way to learn? Sadly that has become increasingly a thing of the past. When Britain ceased, in the wake of the industrial revolution, to be a predominantly rural nation, families lost their links with the country (which is where the roots of good cooking lie). The rationing and shortages imposed by two world wars further interrupted this tradition, till in the end I think almost a whole generation has missed out on the pleasures of cooking—in many cases where women now have to go out to work it has been relegated to the level of a household chore.

My own philosophy is that cooking should be enjoyable, fun even, but that it will never be a pleasure unless you have a good working grasp of the basic principles. These I have tried to explain here; but, more important, I have also attempted to anticipate the question *why* in many cases. For I believe that if you know *why* you should baste meat when it is roasting, or not over-beat egg-whites (for instance), this takes away some of the mystery; and cooking, perhaps more than any other subject, appears to the beginner cloaked in mystery and bedevilled by hearsay opinions voiced by 'authorities' constantly contradicting each other. Mistakes in the kitchen can nowadays be extremely expensive, and more often than not they are caused by anxiety. I feel that if this cookery course can help to remove some of the apprehensions from people's minds, then for them the whole subject of cooking will appear in quite a different light.

This book, and the programmes it accompanies, does not set out to be a course for the professional cook or chef, or even the aspiring *cordon bleu* student. It is aimed at men and women who want to acquire a sound general knowledge of cooking which will stand them in good stead for a lifetime of family meals, entertaining and personal pleasure. I say men, as well as women, because I know from previous television series and books that there are many men with a great interest in cooking. I hope this book will be beneficial to anyone, male or female, who want to simply enjoy cooking.

It is a three-part course, of which this is the first part. We begin by looking at some of the basic ingredients of cooking—like eggs, flour, meat and spices—and at some of the basic techniques of the kitchen, such as making a white sauce and kneading dough. By the end of the course I hope that all the information a non-specialist cook needs to know to cook confidently and well will have been covered, and that he or she will have been provided with a repertoire of recipes from all over the world to meet the demands of almost any occasion, from a quick lunch-snack to a big dinner-party.

The whole idea is that an absolute beginner to cooking can start here. At the same time I hope that the more experienced cook, too, will find new ideas, even inspiration. There is rarely any one correct and unchangeable way of doing something, and my word on the subject is by no means gospel. But what I can offer here is what my own experience tells me is the easiest and best way to achieve results. To that extent this cookery course reflects my personal approach to food and cooking. I also hope it reflects the changing background to cooking today—our dwindling resources and world shortages which in turn have sent prices on a dizzying climb. The really affluent era of food is passing (which is no great disaster if it makes us look again at, say, pulses or some of the less fashionable fish), and it seems to me to be a very salutary thing to go back to cooking the basic dishes *well*.

Diets, fats and cholesterol
It is now an accepted fact that the effects of affluence in the western world are as much to blame for the spread of heart disease as anything—and that our kind of diet is a major factor in this: too much fat, cholesterol, not enough fibre and so on. And while eminent nutritionalists argue the world over and new theories are put forward daily, the layman has now become totally confused as to what he should or should not do about it.

My advice is not to make emotional or drastic overnight changes in your diet simply because of the latest theory. Rather, attempt to set a pattern of more moderate eating overall. We all eat far more than we need to, and *this* is the root cause. I have sometimes been accused of using too much cream, butter or olive oil in my recipes, but the whole point of recipes is that there are very few of us who actually use a 'recipe' every day. We eat grills, omelettes, salads and other plain foods the majority of the time: those occasions when we are going to be bothered to actually cook a recipe are those when it is worthwhile making the end result as delicious as possible. In short, I don't advocate cream, wine or butter in cooking every day, but rather for special occasions.

And a brief word here about slimming and dieting. In my job dieting is harder than it is than for most people! But after a lot of trial and error I have managed to arrive at a simple conclusion: cut out what you don't actually need nutritionally. If the rest of your diet is well balanced, sugar, for instance, is totally superfluous. In fact, sugar is merely a habit, like smoking or drinking. Unless I'm being entertained, I only allow myself wine at the weekends, and again either a pudding or a cake only at weekends. I'm not missing anything—I still enjoy wine and sweet things, in fact rather more now than I did previously. I don't have to count calories or follow boring dietary procedures. While I agree that serious weight problems need serious treatment, all the average person needs to do is to eat in moderation all the time, and to give up for most of the time those items that contain sugar.

Delia Smith

Equipment

It would be quite unthinkable for a carpenter or a dressmaker or even an amateur gardener to attempt to create anything worth while without the right tools for the job. Yet many people try to cook with second-rate, dilapidated, or sometimes with hardly any equipment at all. Whether you have to cook for a family every day or simply want to cook for pleasure, one thing is certain: good results will be achieved far, far more easily with the right kind of basic equipment.

Good kitchen equipment *is* expensive, but most items last a lifetime and will pay for themselves over and over again. I see so many people attempting to cook with battered saucepans with ill-fitting lids, with blunt knives and makeshift scales—often in the homes of those who have spent a small fortune on the kitchen fixtures. But all the matching units in the world can't compensate for having to peel brussel sprouts with a table knife.

I don't suggest you can go out and equip yourself with all the essentials in one go. But they should be your priorities as and when you are able to add to your stock, and they should be distinguished from the mountain of gadgetry which clutters up the shops in the name of labour-saving: a great many of these supposedly convenient gadgets are often more expensive than the basic tool and a lot less efficient (even when they are not going wrong).

General Cooking

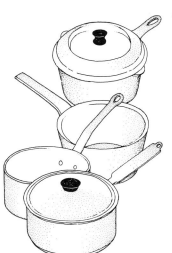

Saucepans Now there's a subject for a start. The market is inundated with them, all shapes, sizes and colours of the rainbow. But they represent a big investment, so how does a beginner know what to choose? I do think some personal preference comes into this, and often what a person is used to is what he or she likes best. It's probably fair to say that no one particular type of saucepan can answer every type of need. I have several different sorts myself, and below are my opinions on them. But first, one important point, how do you prevent cookware sticking? Always follow the manufacturer's instructions on how to season new saucepans, frying-pans and casseroles—this will vary depending on the make, but it makes a world of difference.

Heavy-gauge aluminium These are my personal choice. Not quite so glamorous as the others to look at, they offer all-round reliability and a good, even conducting of heat. They are easy to keep clean— sometimes the aluminium inside them blemishes, but this is easily remedied by boiling up water in them, to which a little lemon juice or vinegar has been added. Very hard-wearing and should last a lifetime. A warning about these saucepans: food should not be allowed to stand too long in them as the metal can react unfavourably on the food.

Enamelled cast ironware These are very heavy and for this reason they hold the heat extremely well—so a much lower heat is needed to keep up a gentle simmer. They come in bright jewel colours and look very attractive. But their heaviness can be a disadvantage: very often two hands are needed to lift a large saucepan full of something. If they are dropped on a hard surface they can chip or even break. I have found that sauces tend to stick and catch if I'm in a hurry and haven't kept the heat as low as it should be. Finally, the inside enamelled surface can become badly stained (though an overnight soak in a biological washing-powder solution does help.)

Stainless steel I know one or two professional cooks who prefer these to anything else. I have found, though, that the contents of the pan nearest the edges (say while boiling milk or making a sauce) get hot quicker than the centre, which means that cooks in a hurry will regularly find the edges of the pan are scorched. The advantages, however, are that they are easy to keep clean, look attractive, and are light to handle.

Copper saucepans I have a set of heavy, handsome copper saucepans hanging up on the wall in my kitchen—and that's where they're staying. I know that the great French chefs swear by them, but I couldn't manage them at all. The brass handles become very hot, and it is easy to forget to use a cloth. Also I found the tinned lining wore down quickly, exposing the copper beneath whose qualities make some foods become rancid more quickly.

Non-stick saucepans For my own cooking I find it essential to use metal implements, and for that reason alone I can never recommend non-stick pans—all the ones I have ever used very soon abandoned their non-stick surface.

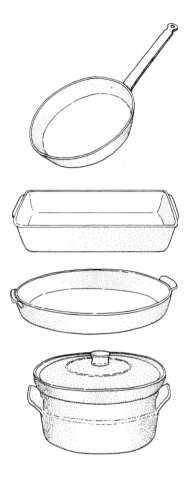

Frying-pans My choice here is definitely for a heavy, cast-iron pan—there is a particularly good French, imported one which has a matt-black inside coating which remains unharmed by metal utensils. Every cook should have two frying-pans, one with an 8 inch (20 cm) base diameter and another a 10 inch (25·5 cm).

Meat roasting tins Solidity is the important thing here—the cheap thin-gauge metal ones, when exposed to very high temperatures, simply buckle. And once the base of the tin has become uneven you might as well throw it away. Also in this category, it is worth mentioning that the oval cast-iron (shallow) gratin dishes are useful.

Casseroles I would definitely recommend cast-iron enamelled ware. One good 4½– 5 pint (2·5–3 l) casserole would be about right for a family of four. The advantage of this kind of casserole is that you can use it on top of the stove as well as inside—and it is attractive enough to be taken straight to the table. The less expensive earthenware casseroles are useful for certain recipes, but these are only suitable for oven cookery.

Baking
For baking you need: a long straight rolling-pin (see Pastry section), a flour dredger which sprinkles a dusting of flour over a flat surface very evenly, a pastry brush (the flat one rather than the round type), and a set of pastry cutters. I always use fluted cutters, but plain ones are available, and they come in sets of seven ranging from 1 inch (2·5 cm) to 3½ inch (9 cm) in diameter.

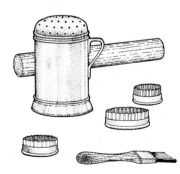

Baking sheets Good, solid and flat, these are a very necessary item as they conduct heat from underneath, so helping to cook the underside of a quiche or tart. Biscuits and scones are also cooked this way.

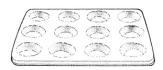

Patty tins If you are buying these for the first time, make sure you buy tins with a dozen sections and not just nine. If you are slogging through a batch of mince pies you save a lot of time cooking twelve in one go.

Quiche tins Should be as solid as possible, with a loose base. The most useful sizes are 8 inch (20 cm) and 10 inch (25·5 cm).

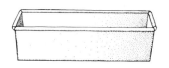

Pies and tarts For these the old-fashioned enamelled pie-plates are the best, because being metal they conduct the heat, and cook the pastry, more evenly. One 8 inch (20 cm) and 9½ inch (24 cm) plate should cover most needs. A deep-rimmed pie-plate with sloping sides, however, is useful for a recipe that calls for depth (like a lemon meringue pie). Here 8 inch (21 cm) diameter is ideal.

Bread tins come in a bewildering variety of sizes, but except for the most ambitious, the old-fashioned bread tins (with pleated corners, rims and double bases) which come in 1 lb (450 g) and 2 lb (900 g) sizes seem to be the most popular. I *do* think a non-stick tin is useful in bread-making. Although it is still must be greased, it is much easier to turn the bread out. For a loaf made from 1 lb (450 g) of flour, the base of the tin should be 7½ inches × 3½ inches (19 cm × 8·5 cm).

Whisking and mixing
Whisks One of the prime functions of a whisk is to get air into something, and a balloon whisk (especially with egg whites) will obtain the largest volume of all: it whisks very evenly and can disperse lumps in a sauce in seconds.

Electric hand whisk I have never felt the need to own a free-standing mixer—partly, I think, because I like to get the feel of the ingredients I am mixing. An electric hand whisk allows me to do this, and its other advantage is that it can be used anywhere in the kitchen—in a saucepan or bowl over heat, for instance. A hand rotary whisk is, of course, cheaper but a lot more hard work.

Kitchen fork I use a wooden kitchen fork for fluffing and separating rice. It is gentler than a metal one, and is also useful for starting off the mixing of bread dough.

Kitchen spoons Apart from the metal teaspoons, dessertspoons and tablespoons which are essential, a cook also needs a variety of wooden spoons, including a very useful one with a pointed edge that can delve into the corners and crannies of a saucepan quickly (e.g. for scrambled eggs). Other handy spoons are: a long-handled draining spoon with perforations in it to separate something solid from its liquid; an unperforated, long-handled spoon which will save you burning your arms when you want to baste something in a hot oven; and a ladle.

Slices and spatulas

Fish slice Something of a misnomer, because this will come in useful when frying all kinds of things. Its flat blade should have plenty of flexibility in it—the rigid ones simply can't slide under such delicate things as fried eggs without damaging them.

Kitchen tongs These will permit you to turn steaks, chops or sausages without piercing them and losing their juices. My husband insists on a pair for his barbecue.

Spatula A flat-edged piece of hard rubber with a wooden handle: it clears a bowl of dough or other mixture in seconds and much more effectively than scraping with a spoon.

Cutting, chopping and grating

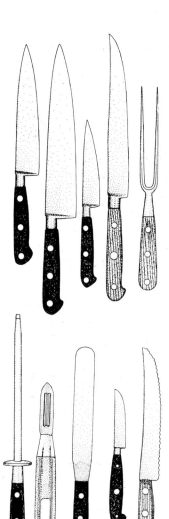

Knives A set of good-quality kitchen knives can transform your culinary life overnight—and by this I mean the stainless steel ones with riveted wooden handles (the Swiss make excellent ones). Carbon steel knives are often recommended but are the devil to stop discolouring. There are endless shapes and lengths of knives available, but you can build up your collection gradually with care. My priorities would be a couple of varying cook's knives (see illustration), a small kitchen knife, a small curved paring knife, a potato peeler, a good carving knife with either a serrated or straight edge (and a carving fork), a palette knife for smoothing icing or cream and lifting biscuits from a baking sheet, and a bread knife (though in fact my palette knife has a serrated edge and cuts bread beautifully).

Keeping knives sharp This is vital. They ought to be sharpened regularly: a sharpening steel is best for this, although it requires a little practice. I was hopeless at first. The butcher's tip to sharpen little and often is a good one, and remember always to sharpen the whole length of the blade, not just one section. (If you really can't manage a steel, there are knife-sharpening gadgets available: they just tend to wear out knives rather more quickly, that's all). It also helps to keep knives sharp (and is a lot kinder on the fingers) if you store them on magnetic racks, which can be attached to the wall, rather than in drawers where they can come into contact with other implements. Perhaps even more important, never use your knives on a plastic or laminated surface—both the surface and the knives will be ruined in no time. Good knives need a *wooden* chopping board with a bit of give in it.

Kitchen scissors A good tightly-riveted pair, kept strictly for kitchen use, will come in handy more often than you might imagine. They are so useful for snipping herbs, cutting string on puddings or scaling fish. My pair, made in Finland, are the best I have come across and (rather enterprisingly) they are manufactured for left-handed people as well.

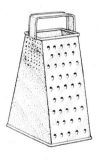

Graters Quite honestly nothing grates as well or as easily as the versatile, four-sided grater with each of its sides offering a different variety of grate. And one of its endearing qualities is that it is so easy to clean. The only other grater I use is a small nutmeg grater, which has a built-in compartment for holding a few whole nutmegs. It hangs on a hook within arm's reach, ready for instant use.

Lemon zester This is a useful, and inexpensive, item which nothing can really replace. It extracts the outer 'zest' from a lemon, leaving the unwanted pith behind, and is so constructed it can get round the awkward curves of a lemon without difficulty.

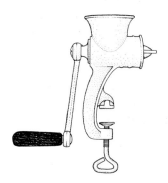

Grinding and mincing

Mincer The cast-iron kind, with a clamp base, is not really an expensive piece of equipment and is virtually indestructible. These come with three different blades for different coarseness of mince and—as we shall see later—are invaluable for dealing with leftover meat, making hamburgers and a dozen other recipes, including chutneys. I emphasise the clamp-base because suction bases never seem strong enough—but make sure you have a suitable table edge to clamp it to.

Pestle and mortar A mortar is a heavy porcelain bowl and a pestle a rounded porcelain tool that crushes or pounds the substances in the bowl—use it for crushing whole spices or pounding garlic and salt together to a cream. I would not be without mine, and suggest the larger and sturdier kind you can buy the better.

Pepper mill There are plenty of pepper mills around that don't work too well, so it is worth investing in a good, wooden one. The taller it is, the less often you will have to refill it with peppercorns. Elsewhere in the book I have enlarged on the virtues of freshly-ground pepper, so let me only say here that it has a hundred per cent more fragrance and flavour than the ready-ground stuff.

Lemon squeezer In this case, the simpler the better. A strong plastic or a tough glass squeezer will do well: some of the plastic ones have a screw-on cup underneath to catch the juice and separate off the pips—so that they are easier to pour.

Sieving, sifting, straining

Sieves I have three sieves at home. Two of them, in varying sizes, are metal ones because I have had to discard so many melted and disfigured plastic ones in the past. The one plastic one I still possess, with its fine mesh, is used almost exclusively for sifting flour.

Colander The same goes for colanders: never get a plastic colander—you are guaranteed a disaster sooner or later when it has been left too near the heat. The small aluminium or enamel ones will be sturdier and safer.

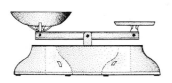

Salad basket Although practically redundant in the winter, my wire salad basket comes into its own in the summer. When salad leaves require washing, you can put them wet inside one of these enclosed baskets then (outdoors) swing the whole thing, using circular movements, and shake off most of the excess water. Then just leave it somewhere to finish drying.

Measuring

Scales If you have cooked for a lifetime with maybe a fairly modest repertoire, then perhaps you don't have to weigh anything—your 'instincts' are well developed. Lucky you. If you're a beginner or, like me, have upwards of 1500 recipes on file and cannot commit even one of them to memory, then you simply *must* weigh everything to be sure of success. My advice is to opt for a proper pair of balance scales (where the weights go on one side, the ingredients on the other): these are far more accurate than the needle-and-spring kind and sturdy enough to outlast you. Look for the largest pair possible. I have some antique balance scales like this that still register perfect balance. You can now buy a set of metric weights, as well as imperial—so the same scales can cope with either.

Measuring jugs A glass measuring jug, with imperial and metric volumes marked on the side, will tell you in seconds what 3 fl. oz is (otherwise it is impossible to know: milk bottles are not advised). Personally I find it useful to have two or three measuring jugs in the kitchen, especially for breadmaking. And I do hope that sooner or later someone will make a glass jug with a 2 pint capacity, as well as the normal 1 pint (please!).

Timing, testing and temperature

Skewers Unassuming little pieces of equipment, but *vital*. Without one I just don't know how to tell if potatoes or vegetables are cooked, but the 'feel' or give of a skewer as it is inserted into the centre is a sure guide. Flat skewers are essential for kebab cookery.

Kitchen timer Very often these are incorporated into modern ovens. But if yours does not have one built in, they can be bought separately. Memories are fallible, and a timer can save a lot of hard work from going out of the window.

Cooking thermometer Sometimes described as a 'sugar thermometer'. Will save a great deal of agonising as to whether the fat is hot enough to put in the chips, or the jam has reached a set. Such information is printed alongside the appropriate temperature on good kitchen thermometers. A *meat thermometer* is a gadget inserted in a joint of meat to help you determine when the joint is ready. However, they can be fallible if they happen to touch and rest against a bone.

There are only two other items I would include in this list. One is a strong solid *tin-opener*, which I suppose everyone needs at one time or another. The other is a *liquidiser*. You might say this is a luxury item, but I would hate to be without one—basically it replaces the hard work involved in sieving soups and purées, by whizzing them up to a smooth consistency in seconds. It also makes breadcrumbs very efficiently. Since it is going to be expensive anyway, don't be tempted to skimp on your liquidiser: buy a solid and reliable one, with a 2 pt (1 litre) capacity.

Eggs

Including recipes for:
Eggs en cocotte
Omelette savoyard
Egg and lentil curry
Poached eggs with cream and watercress
Egg and leeks au gratin
Cheese soufflé
Piperade
Chilli eggs
Zabaglione
Lemon soufflé omelette
John Tovey's quick hollandaise sauce

In this book it's the egg—and not the chicken—that comes first. There are good reasons for starting with eggs, not least because they are such a basic ingredient in our cookery and a real understanding of what they are and what they can do is essential before we progress to, say, pastry later.

But there's another reason. Someone who 'can't even cook an egg' is—to the rest of the world—someone who has either despaired of or totally neglected the art of cooking. Yet there is an assumption here that egg cookery is so basic it needs no practice or experience—it's intuitive. I don't believe that. Cooking *can* be easy, but only when you know the proper way to do it. And that's something I hope to demonstrate by starting with eggs. And anyway imagine—if everyone from the age of nine to ninety could make an omelette correctly, they'd never lack for one delicious, interesting and nutritious meal at their fingertips!

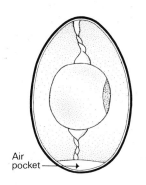

Air pocket

What's in an egg?

Eggs are full of life: they provide nutrients, proteins, fats, vitamins and minerals, nearly everything needed for life. One ingredient that may seem less essential, but as we shall see figures pretty largely in the cooking of an egg, is air. It's that tiny pocket of air (see illustration) that is directly related to the age and quality of an egg.

Nature included this air pocket so that the tiny, developing chicks could breathe. However, when eggs are for consumption rather than hatching, they are cooled and stored, and their water content starts to evaporate—and the air pocket gets bigger. It follows therefore that, generally speaking, the larger the air pocket the staler the egg. (I say generally because sometimes a hairline crack, invisible to the human eye, can let air into a very fresh egg: but this is distinctly rare.)

The freshness of an egg is very important in cooking. Stale eggs, with their flat yolks and watery whites, spread themselves miserably to all corners of the frying-pan. Not to mention the ones whose yolks in poaching water completely part company with their whites—while the whites in turn are reducing the water to a mass of foaming bubbles!

Cholesterol

Cholesterol, a by-product of animal fats and dairy foods which has a tendency to build up in our systems, is often cited as a contributory factor in heart disease. Quite apart from the total diversity of opinion among nutrition experts all over the world on the subject, I am certainly not in a position to expound on medical problems. What I can say is that if we only eat what we actually *need* to eat and in a balanced pattern, all the risks of our modern diet are minimised. The root of the problem is that as a (comparatively) affluent nation we have acquired the habit of over-eating and under-exercising. Perhaps the worry ought to be, not am I eating too many eggs or too much butter, but am I eating too much overall? In the end it may be the old answer about moderation being the cure for most ills.

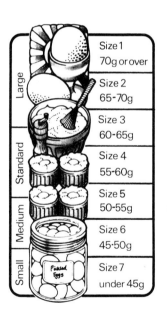

Large	Size 1	70g or over
	Size 2	65-70g
Standard	Size 3	60-65g
	Size 4	55-60g
Medium	Size 5	50-55g
	Size 6	45-50g
Small	Size 7	under 45g

Buying eggs

If there's one thing we can thank our membership of the EEC for, it's the compulsory date-stamp on egg-boxes. Undoubtedly it has meant that fresher eggs are now more widely available, and if the packing-date on the box does happen to say Week 1 and it's already Week 4, you can tell those eggs have been hanging around the supermarket a bit too long. It is not always easy to work out which Week 33 is, in the middle of a crowded supermarket, but if you buy eggs regularly you should be able to check week by week; or you can get little charts from the British Egg Information Service, 37 Panton St., London SW1.

All eggs are classified for quality (A, B or C) at the packing station, by the process called 'candling'—originally quite literally by shining a candle behind the egg to detect defects such as blood spots, cracks and blemishes. Class A and B eggs can be sold in shops. Class A have excellent internal quality; Class B have fair internal quality. Boxes containing Class A eggs could have a red band round bearing the word 'Extra'. This means that the eggs have been packed for less than 7 days (the date of packing must be on the box). Class C eggs are used only for manufacturing.

Then what about all those slightly mysterious numbered codes on the boxes? These designate first the country of origin (the UK is 9), then the region and then the licence number of the packing-station. All this fascinating information would only concern us if we had a complaint to make. More to the point is the continental grading system (size 1–7) which came into force in 1978.

This replaced the original four categories: large, standard, medium and small. Size 1, the largest of them all, doesn't fit into the egg-boxes—and I've got a sneaking feeling there aren't many size 1 hens laying them anyway—so I think that as far as consumers are concerned we can discount that particular size. Sizes 6 and 7 aren't normally available to the public either, because they're far too small (45–50 g or under 45 g respectively). That really leaves us with only four sizes, which is in fact what we had before. I would recommend if you want 'large' eggs you buy size 2, and if you want 'standard' eggs you buy size 3 or 4.

Free-range eggs

Ninety per cent of the eggs sold in Britain are battery-produced. However, if you're lucky enough to live near an old-fashioned farm where the hens scratch about and run free, you probably can get well-flavoured eggs with rich-coloured yolks. A warning though: many farm gates with their Free Range notices are not to be trusted. Many have their own deep-litter units where hens by no means run free. Also the eggs bought there will be ungraded, often with startling degrees of size difference, and blood spots or hairline cracks are all part of the bargain.

Brown or white?

The only difference between brown and white eggs is the colour of the shell. The contents are identical. In this country we tend to find brown eggs aesthetically pleasing and happily pay extra for them. And I admit, if I had a pretty breakfast tray all set with a fine china egg-cup, I would personally choose a brown egg (preferably with speckles) and of course brown bread to match.

How fresh are they?

The best place to buy eggs, at least in a town, is from a supermarket with a quick turnover. But once you've bought your eggs, how do you know if they're fresh or not? One reliable way of telling is to place one in a bowl of cold water: if it sits on the bottom in a horizontal position as in the illustration, the egg is very fresh. On the other hand, if it tilts to a semi-vertical position, it is less fresh; and stale if it pops up into a completely vertical position.

By breaking one out onto a saucer you can tell at a glance. A fresh egg will have a rounded, plump yolk that sits up proudly: the white will consist of an inner gelatinous circle clinging all round the yolk, with a second outer circle of flatter, more liquid white. When an egg is stale the yolk turns flabby and the white loses its gelatinous inner circle—it looks frankly weak and watery. This is what makes eggs, among other things, more difficult to separate.

Storing eggs

It's my opinion that eggs stored in a cool place will remain in good shape for two weeks. During the third week of storage I tend to use them only for cakes or sauces. Eggs in any event don't like extremes of temperature: I prefer not to keep mine in the fridge, if only because most recipes call for eggs at room temperature. This helps to avoid curdling in cake recipes and they are less likely to break if you're boiling them. If you have no practical alternative, then keep your eggs in the lowest part of the refrigerator: near the freezing compartment is usually too cold a position (which is unhappily where most manufacturers of fridges tend to put their egg racks). And remember to remove them several hours in advance to allow them to come to room temperature—for breakfast take them out the night before. The general guidelines then are (i) store them in a spot neither too warm nor too cold, (ii) store them thin end down, and (iii) store them away from strong smells, because the shells are porous and can absorb pungent flavours.

Separated yolks and whites can be kept for a day or two. The yolks, if they're unbroken, can be kept in water: if broken, sprinkle some water on top to prevent a skin forming. The container should be covered closely with foil or cling-film and kept in the fridge. It's interesting to note that chilled egg whites when whisked produce a slightly larger volume (though it's up to you to decide if this is any incentive to go to the trouble of separating and chilling the whites first—I know my life is too busy for such refinements!).

Beating egg whites

The secret of beating egg whites is knowing when to stop, because once they're over-beaten they start to collapse. What happens is this: whisking incorporates air into the whites, making them expand and grow in volume. As you whisk, tiny air bubbles are formed, but like all bubbles (or balloons even) too much air causes them to burst—and naturally with over-beaten egg whites the loss of air will cause a loss of volume.

I find that when you lift the whisk up and the egg stands up in soft peaks, it is time to stop. If you are folding egg whites into another mixture (i.e. for a soufflé or mousse) use just one metal tablespoonful and fold that in first. This slackens the mixture, making it much easier to fold the rest in. For notes on various types of whisk see pages 14 and 15.

Boiled eggs

There seem to be almost as many methods of boiling an egg as there are cooks. The aunt of a friend of mine insists that three verses of 'Onward Christian Soldiers' is the correct timing for a perfect egg (but she takes it a trifle *maestoso*, I think). My recommendations would be rather more precise.

To get the best results the egg should be at room temperature, otherwise the change in pressure within causes them to crack on contact with the heat. (If you find your boiled eggs constantly cracking, try piercing the rounded end first with a needle to release the pressure—it's very easy.) The water for boiling should not be bubbling too fast, just barely simmering. The saucepan should be small enough to prevent the eggs dancing around while cooking. Both these are factors which can also cause cracking.

I have found the most trouble-free method is to carefully lower the eggs (using a tablespoon) into gently simmering water. Simmer for exactly 1 minute, then remove the saucepan from the heat, put a lid on and leave the eggs for a further five minutes for size 4, or six minutes for size 2. This will produce a white that is just set and a soft creamy yolk. If you like them done more or less than this, add or subtract $\frac{1}{2}$ minute from the five or six minutes. This way there's less chance of them cracking by careering about in the bubbling water and less likelihood of overcooking by boiling too fiercely. *Note:* for *really* fresh eggs, that is less than four days old, allow extra cooking time.

Hard-boiled eggs

Place the eggs in a saucepan of cold water, bring them up to a gentle simmer, and simmer for exactly 7 minutes for size 4 eggs or 9 minutes for size 2 eggs. *Always* cool them under cold running water to prevent them cooking further or developing a dark ring between the yolk and the white. If, for a particular recipe, you need to peel the eggs while they're still warm—tap gently to crack the eggs all over, peel the shells, and rinse off any reluctant pieces of shell under a warm running tap.

Poaching eggs

You could assemble a whole catalogue of 'dos and don'ts' on the subject of poaching if you wanted to. French chefs whisk the water to form a sort of whirlpool before dropping the egg in, which is said to help it keep a good shape. Some say add a little salt to the water: others say never, never add salt. Some add a few drops of vinegar, others pour in as much as 3 tablespoons. Salt and vinegar *do* help the white to coagulate, but the method below has proved 100 per cent satisfactory in my experience.

The most important ingredient is really fresh eggs. Start with a small frying-pan, filled to a depth of approximately $1\frac{1}{2}$ inch (4 cm) barely simmering water. No salt, no vinegar. Keep the heat low enough for there to be just the merest trace of tiny simmering bubbles on the base of the pan, and no more.

Break each egg gently into the water (breaking the eggs into a cup first is all right but unnecessary, I think), and don't attempt to poach more than two at a time unless you're a really experienced hand. Three minutes is just right for size 2 eggs, but you can vary this fractionally according to taste. While they are cooking you can help the tops to cook by basting with the water. To remove, use a slotted spoon and have ready a wad of kitchen paper on which to rest the spoon and egg for a few seconds, to absorb any excess water. Always remember to remove the first egg that went in, before the other.

Scrambling eggs

On this I'm a disciple of Escoffier. And what he did was to melt a walnut of butter in a small solid saucepan over a gentle heat, then swirl it around to coat the pan thoroughly. Have ready two large eggs beaten and seasoned, and pour them into the foaming butter. (Whatever you do, don't let it brown.) Now with a wooden spoon—preferably one with a point—stir like mad, getting the point right into the corner of the pan to prevent the egg sticking.

Take the pan off the heat while there's still some liquid egg left, then add another knob of butter which will melt into it as it finishes cooking in the heat of the pan. For a touch of luxury you could stir in a teaspoonful of thick cream along with the second lot of butter!

Frying eggs

A very personal thing, how you like your egg fried—but for
absolute beginners here is my method, which might prove helpful.
For me frying requires a bit more heat than other methods,
because I like a faint touch of crispness around the edge of the egg:
so—a medium heat, a fresh egg and some hot but not smoking
bacon fat or pure lard (butter goes too brown for frying, I think).
Let the egg settle in the pan and start to set; then, using a
tablespoon, tip the pan and baste the top of the egg with the fat
until it's done to your liking. Lift it out carefully with a fish slice.

Baked eggs (eggs en cocotte)

These are deliciously special, and can be cooked with a variety of
other ingredients (such as cheese, cream, lightly-cooked chopped
vegetables) in the base of the dishes. The most important items are
the special dishes in which the eggs are cooked, called ramekins
and looking like small ridged soufflé dishes.

The basic method is as follows. Butter the dishes fairly
generously and break an egg into each one. Season them with salt
and pepper, then put a large knob of butter on top of each yolk.
Now stand the dishes in a meat-roasting tin, pour in enough hot
water to come halfway up the sides of the dishes, then bake on a
high shelf in a pre-heated oven (gas mark 5, 375°F, 190°C) for 15–
20 minutes. Then serve straightaway.

Omelettes

Let me say first that the *size* of your frying-pan is as vital for good
omelettes as for many other things. Ideally every cook should
possess two or three pans of varying size—a two-egg omelette, for
instance, needs a 6-inch (155 cm) pan, while a four- or five-egg
omelette calls for a 10-inch (25·5 cm) pan. Too few eggs in a large
pan make a thin, dry (and probably tough) omelette. Too many
eggs in a small pan make a thick and uncomfortably spongy one.
An omelette pan should be rounded at the sides and, best of all,
made in enamelled cast iron or heavy aluminium.

If your omelette is for one person, break two eggs into a basin
and on no account over-beat them. This is where so many people
go wrong. You don't need an electric whisk or even a hand-
whisk—just a large fork or, as I observed a Breton lady
demonstrating an omelette French-style once, a knife. She simply
stirred the yolks into the whites with the blade of the knife. So—no
vigorous beating or whisking.

Next add a seasoning of salt and freshly-milled black pepper. Now put your omelette pan on a medium heat to warm through, without anything in it (if you're using butter, this pre-heating the dry pan prevents the butter being over the heat too long and therefore browning). When the pan is hot, throw in a good knob of butter, say ¾ oz (15 g), then turn the heat up to its highest and swirl the butter round and round so that it coats the base and sides of the pan completely.

When the butter starts to froth, pour in the eggs and shake the pan to spread them out evenly, then take a fork or a spoon and draw the edges of the omelette towards the centre, allowing the pools of liquid egg on the surface to run into the channels you have made.

Carry on like this until the omelette is almost set but the surface still soft and a little liquid (or as the French say, 'baveuse'). When it's ready, take the pan handle in one hand, tilt the pan onto the edge of a warm plate, then with a fork or spoon in your other hand flip the edge of the omelette over to the centre. Then let it fold over again as you turn it out of the pan.

One tip, if you're using butter, is to add a little of the melted butter to the eggs just before you pour them in. This seems to give the omelette an extra-buttery flavour. The nicest omelettes of all, I believe, are the simplest, and if you're adding a filling, use very little—remembering that the eggs are the most important part. One favourite variation of mine is an omelette made with a few fresh herbs (*omelette fines herbes*): use a level tablespoon of very finely-chopped parsley and a level tablespoon of very finely-chopped leek, or spring onion or chives. Add the herbs to the two stirred eggs 30 minutes before you make the omelette, then proceed as above.

Note: olive oil or a flavoured groundnut oil can be used instead of butter.

Open-faced Omelettes
This is a quite different sort of omelette—it's never folded but served cut into wedges. In Spain they refer to this as 'tortilla' and in Italy 'frittata'. Fillings can be varied: a typical tortilla would contain potatoes, peppers, onions and slices of spiced chorizo sausage. In Italy I've eaten it cooked with cubes of cheese and raw chopped spinach leaves. On the next page is a French version, sometimes known as *Omelette savoyard*.

Omelette savoyard

(serves 2 people)

4 eggs
1 large onion, chopped
3 rashers of bacon, chopped
2 medium-sized potatoes, peeled and cut into small cubes
2 oz Gruyère cheese (50 g), cut into thin slivers
1 dessertspoon butter
1 dessertspoon olive oil
Salt and freshly-milled black pepper

You'll need a medium-sized frying-pan.

Melt the butter and oil together in the frying-pan. Dry the cubes of raw potato thoroughly in a tea towel, then fry them over a medium heat, tossing them around quite often until they're beginning to turn golden and are almost cooked through (about 10 minutes). Then add the bacon and onion to the pan and continue to cook these for a further 10 minutes or so or until the onion is soft.

Meanwhile pre-heat the grill to its highest setting. Arrange the slivers of cheese over the other ingredients in the pan, then beat the eggs with a fork (gently and not too much); season them with pepper but only a pinch of salt.

Turn the heat right up under the frying-pan and pour in the eggs. Now, using a palette knife, draw the outside of the omelette inward, allowing the liquid egg to escape round the edges. Then place the pan under the grill for a few moments to set the top. Serve cut in wedges with a crisp green salad as an accompaniment.

Note: In the summer this tastes just as good served cold.

Egg and lentil curry

(serves 3 people)

If I'm in the mood for a curry but a bit short of time, an egg curry always seems to fit the bill.

6 eggs
1 medium onion, roughly chopped
1 large carrot, thinly sliced
2 sticks celery, chopped
1 clove garlic, crushed

1 small green pepper, chopped
3 oz whole lentils (75 g)
2 tablespoons groundnut oil
1 rounded tablespoon flour
1 rounded teaspoon Madras curry powder
½ teaspoon ground ginger
1 level teaspoon ground turmeric
1 pint boiling water (570 ml)
2 tablespoons natural yoghurt
Salt

To garnish:
Chopped parsley and slices of raw onion

First heat the oil in a thick-based saucepan and fry the onion, browning it a little, then add the celery, carrot and pepper, and continue to fry till these have browned a little too (about 5 minutes). Then stir in the lentils and crushed garlic, and after that sprinkle in the flour and spices. Stir to soak up the juices, and keep stirring whilst you gradually add 1 pint (570 ml) of boiling water. Add some salt, then put a lid on and simmer gently for about 35 minutes or until the lentils are soft.

While the sauce is cooking place the eggs in cold water, bring them up to simmering point and then simmer for 7 minutes exactly. Now run some cold water over them until they're cool enough to handle, then peel and slice them in half.

A minute or two before serving, stir the yoghurt into the sauce and add the halved eggs. Then serve the curry with boiled rice sprinkled with chopped parsley and raw onion slices and have some mango chutney to go with it.

Poached eggs with cream and watercress

(serves 2 people)

The sauce for this recipe is a very attractive speckled pale green colour— and the whole thing goes very well with some plain buttered noodles.

4 fresh eggs
2 bunches watercress, trimmed and chopped
1 oz butter (25 g)

¾ oz plain flour (20 g)
½ pint milk (275 ml)
1 oz mild cheese (25 g), grated
1 level tablespoon Parmesan cheese, grated
2 tablespoons double cream
Lemon juice
½ oz extra butter (10 g)
Salt and freshly-milled black pepper

Make the sauce first by gently melting the 1 oz (25 g) of butter in a saucepan, stirring in the flour and adding the milk by degrees until you have a smooth white sauce. Then season, turn the heat to its very lowest and allow the sauce to cook for about 7 minutes. While that's happening, trim and discard the watercress stalks and chop the leaves roughly. Then melt the extra ½ oz (10 g) of butter in a saucepan, add the watercress and, again with the heat as low as possible and a lid on, allow the watercress to collapse down into the butter—this should take roughly 5 minutes.

Now add the watercress and all its buttery juices to the sauce, adding the grated cheeses. Stir to melt the cheese, then pour the sauce into a liquidiser and blend it at high speed until you have a green speckled sauce. Next return the sauce to the saucepan, adding the cream and a squeeze (½ teaspoonful) of lemon juice and a seasoning of salt and pepper. Keep the sauce warm whilst you now, quickly, poach 4 eggs by breaking them into a frying-pan of barely simmering water and giving them approximately 3 minutes. Lift them out with a draining-spoon, resting each one on a wad of kitchen paper to drain. Serve them on a bed of rice or noodles with the sauce poured over and sprinkled with more grated Parmesan.

Eggs and leeks au gratin
(serves 4 people)

Eggs, leeks and cheese are a really delicious trio and all this needs to go with it is crusty wholewheat bread.

8 eggs
4 medium leeks, cleaned and chopped
3 oz strong Cheddar cheese (75 g), grated
1 tablespoon Parmesan cheese, grated
3 oz butter (75 g)
1½ oz plain flour (40 g)

Right: Omelette savoyard, page 30.

¾ pint milk (425 ml)
Cayenne pepper
Salt and freshly-milled black pepper

To garnish:
Some chopped parsley or watercress

For this you'll need a generously-buttered shallow baking dish.

Select a saucepan that will hold 8 eggs fairly snugly, then cover them with cold water, bring the water to a gentle simmer and allow 7 minutes exactly—then cool them under cold running water.

While the eggs are cooking, make up a sauce using 2 oz (50 g) of the butter and 1½ oz (40 g) of flour, and add the milk gradually till the sauce is smooth. Then leave it to cook very gently for about 6 minutes. (Alternatively, use the all-in-one method, page 144.)

Next melt the other 1 oz (25 g) of butter in a saucepan, stir in the chopped leeks and let them sweat gently (with a lid on) for 5 minutes—they should have cooked in that time but still have a bit of 'bite' to them.

Now arrange the leeks over the base of the buttered baking dish and place the peeled halved hard-boiled eggs on top—roundside up. Next stir two-thirds of the Cheddar cheese and all the Parmesan into the sauce. Season well and, as soon as the cheese has melted, pour the sauce all over the eggs. Sprinkle the remaining Cheddar on top with a dusting of cayenne, then place the dish under a medium grill until the sauce is bubbling hot and the cheese is nicely toasted. Sprinkle with parsley or garnish with watercress before serving.

Cheese soufflé
(serves 3–4 people)

The one and only secret of success in making a soufflé is to *whisk the egg whites properly* (see page 25). Once you have mastered that, soufflés should never be a problem. But do remember it is in the nature of soufflés to start to shrink straight away, and always serve them absolutely immediately.

Left: Aduki bean and brown rice salad, page 222; Sausage rolls, page 91; Courgette and cheese quiche, page 90.

3 oz grated cheese (75 g) (any hard cheese can be used)
3 large eggs, separated
1 oz plain flour (25 g)
1 oz butter (25 g)
¼ pint milk (50 ml)
A pinch cayenne pepper
¼ teaspoon mustard powder
A little freshly-grated nutmeg
Salt and freshly-milled pepper

Pre-heat the oven to gas mark 5, 375°F (190°C)

For this you will need a 1½ pint (850 ml) soufflé dish or a pie-dish, butter it well.

First of all in a medium saucepan melt the butter, then add the flour and stir it over a moderate heat for 2 minutes.

Gradually add the milk to the saucepan—stirring all the time— and simmer gently for 3 minutes, still giving it an occasional stir. Then stir in the cayenne, mustard, nutmeg and a seasoning of salt and pepper, and leave the sauce to cool a little before stirring in the grated cheese. Beat up the egg yolks thoroughly, then stir them in.

Next whisk the egg whites till they are stiff, take a couple of spoonfuls and beat them into the sauce, then fold in the rest very carefully. Transfer the mixture to the soufflé dish, place on a baking sheet in the centre of the oven and bake for 30–35 minutes. The soufflé is cooked when a skewer inserted into the centre comes out clean.

Piperade

(serves 2 people)

This is the famous egg dish from the Basque region of France, where it's served very often with a thick slice of Bayonne ham. I serve it either just with triangles of fried bread or with grilled gammon steaks.

2 green peppers, deseeded and cut into strips
1 lb tomatoes (450 g), skinned, deseeded and chopped

2 medium onions, chopped small
1 or 2 cloves garlic, crushed (how much is up to you)
$\frac{1}{2}$ teaspoon dried basil
4 large fresh eggs
Butter and olive oil
Salt and freshly-milled black pepper

For this you'll need a heavy saucepan.

Melt a knob of butter and a dessertspoon of olive oil in a shallow heavy pan and add the onions, cooking them very gently for 10 minutes without browning. Now add the crushed garlic, tomatoes and peppers, stir everything around a little, season with salt and pepper and basil, and cook without covering for another 20 minutes or so (the peppers should be slightly underdone).

Now beat the eggs thoroughly, pour them into the pan and, using a wooden spoon, stir just as you would for scrambled eggs. When the mixture starts to thicken and the eggs are almost cooked, remove the pan from the heat, continuing to stir, and serve immediately (as with scrambled eggs, do be very careful not to overcook).

Chilli eggs
(serves 2 people)

These are eggs set in a hot spicy tomato sauce. In the summer 1 lb (450 g) of peeled fresh tomatoes would be best, but in the winter the tinned Italian variety have more flavour than imported tomatoes.

4 fresh eggs
3 tablespoons olive oil
1 large onion, chopped
1 green pepper, chopped
2 cloves garlic, crushed
$\frac{1}{2}$ teaspoon hot chilli powder
$\frac{1}{2}$ teaspoon cumin powder
$\frac{1}{4}$ teaspoon oregano
A few drops of tabasco

14-oz tin Italian tomatoes (400 g)

4 oz Cheddar cheese (110 g), grated

Freshly chopped parsley

Salt and freshly-milled black pepper

A heavy medium-sized frying-pan.

Heat the oil in the frying-pan and fry the chopped onion, green pepper and garlic gently for about 10 minutes. Then stir in the chilli and cumin powders and add the oregano along with a few drops of tabasco. Mix thoroughly and then add the contents of the tin of tomatoes.

Turn up the heat a bit and let the mixture cook (uncovered) for about 10 minutes or until the tomatoes have reduced to a thick pulp, then season with salt and freshly-milled black pepper.

Now carefully break the eggs into the pan on top of the mixture. Then sprinkle the cheese all over the eggs, cover the pan with a close-fitting lid or a suitably-sized plate and, lowering the heat, simmer very gently for about 10–15 minutes, or until the eggs are cooked to your liking. Then sprinkle with chopped parsley and serve.

Zabaglione
(serves 4 people)

This very famous Italian classic should be made with Marsala wine, which isn't very expensive, but failing that a sweet sherry or Madeira would do.

8 egg yolks

3 fluid oz Marsala (75 ml)

4 dessertspoons caster sugar

For this you'll need a medium-sized mixing bowl that will sit comfortably over a saucepan containing barely simmering water.

Into the mixing bowl place the egg yolks and sugar and start to whisk them (not on the heat yet) with an electric hand whisk or a balloon whisk until the mixture is pale and creamy. Then gradually whisk in the Marsala bit by bit.

Now transfer the bowl to the saucepan—keep the heat very low— and continue whisking until the mixture thickens. This can sometimes be rather slow (10–15 minutes), but don't be tempted to turn the heat up because, if the mixture becomes too hot, it will curdle.

When it does thicken, pour it into four warmed wine glasses and serve straight away.

Lemon soufflé omelette

(serves 2 people)

This is a light, foamy, lemony pudding literally made in moments.

3 large eggs, separated
1 lemon
2 dessertspoons caster sugar
Butter

A thick-based frying-pan.

First of all, add the grated rind and the juice of the lemon to the egg yolks, together with the sugar, and whisk until the mixture is slightly thick and creamy. Now start to melt a knob of butter in the frying-pan and turn the heat on the grill to its highest. Whisk the egg whites until stiff, then using a metal spoon carefully fold them into the yolks, lightly and quickly.

Now pour the lot onto the heated butter, then fold and stir a bit to prevent anything sticking to the bottom. After about 10 seconds place the pan under the grill, so that the top can brown nicely. Serve immediately straight from the pan.

If you like to make it slightly more spectacular you can warm a small ladle and pour brandy into it. Set light to the brandy, then carry your omelette to the table, pouring the lighted brandy over just before you get there.

John Tovey's quick hollandaise sauce

This recipe is excellent for using up egg yolks, and is equally delicious with plain grilled fish or meat—or as an accompaniment to vegetables like asparagus and artichokes. (For a more traditional version of this sauce, see page 151).

6 oz (170 g) butter
1 tablespoon wine vinegar
2 tablespoons lemon juice
3 egg yolks
$\frac{1}{2}$ teaspoon caster sugar
A pinch of salt

Put the butter into a small saucepan and allow it to melt slowly. Place the wine vinegar and lemon juice in another saucepan and bring to the boil. Meanwhile blend the egg yolks, sugar and salt in a liquidiser—then, with the motor still switched on, gradually add the hot lemon juice and vinegar.

When the butter reaches the boil, start to pour this in very slowly in a thin trickle (with the liquidiser motor running all the time) till all the butter is added and the sauce is thickened. To keep it warm, place it in a basin over some hot water till ready to serve.

Bread

Flour, yeast and breads

You may drive out Nature with a pitchfork, but she will ever hurry back, to triumph in stealth over your foolish contempt.

Horace: *Epistles*

There's a lot of truth in that little Latin quote, and never more so than now when technology tends to dictate, rather than serve, the needs of man. When it comes to the milling of flour and the commercial baking of bread, in this country and others, nature has indeed been driven out, not with a pitchfork but by a mountain of machinery.

In Britain more than 80 per cent of our flour is milled for the convenience of the machines that make factory bread, and not for the pleasure it gives to those who eat it. Alas, the very essence and flavour of the cornfields are contained in that part of the wheat which is discarded by modern millers: even the natural colour of the wheat is bleached out. It's true that the lost nutrients are replaced chemically, but as our modern wrapped-and-sliced white loaf shows only too clearly, nothing can replace the character, texture and flavour of the wheat.

However, it seems that Horace was right—nature is poised for a comeback. It is now quite evident from sound medical opinion the world over that too much 'refined' food isn't very good for us: it lacks the fibre ('roughage') essential to our diet, and it's said to be the cause of serious colonic diseases, not to mention the national preoccupation with constipation. As a result the 'wholefood' movement is losing its cranky image and gathering strength, and more and more people are attempting quite deliberately to adapt to a more wholesome, less refined diet.

First of all we must define what is meant by refined flour as opposed to unrefined 'whole' flour. In the past large bakeries have managed to obscure the real difference: often so-called brown bread has been white with caramel colouring added, and sometimes the odd bit of natural grain was re-incorporated. Now the Trades Description Act stipulates that wholewheat bread *must* be made with 100 per cent wholewheat flour, and so-called 'wheatmeal' bread with 81–85 per cent extraction flour. Nowadays anything brown that is not called either of these is probably of the refined, dyed variety.

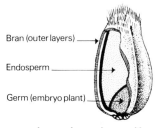

Bran (outer layers)

Endosperm

Germ (embryo plant)

A grain of wheat

Let us examine a grain of wheat, then, and see how it is milled into the various types of flour. Each grain contains three basic components. There is the *germ* (the part that germinates and grows into a new wheat plant), and this contains proteins, vitamins, oil and much of the flavour. Next there is the *endosperm*, containing starch, and all round both these are the protective layers of *bran*. The germ accounts for 2 per cent of the grain, the bran layers 13 per cent and the starch 85 per cent. In the days when the whole grain was ground by hand on stone-mills, the bread contained all the properties above.

Milling old and new

Obviously the bread made with these traditional methods was brown. The trouble started, in my opinion, when white flour (at least, whiter) became fashionable on a wide scale in the late 17th century, as a symbol of status and wealth. This 'refined' flour was sifted, or bolted, through a wool-and-linen fabric which got rid of the toughest layer of bran particles: later an even finer flour was obtained by sifting through silk. This fine flour made lighter bread and was of course more suitable for cakes, biscuits and other confections.

By the 1870s the modern mechanical roller-mill had been invented, which automatically separated the bran and the germ from the starch: the starch was then crushed through fine nylon meshes, and finally bleached with chlorine into our modern whiter-than-white flour. The 'status symbol' was available to all, but ironically it is no longer because we want it but because we have to have it. The vast machinery that makes our national loaf can now only cope with this sort of flour (even the bleaching, which helps to mature the flour, is for the benefit of technology rather than taste; it is banned in several countries because it also happens to destroy the vitamin E content—here this is put back synthetically).

To my way of thinking, if we want an alternative to the whole commercial world of the Sliced White, the only really satisfactory alternative we have is to choose our own flour and make our own bread. It may be that you are one of those few, fortunate people who live near a small baker still using select flour and traditional baking methods. If not, I hope to prove to you how uncomplicated home-baking can be, how even an absolute beginner can produce a loaf infinitely superior in texture and flavour to any factory bread on offer. But before embarking on any of the recipes in this chapter, *please* read the following notes carefully.

Flour
100 per cent stoneground wholewheat flour (wholemeal)
As the name suggests, this is flour ground on a traditional stone-mill. It contains the whole of a grain of wheat. Nothing has been added and nothing taken away. There has been some confusion as to what exactly is the difference between *wholewheat* and *wholemeal*. Whatever terms the millers might use to describe the coarseness of the grinding, so far as consumers are concerned there is *no* difference. I have bought various bags of flour, some labelled wholemeal and others labelled wholewheat: sometimes the texture of one is coarser than the other, sometimes it's identical. Suffice it to say that whatever texture you happen to like is right for you.

80–90 per cent extraction flours
These are unbleached flours in which 10–20 per cent of the grain has been extracted in the milling. Provided these are stone-ground, they are natural flours with the bran partially removed. This type of flour is sometimes referred to as 'wheatmeal' and the loaf made from it is called wheatmeal bread—lighter in texture but still with a wholewheat-flavour. (If you like making wholewheat bread most of the time but occasionally want the lighter wheatmeal, you can make up your own 85 per cent extraction by using half quantity of wholewheat flour and half of strong white.) *Note:* Unless the extraction rate is given on the packet and it carries the magic words 'stone ground', the sort of brown flour distributed by some of the larger firms is usually roller-milled white flour with added colour and part of what has been extracted put back.

Strong white flour
White flours are normally of 70–72 per cent extraction, with hardly any traces of bran or germ left and of course bleached (actually an unbleached variety is available, and this is a pale cream colour).

All flours vary in strength, according to the amount of *gluten* (protein) they contain. This will depend on the variety of wheat, and the type of soil and climate in which it is grown. Strong (or 'hard') wheats are grown in extreme climates, as in Canada or Russia: in this country our wheat, and therefore our flour, is soft.

The stronger the wheat, the higher the gluten content and (as we shall see) the better a dough will stretch and expand—which is exactly what we need for bread.

Plain flour

Plain household flour is usually a soft flour. It won't give such good results as strong flour for bread, but it is cheaper and quite capable of producing a home-made loaf better than many shop-bought varieties. With less gluten in it, it is the very best type of flour for cakes and short pastries (and, along with self-raising flour, is therefore dealt with in the next chapter).

How to store flour

Flour needs a cool, dry place for storage. That's easier said than done in a modern kitchen, I know, but do try to keep it away from a damp steamy atmosphere: a large and roomy enamelled flour-bin is ideal or, failing that, tightly-lidded storage jars will do. Wholewheat flours have a much shorter shelf-life than white flours, because the wheat germ contains oil which can in time develop a rancid flavour. I think six weeks is the maximum storage time for wholewheat (so buy in small quantities), and three months the maximum for white flour.

Yeast

In her splendid book on *English bread and yeast cookery*, published by Allen Lane, Elizabeth David has this to say:

In Chaucer's England one of the names for yeast or barm was goddisgoode 'bicause it cometh of the grete grace of God'. These words simply imply a blessing. To me that is just what it is. It is also mysterious, magical. No matter how familiar its action may become nor how successful the attempts to explain it in terms of chemistry and to manufacture it by the ton, yeast still to a certain extent retains its mystery.

Perhaps one of the reasons yeast seems so mysterious is that it is in fact alive. When we buy it it is alive (one hopes) but inactive: under the right conditions, that is with a little warmth and the addition of some water, it is activated and releases the gas that will raise the dough. All this activity ceases only when the dough is placed in the oven and the extreme temperature kills off the yeast.

Yeast is available in two forms: fresh from some bakers or chemists, and dried (granular) in tins or packets.

Fresh yeast should look firm and moist, cream-coloured and cool to touch. If it's crumbly, dryish and dark in places it is stale and might not do its work. To use it simply mix the required amount into the liquid and mix into the dough straight away. Fresh yeast can be bought in bulk and stored in a deep freezer in, say, wrapped 1 oz (25 g) portions. It will keep in a freezer for three months, or in a refrigerator for three days.

Dried yeast As supplies of fresh yeast are so unreliable nowadays I always use dried. As a matter of fact I think it's a fallacy that bread made with fresh yeast tastes better—I have made simultaneous, identical loaves and found no difference in flavour. However, a word of warning. Dried yeast does become stale just like fresh yeast, so it is very important to store it in a tightly-lidded small container in a cool dry place. It is obvious from the letters I receive (and my own experience) that it's perfectly possible to buy a duff batch. It could have been stored too long before purchase or, in the case of the cellophane packets, kept in a damp place. Therefore if, when you mix it, the yeast doesn't froth (see page 47), discard it and return it to the shop where you bought it. My advice is to try to buy the sealed tins rather than the packets, and replace the plastic cap carefully and firmly after using.

Liquid
Water is most commonly used for bread; occasionally milk or a combination of both. Milk in the mixture gives a softer crust and is better for soft rolls, baps, muffins. Liquid measurements can never be absolutely exact because different types of flour absorb different amounts.

Salt
The quantity of salt you put into bread is determined by two considerations—your own taste, and whether you're in a hurry. Salt does slow down the action of the yeast (too much can actually kill it), so if you want to increase the salt in any of my recipes do allow extra rising time.

Sugar
Sugar is always needed to activate dried (but not fresh) yeast. For dried yeast use brown sugar for wholewheat loaves, and white for white bread mixes. Molasses are sometimes used to give a different flavour and a moister loaf.

Fats

Adding a small proportion of fat can very slightly enrich a dough and help it to stay fresh longer. Personally I find butter is best of all, but vegetable fat or lard if you prefer can be used instead. Proper enriched doughs are those that have quite a lot of fat in them, sometimes plus eggs and dried fruit (e.g. hot cross buns, malt loaves). The extra fat retards the growth of the yeast, so an extra quantity of yeast is used in this type of recipe.

How a loaf of bread is made

These notes apply to the traditional method of breadmaking. However, later in this chapter, I have also given recipes for quick and simple loaves, dispensing with some of these stages.

Flour should be at room temperature, even slightly warmer, to speed things up. If your flour feels chilly, warm it in a low oven for 10 minutes (and if the bowl it's in gets too hot, tip it into another).

Dried yeast The water for mixing with the yeast should be hand-hot, i.e. you can place your little finger in the water for a few seconds without it hurting. Measure it out and pour approximately one-

third of it into another jug, add the sugar to this, then sprinkle in the dried yeast. Stir once and leave it until it forms a frothy head—this will probably take 10 minutes but might take a little longer. In order to raise the dough it must have at least $\frac{3}{4}$ in. (2 cm) of froth.

Mixing Add the salt to the flour and blend it in thoroughly—remember if you add extra salt to allow for extra rising time. Pour the yeast liquid in and mix to a dough, gradually adding the rest of the water, bearing in mind that as flours vary you may not need it all or you may well need a spot more. Add enough to make a smooth dough that will leave the bowl clean. If you've overdone the liquid and it's too slippery it doesn't matter a scrap: just sprinkle in some more flour.

Kneading For bread dough that has to be kneaded, simply place it on a flat work surface then stretch it away from you, using the heel of one hand (see illustration) to push from the middle and the clenched knuckles of your other hand to pull the other half of the dough towards you—both hands should move simultaneously to stretch out the dough. Then lift the edges over and back to the middle. Give it a quarter-turn and repeat the process. It soon becomes a rather rhythmic operation, and the dough will then start to become very elastic. This is the gluten at work. In simple language, the water meets the gluten and what makes it become springy and alive is a good pummelling. That's why if you're feeling angry bread-making can be most therapeutic! One point to bear in mind here is that refined flour has a larger proportion of gluten, so white bread dough will become more elastic and rise much more than a wholewheat dough. A properly kneaded piece of dough will look plump and rounded with a very smooth surface.

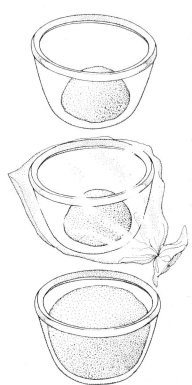

Rising This is the period the dough must be left for the yeast to do its work: all yeast doughs need at *least an hour at room temperature before* baking or less in a warm place. I used to think how annoying it was that slower rising times produce better bread, though now I do feel it is *sometimes* more convenient to go away and leave it for a couple of hours. In the end it is best to make the sort of bread that fits into your own timetable. To speed up the rising it is best to leave the dough in a so-called 'warm' place. I use the plate-warming compartment of my cooker—but others may be too hot for this and care has to be taken because too high a temperature can kill off the yeast. Always cover the dough, either with a folded damp tea-towel or by completely encasing the bowl inside a polythene bag (such as a bin-liner)—put a few drops of oil in the bag first to prevent the dough sticking. The Flour Advisory Bureau recommend that if no suitable warm place is forthcoming you wrap the bowl in a polythene bag, seal it and sit the whole thing in a larger bowl of warm water. (If you don't cover the dough, heat is lost and a skin can develop and, when you knead again, the dough will be lumpy.)

If you have more time to spare, the dough will rise at room temperature and perhaps be the better for it. You can even allow the dough to rise at a cold temperature, in the lower part of the fridge, covered in the same way. This is useful if you want to mix and knead the dough the night before, leave it to rise in the fridge, and shape and bake next morning. Dough, when risen properly, should have doubled in size and should spring back and feel very slightly sticky when lightly touched with the finger. Remember, the slower the rising time, the more uniformly the yeast will work and the more evenly textured the finished bread will be.

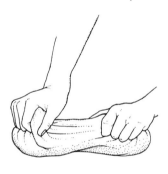

Knocking down and proving Some recipes call for a second rising or 'proving', which is exactly what it is: the yeast proving it is still alive and active. The experts say that sometimes during the first rise a dough will expand unevenly (with a resulting loaf that is partly too open-textured, partly too close-textured). The proving ensures there will be an even rise. *Knocking down* is simply punching all the gas out of the dough and bringing it back to its original size, to allow it to rise a second time in the bread tin.

Baking Bread tins should always be generously greased. I always use butter for this, and a piece of kitchen paper to spread it evenly all round the tins—especially in the ridges and corners. Always bake bread in a hot oven (from gas mark 6, 400°F (200°C) min., to gas mark 8, 450°F (230°C) max.). Bear in mind it's always better to over-cook rather than under-cook bread: to test if a loaf is cooked, tap it on the under-side with your knuckles and, if it sounds

hollow, it's done. If you like very crusty bread, then after you've turned the loaves out of their tins, pop them back in the oven upside down for 5—10 minutes (to bake the underneath and sides). *Always* cool bread on a wire cooling tray, otherwise, on a flat surface, the steam will be trapped and the crust will become wet and soggy.

Storing bread

The best way to store a loaf for any length of time is in a freezer. I have a small 4-star freezing compartment above my fridge and I sometimes freeze bread for as little as three days—because once defrosted it really is fresher than one kept in the bread bin for the same time. Otherwise I would recommend a stainless steel or aluminium bread bin, or roll-top container. But all these must have tiny air holes in them to keep bread for a reasonable period: if the moisture is not allowed to escape, mould can develop. That is why sealed polythene bags or lidded boxes are *not* suitable.

So much for the essential principles of bread-making, which I hope will answer most everyday queries. At the same time I wouldn't want anyone to be side-tracked into too many paths of perfection. The quick and easy wholewheat bread recipe below will give even a first-time bread-maker a really delicious, crusty loaf with a proper wheat flavour. Similarly the simple hot cross buns recipe will produce buns far superior to anything that came out of a factory. The point is, your loaves, buns and rolls may not win a prize at a Master Bakers' contest (I know mine wouldn't), but the pleasure they will give you and your family will make the small amount of effort thoroughly worth while.

Quick and easy wholewheat bread

(makes 1 large or 2 small loaves)

This recipe was inspired by Doris Grant in her excellent book *Your daily food* (Faber and Faber). Although it's quick and easy, I have never found a shop-bought wholewheat loaf nearly as good. For those of us who simply don't have the sort of timetable that kneading, knocking down and proving fits into, this loaf is an absolute gem and the one that I, personally, make most often.

1 lb stoneground wholewheat flour (450 g)
2 teaspoons salt
Approximately 12–13 fl. oz hand-hot water (355–380 ml)
1 teaspoon brown sugar
2 level teaspoons dried yeast
A little extra flour

(For 3 lb (1 kg 350 g) flour simply multiply the rest of the ingredients by 3.)

You'll need one 2 lb (900 g) bread tin with a base measurement of $6\frac{1}{2} \times 3\frac{1}{2}$ inches (16·5 × 9 cm) or two 1 lb (450 g) bread tins $5\frac{1}{4} \times 3$ inches (13·5 × 8 cm). The tin or tins should be buttered fairly thickly.

Begin by weighing the flour and mixing the salt into it so that it is fairly evenly distributed. Then warm the flour slightly in a low oven for about 10 minutes.

While the flour is warming, prepare the yeast by measuring 3 fl. oz (75 ml) hand-hot water in a measuring jug. Stir the sugar in and sprinkle in the 2 teaspoons of yeast as well, stir once, then leave it for 10–15 minutes until a good 1 inch (2·5 cm) of froth has formed.

Now tip the warm flour into a large mixing bowl, make a well in the centre, stir the yeast liquid once—to make sure it's dissolved—then pour it into the well and, starting with a wooden spoon, begin to mix the yeast liquid into the flour to form a dough, gradually adding the rest of the measured water. Finish off the mixing with your hands until you have a smooth dough that leaves the bowl clean, i.e. no bits of flour or dough remain on the side of the bowl. The exact amount of water you need depends on the flour. If you like you can do the mixing with the dough hook of an electric hand whisk (or even in a mixer).

Now transfer the dough to the tin (or tins) by stretching it out to an oblong and folding one edge into the centre and the other edge over that. Fit the dough into the tin, pressing all round the edges so that the surface will already be slightly rounded. Next sprinkle the surface with a generous dusting of flour. Cover the tin with a damp tea towel and leave it to rise in a warm place for 30–40 minutes or at room temperature for approximately an hour.

Meanwhile pre-heat the oven to gas mark 6, 400°F (200°C), and
when the dough has risen to within $\frac{1}{4}$ inch ($\frac{1}{2}$ cm) of the top of the
bread tin (or to the very top if you are using a shallower loaf tin),
then bake the bread for 45 minutes if it's the large size or 35
minutes for the smaller size. After that turn out the bread and
return it to the oven, upside down, for a further 5–10 minutes to
crisp the base and sides.

The loaves, if cooked, will sound hollow when tapped underneath.
Cool the bread on a wire cooling tray and *never* put it away or
freeze it until it's absolutely cold. *Note:* If you want to make a
lighter textured loaf by the same method, all you do is use $\frac{1}{2}$ lb
(225 g) 100 per cent wholewheat flour and $\frac{1}{2}$ lb (225 g) strong white
flour and prepare it in exactly the same way as above.

Plain white bread
(makes 2 loaves)

This is, for those who prefer the lighter
texture of a plain white loaf (and indeed
most people prefer it for toast), a basic
white loaf recipe.

2 level teaspoons of dried yeast
$\frac{3}{4}$ pint of hand-hot water
1 teaspoon of white sugar
1$\frac{1}{2}$ lb of strong white flour (warmed slightly)
1 level tablespoon of salt
$\frac{1}{2}$ oz of butter
A little extra flour

Two 1 lb loaf tins, well buttered

Pour $\frac{1}{4}$ pint of the measured hand-hot water into a bowl, then with
a fork whisk in the sugar, followed by the dried yeast—and leave
this mixture on one side to froth.

Meanwhile sift the flour and salt into a bowl and rub in the butter.
When the yeast is ready, pour it into a well made in the centre of
the flour, then pour in the remaining $\frac{1}{2}$ pint of warm water. Now
mix to a dough, starting off with a wooden spoon and using your
hands in the final stages of mixing.

Wipe the bowl clean with the dough—adding a spot more water if
there are any dry bits left—and transfer it to a flat work-surface
(there shouldn't be any need to flour the surface). Knead the

dough for ten minutes or until it develops a sheen and shows a slight blistering under the surface (it should also be springy and elastic).

You can now either leave the dough on the surface covered by the upturned bowl or return the dough to the bowl and cover with polythene or clingfilm. Leave it until it looks as though it has doubled in bulk—1½ to 2 hours at room temperature or 45 minutes to an hour in a warm place.

After that knock the air out, then knead again for 5 minutes. Now divide the dough in half, pat each piece out to an oblong, then fold one end in to the centre and fold the other end in on top. Put each one into a buttered tin, sprinkle each loaf with a dusting of flour then place them side by side in an oiled polythene bag until the dough rises above the tops of the tins (30 minutes in a warm place or an hour at room temperature).

Now pre-heat the oven to gas mark 8, 450°F and bake the loaves for 35–40 minutes or until they sound hollow when their bases are tapped. Return them, out of their tins, upside down in the oven to crisp the base and side crust. Then cool on a wire rack.

Oatmeal bread

(makes 2 small loaves)

This bread has a lovely wholesome flavour, just the thing for a snack lunch with some strong Cheddar cheese; it also makes delicious bacon sandwiches.

4 oz medium oatmeal (110 g)
½ pint milk (275 ml)
2 teaspoons dried yeast
¼ pt hand-hot water
10 oz wholewheat flour (275 g), warmed slightly
10 oz strong white flour (275 g), warmed slightly
1 tablespoon salt
1 teaspoon honey
2 oz butter (50 g)
1 teaspoon sugar

A floured baking sheet.

Start this about 4 or 5 hours ahead by combining the oatmeal and the milk in a bowl and leaving them to soak. Then to make the loaves, start by pouring $\frac{1}{4}$ pint (150 ml) of hand-hot water into a jug. Whisk in the sugar and then the yeast, and leave it for 10 minutes to get a good frothy head.

Then mix the two flours and the salt in a mixing bowl, making sure you mix them together very thoroughly. Then make a well in the centre of the flour.

Next gently warm the butter and honey together in a small saucepan until the butter becomes liquid, then pour this into the well in the flours, followed by the frothed yeast. Finally add the soaked oatmeal mixture, then mix everything together to form a smooth dough that leaves the bowl clean. If it's very stiff you may need a drop more milk. Now transfer the dough to a flat working surface and knead it for about 10 minutes: after that return it to the bowl and cover with a damp cloth or cling-film. Leave it like this until the dough has doubled in bulk (about 90 minutes at room temperature or rather less in a warm place). Then knock and punch the air out and knead again for 5 minutes.

Next, divide the dough in half, and make each half into a round shape. Roll each loaf gently in some wholewheat flour, pressing in a light coating, then place both on a floured baking sheet. Use a sharp knife to make $\frac{1}{4}$ inch ($\frac{1}{2}$ cm) deep slashes across the top of each loaf.

Place the baking sheet (and contents) inside an oiled plastic bag and let the dough prove for a further 1–1$\frac{1}{2}$ hours (or 45 minutes in a warm place). Bake in a pre-heated oven, gas mark 8, 450°F (230°C), for 10 minutes, then turn down the heat to gas mark 4, 350°F (180°C), and bake for a further 30 minutes.

Soured cream soda bread

(makes 1 loaf)

This is a good loaf to make if you're in a hurry or need some bread unexpectedly. It doesn't need yeast, as the soured cream and soda are the raising agents. It is best eaten slightly warm from the oven.

1 lb wholewheat flour (450 g)
2 teaspoons salt
1 teaspoon bicarbonate of soda

¼ **pint soured cream (150 ml)**

¼ **pint water (150 ml) (plus 2–3 extra tablespoons)**

Pre-heat the oven to gas mark 7, 425°F (220°C)

A greased baking sheet.

Begin by mixing the flour, salt and bicarbonate of soda thoroughly in a bowl. Then in a jug whisk the soured cream and water together and stir this mixture into the flour together with 2–3 further tablespoons of water, if it needs it.

Knead the dough lightly (into a round ball) so as to get the surface smooth, then put it onto the prepared baking sheet and cut halfway through the loaf with a sharp knife, one way, then do the same the other way forming a cut cross, which will form the loaf into four crusty sections.

Bake the loaf in the top half of the oven for 30 minutes—covering the top with foil for the last 5 minutes of the baking time, if the crust looks like getting too dark. Cool on a wire rack for a minimum of 15 minutes before eating. This is delicious cut in thick slices, buttered and spread with home-made lemon curd or some really good honey.

If you don't like a very crisp crust, wrap the bread in a tea-towel whilst it cools, so that the steam it gives off softens the crust a little.

Note: Soda bread is best eaten as fresh as possible: it's not a keeping loaf at all—though I'm sure there won't actually be any left to keep! If you can't get soured cream use ½ pint milk and 2 teaspoons of cream of tartar.

Quick wheatmeal rolls

(makes 12 rolls)

The quick wholewheat bread on page 48 is not suitable for individual rolls because, without kneading, there's no elasticity in the dough and, during the rising time, it spreads itself out too much. This recipe does require 5–6 minutes kneading but only one rise, so it's still relatively quick.

| 8 oz wholewheat flour (225 g) |
| 8 oz strong white flour (225 g) |
| 1 teaspoon butter |
| 1 level teaspoon brown sugar |
| 2 level teaspoons salt |
| 2 level teaspoons dried yeast |
| ½ pint hand-hot water (275 ml) |
| A little extra flour |

One large or two small well-greased baking sheets.

Measure the flours into a bowl, add the salt and mix thoroughly together. Then warm the flour slightly in a low oven.

To prepare the yeast measure ½ pint (275 ml) hand-hot water in a jug, then pour half of it into another jug or bowl. Sprinkle in the sugar and then the yeast, stir and leave it aside till a good 1 inch (2·5 cm) frothy head has formed.

Now remove the flour from the oven, rub in the fat, then make a well in the centre, stir the yeast liquid and pour it into the well. Pour the other liquid into the yeast jug, to rinse it out, then add this to the flour gradually stirring with a wooden spoon at first and then finishing off with your hands until you have a smooth dough that leaves the bowl cleanly.

Now transfer the dough onto a flat working surface and knead it thoroughly for about 6 minutes, by which time it will have become very elastic and springy.

Next divide the dough into 12 portions to form the rolls. If you want your rolls to be absolutely the same size, you can weigh the dough, divide the total weight by twelve and then weigh each individual piece. Stretch each piece into an oblong and fold one end into the middle and the other end over that. Then, with the folds underneath, slap the roll into a round ball. Place the rolls onto the well-greased baking sheets, cover with a sheet of oiled polythene, or encase the baking sheet inside an oiled pedal-bin liner. Leave the rolls to rise until they have doubled in size: 35–40 minutes in a warm place or 1–1½ hours at room temperature.

Meanwhile pre-heat the oven to gas mark 7, 425°F (220°C).

When the rolls have risen, sprinkle them with flour and bake them on a high shelf of the oven for 20–25 minutes. They should sound hollow when you tap them underneath if they are cooked enough. Cool the rolls on a wire cooling rack.

Poppyseed rolls
(makes 16 rolls)

Basically these are the familiar soft Vienna rolls—improved, I think, by a liberal sprinkling of poppy seeds.

1 lb strong white flour, warmed slightly
2 teaspoons salt
½ pint milk (hand-hot)
2 teaspoons dried yeast
1 teaspoon white sugar
4 oz butter (room temperature)
1 beaten egg
2 tablespoons (approx.) poppy seeds

1 large (or 2 small) baking sheets, well-greased

Start by pouring ¼ pint of the warm milk into a bowl and whisk the sugar into it with a fork, followed by the dried yeast. Leave this on one side for 10 minutes to froth. Meanwhile sift the flour and salt into a bowl, make a well in the centre, and (when it's ready) pour in the frothed yeast-and-milk. Mix to form a smooth dough, then turn out onto a flat working surface and knead for 10 minutes.

After that put the dough back in the bowl, cover with clingfilm and leave it to rise until doubled in bulk (which will take 1½–2 hours at room temperature or 45 minutes to an hour in a warm place). Then punch the dough down in the bowl to knock the air out, and then gradually work in the softened butter. The dough will now be very sticky, but ignore this and carry on until the butter is evenly worked into the dough.

Next, turn it out onto a lightly-floured work-surface and knead into a round shape—divide this into sixteen sections. Roll each piece out into a long roll, and literally tie each roll into a knot. Place each roll on the baking sheet and brush with beaten egg. Now pop the baking sheet and rolls into an oiled polythene bag, and leave them to prove until puffy and risen again—about half an hour in a warm place or an hour at room temperature. Then pre-heat the oven to gas mark 5, 375°F (190°C), sprinkle the rolls with the poppy seeds and bake for about 20 minutes or until golden brown.

Breakfast baps
(makes 12)

These are indeed good at breakfast, also they're good for hamburgers or for putting delicious fillings in and taking on a picnic or car journey.

1 lb plain white flour (450 g)
1½ teaspoons salt
2 oz butter (50 g)
¼ pint hand-hot water (150 ml)
¼ pint milk (150 ml)
1 teaspoon granulated sugar
2 teaspoons dried yeast

Lightly grease 2 baking sheets.

Sift the flour and salt into a bowl, and rub the butter in until thoroughly blended. Now blend the water, milk and sugar together in another bowl, whisk in the yeast and leave on one side for 10 minutes to form a good head of froth. Now make a well in the flour, stir the liquid into it until the mixture forms a smooth dough, then turn the dough onto a lightly-floured surface and knead for about 10 minutes—or until the dough is silky smooth and feels very springy and elastic. Return it to the bowl, cover with a damp cloth or cling-film and leave it until it's doubled in bulk (about 1½ hours or 50–60 minutes in a warm place).

Then pre-heat the oven up to gas mark 9, 475°F (245°C). Knead the dough lightly and divide it into 12 equal pieces. Form each one into a ball and place them on a baking sheet—you should manage to get six on each baking sheet. Flour your hands and flatten the balls slightly into disc shapes. Then press a deep hole with your thumb in the centre of each bap (this prevents any blistering whilst it's cooking). Now brush each one with milk and sprinkle on a generous dusting of flour. Then put the baking sheets inside large plastic bags for 20–25 minutes to prove. Bake for 10 minutes so they are golden brown under the floury tops. Transfer to a wire rack to cool, and eat them very fresh.

Chapattis
(makes 12)

This is an anglicised version of the flat bread served with curry in India. Don't be put off because it sounds complicated. It's actually much easier and quicker than it sounds.

½ lb wholewheat flour (225 g)
1 teaspoon salt
About ¼ pint cold water (150 ml)
A little lard

Simply mix the flour and salt in a bowl, then gradually add enough water to combine the mixture to a non-sticky dough. Transfer the dough to a work surface and knead for about 10 minutes. Then leave it, covered by the upturned bowl, to rest for 30 minutes.

After that pre-heat the grill to high, then break up the dough and roll it into walnut-size pieces. Now roll out each piece on a lightly-floured surface as thin as possible; just less than ⅛ inch (3 mm).

Next heat a frying-pan or griddle over a medium heat and grease lightly with a piece of lard paper. Put the pancakes on the hot surface, one at a time, and wait until bubbles start to rise in them, rather like cobblestones. Flip over and cook for about 15 seconds, then transfer each one to cook under the grill about 6 inch (15 cm) from the heat. They should immediately inflate to virtually a round ball. Then, when lightly browned, turn and cook the other side. To serve, as the bread collapses, transfer it to a warmed dish, lined with a napkin. Cover and take to the table.

Each chapatti should take about ½ minute to cook, so the total cooking time is only about 6 minutes.

Muffins
(makes 12)

Muffins always remind me of fireside teas in the depth of winter. I like to cook them on top of the stove, which is the traditional method, but if you haven't got a griddle, a heavy-based frying-pan will do.

1 lb strong plain flour (450 g)
1 rounded teaspoon salt
8 fl. oz milk (225 ml)

2 fl. oz water (55 ml)
1 teaspoon caster sugar
2 level teaspoons dried yeast
A little lard

Measure the milk and water in a small saucepan and heat until just hand hot. Pour it into a jug, add the sugar and dried yeast, mix it with a fork and leave it about 10 minutes to get a real frothy head.

Meanwhile sift the flour and salt into a large mixing bowl, make a well in the centre, then pour in the frothy yeast mixture and mix it to a soft dough—it should leave the bowl cleanly, but if it seems a bit sticky add a spot more flour. On the other hand, if it seems a little dry add just a spot more water.

Now transfer the dough to a flat surface and knead it for about 10 minutes, by which time it should be very smooth and elastic. The dough can go back into the bowl now. Just slip the bowl inside a large, oiled polythene bag, and leave it in a warm place until the dough has doubled in size. This will take about 45 minutes or longer, depending on the temperature.

When the dough has risen, lightly flour the work surface, then tip the dough out and roll it out to about ½ inch (1 cm) thick, then using a 3-inch (7·5-cm) plain cutter cut out 12 rounds, re-rolling the dough a couple of times again if it starts to get puffy. Mix the scraps and re-roll as well to use it all up.

Now place the muffins on an ungreased lightly-floured baking sheet, sprinkling them with a little more flour, then leave them to puff up again for about 25–35 minutes in a warm place.

When they are ready to be cooked, grease a thick-based frying-pan or griddle with just a trace of lard. Then heat the pan over a medium heat, add some muffins and cook them for about 7 minutes on each side, turning the heat down to low as soon as they go in. You'll need to do this in three or four batches, but they can be made well in advance.

If you want to serve them in the traditional way, all you do is break them just a little around their waists without opening them, then toast them lightly on both sides. The correct way to eat them is just to pull them apart without cutting and insert a lot of butter. You can store them in an airtight tin for about two days before toasting if you have any left over.

Bara brith

(makes 1 loaf)

There are several different versions of this Welsh 'speckled bread'. Many of them don't contain yeast; but, for me, this version is the nicest and if there's any left over it's delicious toasted.

1 lb strong plain flour (450 g)
4 teaspoons dried yeast
8 fl. oz milk (225 ml)
2 oz brown sugar (50 g) plus 1 teaspoon
1 teaspoon salt
3 oz butter or margarine (75 g)
1 standard egg
1 teaspoon mixed spice
12 oz mixed dried fruit (350 g)

A 2 lb (900 g) loaf tin well greased.

First warm the milk in a small saucepan till it's hand-hot, and then pour it into a bowl. Whisk in 1 teaspoon of sugar, followed by the yeast, then leave it in a warm place to froth for about 15 minutes.

Now sift the flour and salt into a large mixing bowl, stirring in the sugar as well. Then rub the fat into the dry ingredients until the mixture looks like fine breadcrumbs. Stir in the mixed spice next, then pour in the beaten egg and frothed yeast, and mix to a dough. Now turn the dough onto a floured surface and knead until smooth and elastic (about 10 minutes), then replace the dough in the bowl and cover with a cloth or some clingfilm. Leave in a warm place to rise until it has doubled in size—about 1½ hours.

After that turn the dough out and knock it down to get the air out, then gradually knead the fruit in and pat out to a rectangular shape. Roll it up from one short side to the other and put it in the loaf tin (seam-side down). Place the tin inside an oiled plastic bag and leave it to rise, until the dough has rounded nicely above the edge of the tin (about 30–45 minutes). Meanwhile pre-heat the oven to gas mark 5, 375°F (190°C).

When the dough has risen and springs back when pressed lightly with a floured finger, remove the polythene bag and transfer the loaf to the oven and bake on the shelf below centre for 30 minutes. Then cover the top of the loaf tin with foil to prevent it over-browning, and continue to bake for a further 30 minutes. Turn the loaf out, holding it in a teacloth in one hand and tapping the base with the other. It should sound hollow—if not pop it back upside down (without the tin) for 5 minutes more. Cool the loaf on a wire rack, and brush the top with clear honey, to make it nice and sticky, before the loaf cools. Slice thinly and serve buttered.

Hot cross buns
(makes about 12)

It's hard to believe the difference in home-made hot cross buns—they really are far better than any bought from a shop and a lot cheaper into the bargain!

1 lb plain flour (450 g)
1 teaspoon caster sugar
$\frac{1}{4}$ pint hand-hot water (150 ml)
1 level teaspoon salt
2 oz cut mixed peel (50 g)
2 oz butter (50 g), melted
1$\frac{1}{2}$–2 fl. oz warmed milk (40–50 ml)
1 level tablespoon dried yeast
1 rounded teaspoon mixed spice
3 oz currants (75 g)
2 oz caster sugar (50 g)
1 egg beaten

For the glaze:
2 tablespoons granulated sugar
2 tablespoons water

Pre-heat the oven to gas mark 7, 425°F (220°C)

A greased baking sheet.

First stir 1 teaspoon of caster sugar into the $\frac{1}{4}$ pint (150 ml) of hand-hot water, then sprinkle in the dried yeast and leave it until a good frothy 'beer' head forms.

Meanwhile sift the flour, salt and mixed spice into a mixing bowl and add the sugar, currants and mixed peel. Then make a well in the centre, pour in the yeast mixture plus 1$\frac{1}{2}$ fl. oz (40 ml) of milk (again hand-hot), the beaten egg and the melted butter. Now mix it to a dough, starting with a wooden spoon and finishing with your hands (add a spot more milk if it needs it).

Then transfer the dough onto a clean surface and knead it until it feels smooth and elastic—about 6 minutes. Now pop it back into the bowl, cover the bowl with a lightly oiled plastic bag (a pedal-bin liner is ideal), and leave it in a warm place to rise—it will take about an hour to double its original size. Then turn it out and knead it again, back down to its original size.

Divide the mixture into 12 round portions, arrange them on the greased baking sheet (allowing plenty of room for expansion), and make a deep cross on each one with a sharp knife. Leave them to rise once more, covering again with the oiled polythene bag for about 25 minutes. Then bake the buns for about 15 minutes.

Then, while they're cooking, melt the sugar and water over a gentle heat, and brush the buns with it, as soon as they come out of the oven, to make them nice and sticky.

Note: If you like you can make more distinctive crosses with strips of dampened short-crust pastry lightly pressed into each bun before baking.

Pizza

One of the very nicest ways of eating bread is as a 'pizza'—freshly-baked bread dough with delicious fillings melting and bubbling on top. There are, of course, hundreds of variations—tomatoes, cheese, olives, anchovies, chopped peppers, capers, sliced mushrooms, salamis—anything and everything can be used. Below is a recipe for a plain pizza dough and then two with my own favourite fillings.

Pizza dough

8 oz plain flour (225 g)
1 level teaspoon salt
$\frac{1}{4}$ teaspoon sugar
1½ teaspoons dried yeast
1 standard egg, beaten
3–4 fl. oz water (75–110 ml), hand-hot
1 teaspoon oil

First pour 3 fl. oz (75 ml) of hand-hot water into a basin and whisk in the sugar, followed by the yeast; then leave this mixture on one side for about 10–15 minutes until it gets a nice frothy head on it.

Meanwhile sift the flour and salt together in a mixing bowl. Then pour in the frothy yeast mixture and the beaten egg, and mix to a dough. (You may need to add just a spot of extra warm water—it depends on the flour—but, at the end, you should have a soft, pliable dough that leaves the bowl clean.) Then transfer the dough to a working surface and knead for about 10 minutes until it's silky smooth and fairly elastic.

Now replace the dough in the bowl and rub the surface all over with the oil. Then seal the top of the bowl with cling-film—or cover with a clean, damp cloth—and put the dough in a warmish place to rise for about an hour, or until it has doubled in size.

Once the dough has 'proved' (that is, doubled in size), knead it again for about 5 minutes, and then it's ready to use.

Pizza with salami and mushrooms (serves 2–4 people)	An 8-oz (225 g) tin Italian tomatoes, drained
	1 tablespoon tomato puree
	1 teaspoon dried basil
	4 oz salami or Italian pepperoni sausage (110 g)
	1 tablespoon capers
	1 small pepper, deseeded and finely chopped
	2 oz mushrooms, thinly sliced (50 g)
	2 tablespoons grated Parmesan
	Oil
	Salt and freshly-milled black pepper

Prepare the pizza dough as above and line a tin as in the previous recipe. Pinch out a narrow border and brush the base with oil.

Pre-heat the oven to gas mark 7, 425°F (220°C).

Now either liquidise the tomatoes or simply rub them through a sieve into a bowl. Then stir in the tomato purée and basil, taste, and season with salt and freshly-milled black pepper. Now pour the mixture on to the pizza base and spread it all over.

Next, skin and thinly slice the salami and halve the slices. Then arrange them over the top of the pizza, sprinkle on the chopped pepper, capers, sliced mushrooms and grated Parmesan, and again trickle a little oil over the top. Leave the pizza on one side for about 10 minutes before baking in the oven for 15–20 minutes.

Pizza with Mozzarella, olives and anchovies

(serves 3–4 people)

Mozzarella cheese, or similar types, are sometimes available at delicatessens and specialised food shops, but if you can't get hold of it, make this with thinly sliced Dutch Gouda cheese.

For the tomato sauce:

2 tablespoons oil

1 Spanish onion, peeled and chopped

2 cloves garlic, crushed

2 14-oz (400-g) tins Italian tomatoes

¾ teaspoon dried basil (or fresh if you have it)

1 large bayleaf

Salt and freshly milled black pepper

For the garnish:

4 oz Mozzarella cheese (110 g), cut in small pieces

2-oz (50-g) can anchovy fillets, drained and chopped

1 dozen black olives, pitted and halved

1 teaspoon dried oregano

1 tablespoon grated Parmesan

Oil

A shallow oblong tin, measuring 10 inches × 11 inches (25·5 cm × 28 cm) ungreased.

First prepare the sauce. Heat the oil and fry the onion until softened and golden; then stir in the remaining sauce ingredients and simmer gently (uncovered) for about an hour, or until the tomatoes have reduced to a jam-like consistency. Then take the pan off the heat, discard the bayleaf and leave the sauce to cool. Now place the dough in the tin and push it out with your hands to line it completely, bringing it up at the edges and pinching it to make a sort of border to contain the filling. If the dough is very springy, be determined with it.

Then brush the base of the dough with oil, cover with the tomato filling and spread it right up to the pinched edge. Next sprinkle the surface with the cheese, anchovies, halved olives, dried oregano and Parmesan, drizzle a tablespoon of oil over the top and leave the pizza at room temperature for 10–15 minutes before baking.

Meanwhile pre-heat the oven to gas mark 7, 425°F (220°C).

Then bake the pizza for 15–20 minutes. Check that the bread base is cooked through in the centre by lifting the pizza up with a fish slice and taking a look, and remember it's better to slightly over-cook than under-cook a pizza and always serve it fresh straight from the oven if possible.

Quick wholewheat pizza

(serves 2–4 people)

Wholewheat dough gives a different, somewhat more substantial pizza—every bit as good as the traditional kind.

½ lb wholewheat flour (225 g)
½ teaspoon salt
1 teaspoon yeast
1 teaspoon mixed herbs
6 fl. oz hand-hot water (170 ml)
1 teaspoon sugar
Freshly milled black pepper

For the filling:
14-oz tin Italian tomatoes (400 g)
1 tablespoon olive oil
1 large onion, chopped
1 clove garlic, crushed
1 teaspoon dried basil
1 tablespoon tomato purée
3 thinly-pared slices Cheddar cheese
1 small tin anchovies, drained
2 oz mushrooms (50 g)
6 black olives
A little more mixed herbs

A well-buttered 8-inch (20-cm) sandwich tin.

Combine the flour, salt, herbs and pepper in a bowl, then in a jug measure 6 fl. oz (170 ml) of hand-hot water and whisk in the sugar and yeast. Leave it to get a frothy head (about 10 minutes), then stir the frothed yeast into the dry ingredients and mix to a smooth dough. Then press it down into the well-greased sandwich tin,

Right: Soured cream soda bread, page 54; Muffins, page 59; Quick wheatmeal rolls, page 55; Quick wholewheat pizza, this page.

bringing the dough up the side of the tin. Now leave to rise, covered with a damp cloth, for about 25 minutes.

While that's happening heat the oil in a saucepan and soften the onion. Stir in the contents of the tin of tomatoes, followed by the basil and garlic, and simmer (uncovered) for 25 minutes or until the sauce has reduced to a very thick jam-like consistency. Then add the tomato purée.

Now push the dough lightly back up the side of the tin, if it has slipped during the rising, then spread the tomato sauce over the base of the bread. Scatter the thinly-sliced mushrooms over the top; lay the pieces of cheese over the mushrooms, then add the anchovies, making a faint criss-cross pattern. Next, drizzle a little more olive oil over everything and sprinkle with a few more mixed herbs and the olives.

Bake on a high shelf at gas mark 7, 425°F (220°C), for about 20 minutes. Then serve piping hot with a crisp salad and some Italian wine to drink.

Pissaladiere

(serves 2–4 people)

Just over the border from Italy, in the south of France, they have their own version of pizza—Pissaladiere. In this recipe I have sacrificed total authenticity by using a wholewheat dough (because it's quicker), but you can use a white dough if you prefer.

2 lb large onions (900 g), thinly sliced
4 tablespoons (approx.) olive oil
1 fat clove of garlic, crushed
A 2-oz (56-g) tin of anchovy fillets in oil
1 doz. (approx.) black olives, pitted and halved
1 teaspoon mixed dried herbs
Salt, freshly-milled black pepper
For the dough:
8 oz wholewheat flour (220 g)
1 teaspoon mixed dried herbs
6 fl. oz hand-hot water (175 ml)

Left: Fish kebabs, page 110; Italian baked fish, page 107; Soused herrings, page 115.

1 teaspoon brown sugar
1 teaspoon dried yeast
1 teaspoon of salt
Freshly-milled black pepper

Pre-heat the oven to gas mark 7, 425°F (220°C)

A swiss-roll tin 13 × 9 inches (33 × 23 cm) brushed with oil.

Make the filling first by heating the oil in a large saucepan. Stir in the onions and crushed garlic, then cook them over a gentle heat (uncovered) for about 30 minutes, stirring occasionally, or until the onions have just about formed a soft mass and show a tendency to stick to the base of the pan. Then take the pan from the heat and taste and season with salt and freshly-milled pepper

While the onions are cooking you can combine the flour, salt and herbs, and some freshly-milled pepper together in a bowl. Pour 5 fl. oz (150 ml) of hand-hot water into a separate bowl and, using a fork, whisk in the sugar followed by the yeast. Leave on one side for 10 minutes to froth, then pour this into the flour mixture. Add a further 1 fl. oz (25 ml) of hand-hot water and mix to form a dough.

Then turn the dough out into a lightly floured surface and roll out roughly to a shape 13 × 9 inches (33 × 23 cm). Place it in the tin, pushing it up the sides and into the corners with your fingers. Then brush the dough with olive oil, cover with a clean cloth and leave in a warm place for 20–30 minutes to rise a little.

Now spread the cooked onion filling over the base. Drain the tin of anchovies: reserve the oil and slice the fillets in half lengthways. Arrange them in a diamond-shaped pattern (like lattice-work) all over the onion filling, and stud each diamond with a halved, pitted olive. Sprinkle with the herbs and drizzle the reserved anchovy oil over the lot. Bake on a high shelf of the oven for 20–25 minutes. Serve hot or cold.

Pastry

Of all the cooking skills pastry-making, it seems, is the one that causes most problems. Pondering on why this should be, I think I detect two main reasons: first there are too many conflicting and confusing rules, and secondly pastry-making is one of those skills that needs to be *taught*. It's not an instinct you're either born with or not—it's a technique that needs proper explanation and a little bit of patience and practice. Unfortunately practice is rarely something that is allowed for in cooking. People spend money on driving lessons or learning a foreign language, but when it comes to food—if it doesn't work the first time, it's a 'wicked waste'.

Pastry psychology

Yes, there is a sort of psychology involved. Attitude is the word I think sums it up, your attitude towards pastry-making. Once you've been shown how to do it, you must be bold and self-assertive! Go to it with confidence—I almost think that pastry dough can sense anxiety and then start to play up! True, you need to be light-handed, but in this section you'll learn how to be light-handed. Also true, pastry must not be overhandled, and overhandling is a symptom of nervousness: just as people who lack confidence insist on stirring, prodding or peeping at things, so it is with pastry. So approach this subject with a confident attitude, and I'm sure perfect pastry is just a few pages away.

Pastry perversity

Although there is a set of basic rules for making pastry, there will always be those infuriating people who appear to break or ignore the rules and still turn out perfect pastry. Well . . . other people's cooking often tastes better than your own, if only because you haven't had to do it. If you are a beginner, don't be side-tracked away from the basic ground rules: a hundred and one versions from friends and family will only confuse you.

There are quite a number of different pastries, but here we will be concerned with instructions and recipes for just three: shortcrust, quick flaky, and suet crust. These will suit most purposes for beginners, and later on we will move to the more advanced types of pastry.

Shortcrust pastry

What is shortcrust? There is no such thing—in answer to an 8-year-old who once asked me—as longcrust. Short in this context actually means friable or easily crumbled, so the shorter the pastry

Pastry 73

the crumblier it is. It is the most useful and versatile of all pastries (the kind that crops up in your apple pies or jam tarts), and once this one is mastered the others will be easy to learn.

Flour

Ordinary plain flour is best for shortcrust pastry. Self-raising flour is used by some people, but I think it produces a more 'cakey' texture, being slightly aerated: the finished pastry is softer, less crisp than with plain flour. Air, however, is a vital ingredient, and all flour must be sifted. Sifting is done not only to disperse the lumps, but also to give the flour an airing—so the higher you hold your sieve over the bowl, the further the flour travels and the more air it incorporates. (Because I always sift white flour, I never pay the extra money for superfine or supersifted flours: the ordinary 'own-brand' in a reliable supermarket is perfectly good, so sifting yourself saves money.)

Wholewheat flour can also be used for shortcrust. Because this flour is coarse-textured, the pastry can sometimes seem heavy or difficult to roll. Therefore to combine the flavour of the wholewheat with a lightness of texture, I use the proportion of half wholewheat flour to half white self-raising.

Salt

A generous pinch of salt is often found in many pastry recipes. For my own part I only use it in savoury ones, in which case I season with salt *and* freshly-milled pepper.

Fats

The choice of fat will determine the flavour as well as the texture of your pastry, and here any differences of opinion can probably be only resolved in the end by personal taste, and the type of recipe the pastry is intended for (for instance, to me in a bacon-and-egg pie or a Cornish pasty lard seems to give the 'right' flavour). Below are my own comments on different combinations:

All margarine (block, not soft margarine which is not suitable). This gives a fairly flaky texture, but cooked at a high temperature, gas mark 7, 425° F (220° C) it had a pronounced margarine flavour.

All butter This produces the crunchiest, crispest shortcrust, but although the flavour is good it is also richer and rather more fatty. So I wouldn't choose this for a recipe with a rich, creamy filling. Butter is also a little more difficult to rub in.

All lard makes a shorter and flakier pastry, but it does have a distinctive flavour which is good for savoury recipes and not so good for sweet. Because lard reaches room temperature more quickly than butter or marge, if too soft it can be more difficult to rub in. All-lard pastry also needs less water for mixing.

Half-butter: half lard This is very easy to rub in and handle. The pastry has a good texture with the right amount of crispness, and a good flavour.

Half margarine: half lard Again easy to rub in and roll out—and my personal favourite for most of my own pastry-making. A few experiments will soon reveal your own preferences.

As a rule fat should be used at room temperature. If it is too cold, it will be inconvenient to rub in: if it is too warm, it will be already slightly oily and the additional heat of your hands will make it too soft to rub in correctly (this will only worry you in a heat-wave or a particularly hot kitchen, in which case don't take it out of the fridge too soon). Fat removed from the refrigerator 2 hours before needed is generally about right.

Liquid

Cold water, as cold as possible in fact, is best for shortcrust pastry. The amount you use can vary enormously, because (as we discovered with bread) different flours absorb different amounts. It is best to add a little at first, and a little more as you need to. What you are aiming for in the end is a dough that's smooth without any dryish bits or cracks in it, moist enough to incorporate all the flour and fat and leave the bowl fairly cleanly. Remember that too much water will produce a hard crust, and too little will make the dough difficult to roll out—but having said that, you will find it easy enough to get the right balance.

Shortcrust pastry—basic principles

(1) *Making the dough: keeping cool* It is true everything should be as cool as you can manage for pastry-making, because if the ingredients—and your hands—are too warm the fat becomes too soft, even oily, and it coats more flour grains than it should. The flour is then unable to absorb enough water and the pastry will be too crumbly. However, don't be put off if your kitchen is typically hot and steamy. Open a window and make the pastry as near to the window as possible.

(2) Rubbing in Once the flour is sifted into a bowl, you then divide the fat into smallish lumps and add them to the flour. Start off with a knife and 'cut' the fat into the flour. Then use your finger-tips only: start to lift the pieces of fat up with the flour and rub them gently through your fingers. Now it's well known that light hands make good pastry—that means, in a word, be as *gentle* as you can. Keep lifting your hands high above the bowl to let in the air and, therefore, lightness. Although this process is called 'rubbing in', I'd prefer to call it 'mingling in', which is nearer what it should be.

(3) Mixing We've established that coolness is important, so here speed is what is needed. The less you handle it, the less likely the warmth of your hands will affect it. Once the fat has been evenly distributed and the mixture looks crumbly, you can start to add the water. Run the cold tap for a minute to get it really cold, half-fill a jug and sprinkle in the water all over (for 4 oz of flour start with 3

tablespoons of water). Now use a round-bladed knife to start to mix to a dough, and finish off with your hands to bring it all together, adding more water till you have enough. (I find *sprinkling* the water all over brings it together more quickly than pouring it into the centre and having to work the wet out towards the dry edges.)

(4) Resting It's a bore, but if you don't want your pastry to break as you roll it out or shrink while it is cooking, you must allow it at least 20–30 minutes before you roll it out. Why? Because, as we discovered with bread, the gluten in the flour reacts to water and develops in time, becoming more pliable and elastic (and so easier to roll and less likely to shrink). Wrap the dough carefully in foil or a polythene bag, and leave it to rest in the refrigerator to keep it cool—this covering is important, to prevent the pastry acquiring a tough skin which will break and crack as you start to roll it out.

(5) Rolling What you need for this is a flat surface, a table-top, laminated work-surface or a proper pastry board. Also the length of the rolling-pin is important: the longer it is, the more evenly it

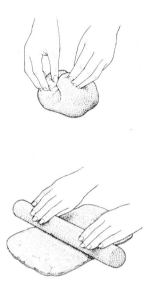

will roll (I find the 18 inch one ideal, and without handles it is far easier to control). A flour dredger is not an expensive item and will sprinkle flour lightly and evenly. Place the dough on a lightly-floured surface, and first shape it with your hands (to a round, or oblong, or whatever your final shape must be).

Give the rolling-pin a dusting of flour, and start to roll with both hands positioned flat at each end of the pin (see illustration), keeping the pressure even and being *gentle*. Save all your aggressions for making bread dough! If the pastry starts sticking to the pin, dust the pin (rather than the pastry) with more flour.

Don't turn the pastry over while you're rolling. It is totally unnecessary, and the pastry you've rolled out will only shrink back and possibly break. When you are rolling a specific shape, always revolve the pastry rather than the rolling-pin. To roll out to a round shape, all you do is keep giving the pastry a quarter-turn after each rolling. Any shape should be rolled fractionally larger than you actually require to line the tin.

(6) Transferring pastry to a tin
The best way is to place the rolling-pin at either end of the pastry, and lightly roll the pastry round the pin, then transfer it to the waiting tin—place the tip of the pastry over one edge of the tin and unroll. Now start to ease the pastry gently into position to line the tin (what you need to keep in mind at this stage is that it is better for the pastry to shrink at the lining stage than to be stretched (otherwise it will shrink in the oven). So ease back any overlapping bits into the tin, leaving yourself as little to trim off as possible. Take care, as well, to press it into position firmly so that no air can be trapped underneath.

Cutting out

Whenever you need to cut out tartlets or pastry shapes, remember to dust the edge of the cutter with flour first. Then place it on the pastry and give it a sharp *tap*. It's very tempting to want to twist the cutter, but my advice is don't, unless you want your round tartlet shapes to turn out oval.

Baking blind

Baking something 'blind' means cooking the pastry on its own in the oven, before the filling goes in. There is a tendency, when this is done, for the base to balloon up during the cooking if there is any air trapped under the pastry. Various remedies for this are used, like lining papers and baking beans to weight the pastry down—but if you have lined the tin properly (see above) these things are redundant. And an extra precaution is to prick the base all over with a fork to release any trapped air (no, the filling won't run through the holes, because as the pastry sets they'll close up again). A final way of making sure is simply to open the oven after 7–8 minutes, have a look and, if the pastry is puffing up, press it back down and prick it once more.

Oven temperatures

These will vary according to the recipe, but most pastry recipes need a pre-heated hot oven (from 375°F to 425°F). A pre-heated baking sheet, too, is essential for anything that needs a crisp base, as this will conduct the heat more efficiently under the tin.

Baking tin, trays, etc.

I cannot stress enough that metal is a so much better conductor of heat than either glass or porcelain. I admit those white fluted porcelain dishes look extremely pretty and many women's magazines show tempting pictures of quiches and flans made in them. But alas, what looks good from the outside is often watery and soggy within—so for crisp, evenly cooked pastry, use metal.

Using shortcrust pastry

So far I have been setting out my own personal notes on ingredients and preferences. However, in the following recipes, the type of fat you use is up to you. If you're a vegetarian, for instance, you will obviously want to use vegetable fat or margarine: similarly any recipe for shortcrust pastry can easily be changed to wholewheat shortcrust if you prefer it.

Basic shortcrust pastry

Since confusion regularly arises over the term '4 oz of shortcrust pastry' (does it mean 4 oz total weight of pastry, or shortcrust made with 4 oz flour?) I have given the required quantities of flour *and* fat.

4 oz flour
1 oz margarine at room temperature
1 oz lard (also at room temperature)
1 pinch of salt
Cold water

Sift the flour and salt into a large mixing bowl, holding the sieve up as high as possible to give the flour an airing. Then cut the fat into small cubes and add them to the flour. Now, using your fingertips, lightly and gently rub the pieces of fat into the flour—lifting your hands up high as you do this (again to incorporate as much air as you can) and being as quick as possible.

When the mixture looks uniformly crumbly, start to sprinkle roughly 2 tablespoons of water all over. Use a round-bladed knife to start the mixing, cutting and bringing the mixture together. Carefully add more water as needed, a little at a time, then finally bring the mixture together with your hands to form a smooth ball of dough that will leave the bowl clean. (If there are any bits that won't adhere to it, you need a spot more water.) Now rest the pastry, wrapped in foil or polythene, in the refrigerator for 20–30 minutes before rolling out.

For *wholewheat pastry*, follow the method above, using 2 oz (50 g) of wholewheat flour and 2 oz (50 g) of white self-raising flour.

Clearly these quantities will vary with each recipe (i.e. you may find you need 8 oz (225 g) of flour and 4 oz (110 g) of fat), but generally speaking the proportion of fat is always half that of the flour.

Deep fruit pies

These are made in the traditional deep, oval, rimmed pie-dishes and only have a crust over the top. The advantage with this type of pie is that you retain all the fragrant juices of the fruits, leaving the top crust crisp and separate.

Apple and blackberry pie

(serves 6 people)

This is best of all made with wild brambles, which seem to have twice as much flavour as the cultivated kind.

For the filling:

1 lb cooking apples (4 medium-sized apples) (450 g)

½ lb brambles, (225 g) washed

3 oz sugar (75 g)

For the shortcrust pastry:

6 oz plain flour (175 g)

1½ oz lard (40 g)

1½ oz margarine (40 g)

A pinch of salt

Cold water to mix

For the glazing:

Milk and caster sugar

Pre-heat the oven to gas mark 7, 425°F (220°C)

You'll also need a 1½ pint (845 ml) rimmed pie-dish.

Start by making the pastry, then leave it to rest while you peel and slice the apples straight into the pie-dish. Then sprinkle in the brambles and then the sugar.

Now roll out the pastry, about 1 inch (2·5 cm) larger than the pie-dish, then cut out a 1 inch (2·5 cm) strip to fit the edge of the dish. Dampen the edge, then fit on the strip of pastry, pressing it firmly and dampen that too. Then press the rest of the pastry over that to form a lid, knock up and flute the edges and make a steam hole in the centre.

Now brush the pastry with milk and sprinkle on a light dusting of caster sugar. Place the pie on a baking sheet on a high shelf and bake for 10 minutes, then reduce the heat to gas mark 5, 375°F (190°C), and continue baking for a further 30 minutes. Then, using a skewer, take out a piece of apple from the centre to test if it's cooked—if not, give it another 5 minutes or so.

Serve hot with chilled pouring cream to mingle with the juices.

Alternatives for deep fruit pies

Here are three different fillings, bearing in mind that the pastry method and cooking times are as in the previous recipe.

English gooseberry pie
For this you'll need 2 lb (900 g) young green gooseberries, 6 oz (175 g) caster sugar and a 1½ pint (845 ml) pie-dish.

Fresh cherry pie
1½ lb (700 g) fresh cherries, 3 level tablespoons Demerara sugar, ½ teaspoon ground cinnamon and a 1½ pint (845 ml) pie-dish.

Damson plum pie
1½ lb (700 g) damsons or damson plums, 4 oz (110 g) sugar and a 1½ pint (845 ml) oval pie-dish.

Basic double-crust fruit pie

The quantities for the recipe below are for any basic fruit pie with a double crust using either pie or wholewheat shortcrust. That is to say the pastry for a 9½ inch (24 cm) enamel pie-plate is always 8 oz (225 g) flour, 4 oz (110 g) fat. The filling is usually 1½ lb (700 g) fruit (see below).

Spiced apple and raisin pie

(serves 6 people)

For the pastry:

4 oz wholewheat flour (110 g)

4 oz self-raising flour (110 g)

2 oz margarine (50 g)

2 oz lard (50 g)

1 pinch salt

Cold water

For the filling:

1½ lb Bramley apples (700 g)

1 oz soft brown sugar (25 g)

¼ teaspoon ground cloves

½ teaspoon ground cinnamon

3 oz raisins (75 g)

2 tablespoons water

¼ whole nutmeg, grated

For the glaze:

Milk and caster sugar

Pre-heat the oven to gas mark 6, 400°F (200°C)

A 9½ inch (24 cm) enamel pie-plate, lightly greased

First quarter, core and peel the apples, then slice them thinly into a saucepan and mix them with the sugar, spices and raisins. Next sprinkle in the water and cook gently (with a lid on) for about 10 minutes or until the apples are soft and fluffy. Then empty the mixture into a bowl to cool.

Next make up the pastry and leave it to rest whilst you pre-heat the oven—putting in a baking sheet—and lightly grease the pie plate.

Roll out a *little more* than half the pastry to a round, then transfer it to line the plate, pressing it gently and firmly all round. Now spoon in the filling, then roll out the other half of the pastry to form a lid. Dampen the bottom layer of pastry round the edge with water, then fix the lid into position, pressing it very firmly all round. Now trim the edges with a knife and use the broad edge of the blade to knock the edges all round, making a layered effect. Then flute the edges by making an impression with your thumb and, using the back of the knife, draw in the edges of the pastry to make a fluted, scalloped effect. Now decorate with the trimmings made into leaves and make a hole in the centre (alternatively, just snip the pie all along the centre with a pair of scissors to make holes) for the steam to escape.

Brush with milk next, then sprinkle on a dusting of caster sugar, which will give a nice crisp sugared surface when the pie is baked.

Place the pie on the baking sheet and bake for 30 minutes.

Alternative fillings for double-crust pies
To get the correct balance of filling, I find it's always best to cook it a little first as the ripeness and sharpness in fruit varies. You can then gauge just the right amount of sugar. Also I've found that cooking the fruit first allows you to get rid of some of the excess juice, i.e. with rhubarb or plums. Alternatively, as with apples, water can be added to make a moister filling.

Apple pie
For the very best flavour use 1 lb (450 g) Bramleys and ½ lb (225 g) Cox's, 1 oz (25 g) sugar and 2 tablespoons water.

Rhubarb

A little ginger always brings out the flavour of rhubarb, so place 2½ lb (1 kg 125 g), cut in chunks, in a saucepan with 1 rounded teaspoon ground ginger and 3 oz (75 g) dark brown sugar but *no* water. Then cook gently, stirring now and then, for about 10 minutes and drain well in a sieve set over a bowl before using.

Summer fruits

A delicious combination: ¾ lb (350 g) raspberries, ¼ lb (110 g) redcurrants, ¼ lb (110 g) blackcurrants, 5 oz (150 g) caster sugar. Place the fruits and sugar in a saucepan and cook, very gently, for just 4 minutes, then drain in a sieve set over a bowl.

Mince pies

(makes 3 dozen)

One tip I may be able to pass on, as a result of years of fraught Christmas preparations—that is, to invest in at least 4 tins which make a dozen tarts each. It's infuriating when a tin only holds nine and it's impossible to place them both on the same shelf. What I now do is bake 2 dozen, a dozen on each shelf, changing over at half-time, and prepare another 2 dozen while they're cooking.

For the pastry:
12 oz plain flour (350 g)
3 oz lard (75 g)
3 oz margarine (75 g)
A pinch of salt
Cold water

Filling:
1½ lb mincemeat (700 g)

For the top:
Milk
Icing sugar

Pre-heat the oven to gas mark 6, 400°F (200°C)

For the normal $2\frac{1}{2}$ inch (6 cm) patty tins
you'll need one fluted 3 inch (7·5 cm)
pastry cutter, one fluted $2\frac{1}{2}$ inch (6 cm)
cutter.

Make up the pastry and allow it to rest for 20–30 minutes. Then
roll half of it out to about $\frac{1}{8}$ inch (3 mm) thick and cut it out into
3 dozen 3 inch (7·5 cm) rounds, gathering up the scraps and re-
rolling again. Then do the same with the other half of the pastry,
this time using the $2\frac{1}{2}$ inch (6 cm) cutter.

Now grease the patty tins lightly and line them with the large
rounds; fill these with the mincemeat (not too much—only to the
level of the edges of the pastry).

Now dampen the edges of the smaller rounds of pastry with water
and press them lightly into position to form lids, sealing the edges.
Brush each one with milk and make about three snips in the top
with a pair of scissors.

Bake near the top of the oven for 25–30 minutes until they're a
light golden-brown. Then cool them on a wire tray and sprinkle
with sifted icing sugar. Store the cooled mince pies in an airtight
tin and warm them slightly before serving.

Lancaster lemon tart

(serves 4–6 people)

This is a first cousin of a Bakewell tart,
using home-made lemon curd instead of
jam, which I think goes very well with
the flavour of almonds.

**Shortcrust pastry made with 3 oz (75 g)
flour and $1\frac{1}{2}$ oz (40 g) fat**

For the filling:

3 rounded tablespoons lemon curd

3 oz butter (room temperature) (75 g)

4 oz self-raising flour (110 g)

3 oz caster sugar (75 g)

1 egg, beaten lightly

1 oz ground almonds (25 g)

The grated zest and juice of a large lemon

**1 oz whole almonds (25 g), peeled and
halved**

Pre-heat the oven to gas mark 6, 400°F (200°C)

You'll need a 7 or 8 inch (18 or 20 cm) enamel pie-plate, lightly greased.

First roll out the pastry and line the pie-plate, crimping the edges, then spread the lemon curd all over the pastry.

Now cream the butter and sugar together till pale and fluffy, then gradually beat in the egg about a teaspoonful at a time. Gently and carefully fold in the ground almonds and flour, followed by the lemon juice and grated zest.

Now spread this mixture evenly over the lemon curd, smoothing it out with a palette knife. Then sprinkle the halved almonds over the surface. Bake it, on a baking sheet, in the centre of the oven for 15 minutes, then reduce the heat to gas mark 2, 300°F (150°C), and continue cooking for a further 25–30 minutes.

This can be served either warm or cold with cream.

Lemon meringue pie
(serves 6 people)

This is one sweet, with its three distinct elements, that needs a careful balance of textures and quantities. The filling has to be lemony enough, neither too stiff nor too oozy. The meringue should be wafery crisp on the outside and soft and marshmallowy within.

For the pastry:
4 oz plain flour (110 g)
1 oz margarine (25 g)
1 oz lard (25 g)

For the filling:
2 large lemons (the grated rind and the juice)
$\frac{1}{2}$ pint cold water (275 ml)
3 level tablespoons cornflour
1$\frac{1}{2}$ oz butter (40 g)
2 large egg yolks
2 oz caster sugar (50 g)

For the meringue:
2 large egg whites
4 oz caster sugar (110 g)

Pre-heat the oven to gas mark 5, 375°F (190°C)

The best dish for this recipe is a deep enamel pie-plate with sloping sides and a rim (measuring 6 inch (16 cm) at the base and 8 inch (20 cm) at the top). Start by making up the pastry and chilling it in the fridge for 20 minutes. Then roll it out to a round about $\frac{1}{3}$ inch larger all round than the rim of the tin. Cut away a narrow ($\frac{1}{3}$ inch) strip all round, dampen the rim of the tin with water and fix this pastry strip on it all round, pressing down well. Next dampen the pastry strip and transfer the pastry round to line the tin—making sure you don't trap any air underneath it. Then flute the edge of the pastry and prick the base all over with a fork. Bake on a high shelf of the oven for 20–25 minutes or until cooked through.

Remove the pastry case from the oven, and immediately lower the heat to gas mark 2, 300°F (150°C) (for the meringue).

Next the filling: measure $\frac{1}{2}$ pint of cold water into a jug and spoon the cornflour and sugar into a bowl. Add enough of the measured water to mix the cornflour to a smooth paste, then pour the rest of the water along with the grated lemon into a small saucepan. Bring this up to the boil, then pour it onto the cornflour paste and mix till smooth.

Transfer the mixture back to the saucepan and bring back to the boil. Then simmer gently for 1 minute—stirring all the time to prevent it from catching. Remove the pan from the heat and beat in the egg yolks, lemon juice and finally the butter. Pour the lemon mixture into the pastry shell and spread it out evenly.

Finally the meringue: for this use a large roomy bowl and in it whisk the egg whites till they form stiff peaks. Beat in a quarter of the caster sugar at a time until it is all incorporated, then spread the meringue mixture all over the filling. Use a broad-bladed knife to spread the meringue to the very edge of the pastry rim, so it seals the top completely. (With your knife you can also make a few decorative swirls.) Cook in the oven for 45 minutes, by which time the meringue will have turned pale beige, and be duly crisp on the outside and squashy within. Serve warm or cold.

Wholewheat treacle tart

(serves 6 people)

I think the crunchiness of wholewheat pastry, and wholewheat breadcrumbs too, make a nicer treacle tart than the traditional version.

For the pastry:
2 oz wholewheat flour (50 g)
2 oz self-raising flour (50 g)
A pinch of salt
1 oz lard (25 g)
1 oz margarine (25 g)
Water to mix

For the filling:
4 oz wholewheat breadcrumbs (110 g)
5 tablespoons golden syrup
1 tablespoon black treacle
Some milk

Pre-heat the oven to gas mark 5, 375°F (190°C)

An 8 inch (20 cm) fluted flan tin with a loose base (lightly greased).

If you place both treacle tins in the oven whilst it's pre-heating, you'll find the treacle easier to measure.

Meanwhile make the pastry and allow it to rest for 20–30 minutes. Then roll it out thinly and line the flan tin with it, cutting off and keeping the pastry trimmings on one side.

Then measure out the warmed treacle and syrup into a bowl, and stir in the breadcrumbs quite thoroughly before pouring the whole lot into the prepared pastry case.

Now roll out the pastry trimmings and cut strips long enough to make a criss-cross pattern all over the surface of the tart. Then brush the strips and edges lightly with milk and place the tart on a baking sheet in the oven. Bake it for about 30–35 minutes. Serve still warm with some chilled whipped cream.

Cornish pasty pie

(serves 6 people)

I find Cornish pasties often have too much pasty and not enough filling. However, the traditional filling of steak, potato and turnip is so delicious I now make one big pie using this filling— which is also a lot quicker than making individual pasties.

For the pastry:

6 oz lard (175 g)

12 oz plain flour (350 g)

Water, to mix

Salt and freshly-milled pepper

For the filling:

1¼ lb chuck steak (560 g)

1 medium to large turnip

1 medium to large potato

1 large onion, finely chopped

½ teaspoon mixed herbs

1 tablespoon water

Salt and freshly-milled pepper

To glaze:

Beaten egg

Pre-heat the oven to gas mark 6, 400°F (200°C)

A well-greased 10 inch (25·5 cm) fluted metal quiche tin.

Make the pastry first, adding a little salt and pepper to season it, then pop it into a plastic bag and leave it in the fridge for 10–15 minutes. Meanwhile, slice the meat into very thin strips about 2 inch (5 cm) long (it's important to keep them very thin— in order that they cook in the time given).

Place the meat in a mixing bowl, with the chopped onion and mixed herbs. Then peel the potato and turnip and slice these as thinly as possible too (the slicing edge on a four-sided grater does this thin slicing job in moments). Now add the turnip and potato to the meat, season with salt and pepper, and mix very thoroughly.

Next roll out half the pastry, large enough to line the tin with about ½ inch (1 cm) overlapping. Spoon the filling in, spreading it evenly all over, then sprinkle in 1 tablespoon of water.

Roll out the other half of the pastry, dampen the edge all round, then fit it over the top of the pie. Then seal the edges, folding them inwards and pressing gently to make a rim just inside the edge of the tin. Make a steam-hole in the centre (about the size of a 10p piece), brush the surface with beaten egg, and bake the pie on a baking sheet, on a high shelf, for 15 minutes. Then turn the heat down to gas mark 4, 350°F (180°C), and continue to cook on the centre shelf for a further 1½ hours. This is still very good eaten cold, so it's a good idea for a picnic.

Quiches and open tarts

For years I've been experimenting with this type of recipe to eliminate—for ever—the problem of the soggy pastry base that seems to plague so many people, myself included. I'm happy to announce that the problem seems largely solved by (a) pre-baking the pastry case, (b) *always* using a baking sheet underneath the tin, (c) painting the inside of the pre-baked pastry shell with beaten egg and allowing it to rest for 5 minutes in the oven before the filling goes in. I have already said (but will stress again) that the container must be *metal*, not porcelain or glass.

Quiche pastry

4 oz plain flour (110 g)
Pinch of salt
1 oz lard (25 g)
1 oz margarine (25 g)
Cold water

This will be enough for a lightly-greased 8 inch (20 cm) quiche or flan tin with fluted edges and a removable base.

Make up the pastry, then rest it for 20–30 minutes in a polythene bag in the fridge.

Meanwhile, pre-heat the oven to gas mark 4, 350°F (170°C), with a baking sheet placed on the centre shelf.

Then roll out the pastry and line the tin with it, easing any overlapping pastry back into the sides if you can. Be careful to press firmly on the base and sides, then prick with a fork all over. Bake the pastry case for 15 minutes on the centre shelf, then remove it from the oven and paint the inside of it, all over, with some of the beaten egg in the filling ingredients, and pop it back into the oven to set for a further 5 minutes.

Now add the filling and bake for a further 30–40 minutes until the quiche is set in the centre and has turned golden-brown and looks puffy.

Mushroom and onion quiche

This is made with what the French called 'duxelles', a paste made with chopped mushrooms and onion. For the lightest and best quiche filling use double cream or single. If you're economising, milk will do.

$\frac{1}{2}$ lb flat mushrooms (225 g), chopped very, very small
1 medium onion, also chopped very small
2 large eggs
$\frac{1}{2}$ pint double cream (275 ml)
1 oz butter (25 g)
Freshly-grated nutmeg
Salt and freshly-milled black pepper

Heat the butter in a saucepan and soften the onion in it for 5 minutes or so. Now stir in the chopped mushrooms and let it all cook gently (uncovered) for half an hour or until most of the juice has evaporated—giving it a stir quite often. Transfer the filling to the tart with a draining spoon, and arrange it evenly over the base.

Whisk the eggs thoroughly, then whisk the cream into them and season with salt, pepper and a small grating of nutmeg. Pour this mixture over the filling, put the flan on the baking sheet in the oven and bake for 35–40 minutes, or until the centre is set and the filling golden and puffy.

Serve straight from the oven, if possible (though this does re-heat quite well).

Courgette and cheese quiche	$\frac{1}{2}$ lb courgettes (225 g)
	1 oz butter (25 g)
	2 oz grated cheese (preferably Gruyère) (50 g)
	1 small onion, finely chopped
	2 large eggs
	$\frac{1}{2}$ pint single or double cream (275 ml)
	1 tablespoon grated Parmesan cheese
	Salt and pepper

Slice the courgettes fairly thinly. Soften the onion in the butter in a frying-pan for 5 minutes, then add the courgettes and brown them a little, turning them frequently. Now transfer both onions and courgettes to the pastry case, sprinkle the grated cheese over them, and proceed as in the previous recipe (and sprinkling the Parmesan over the top before baking).

Kipper quiche
For this use 8 oz (225 g) cooked, flaked kippers, add 2 teaspoons mustard, some freshly-grated nutmeg and a couple of pinches of cayenne pepper to the egg and cream mixture and proceed as above.

Quick flaky pastry
This pastry is surely heaven-sent. It's uncomplicated, no trouble to roll out and handle, and tastes really crisp and flaky. That doesn't sound like the flaky pastry you've heard about? Probably not—the advanced version certainly calls for time and effort, which few of us can spare. In this one, a much higher percentage of fat than in shortcrust is *grated* directly into the flour, so eliminating the repeated processes of rolling out, folding over and half-turning which make the traditional flaky pastry so time-consuming. The results, I'm quite certain, will speak for themselves.

Quick flaky pastry	8 oz plain flour
	6 oz margarine
	A pinch of salt
	Cold water

The margarine has to be block (not soft 'tub' margarine, which is not suitable). Take it hard from the fridge, weigh out the required amount, then wrap it in a piece of foil and return it to the freezing compartment of the refrigerator for half an hour. Meanwhile sift the flour and salt into a mixing bowl.

When you take the margarine out of the freezer hold it in the foil, dip it into the flour, then grate it on a coarse grater placed in the bowl over the flour. Keep dipping the margarine down into the flour to make it easier to grate. At the end you will be left with a lump of grated fat in the middle of the flour, so now take a palette knife and start to cut it into the flour—don't use your hands—until the mixture is crumbly. Now add enough water to bring it to form a dough that leaves the bowl clean, using your hands. Pop the dough into a polythene bag and chill it for half an hour—this time in the main body of the fridge.

Sausage rolls with quick flaky pastry

(makes about 24)

Quick flaky pastry made with 8 oz flour and 6 oz margarine
1 lb good pork sausage meat (450 g)
1 medium onion, grated
1 teaspoon sage
1 egg beaten with 1 tablespoon milk

Pre-heat the oven to gas mark 7, 425°F (220°C)

Make up the pastry as above, and leave it to rest in the refrigerator for half an hour. Mix the sausage meat, onion and sage together thoroughly in a mixing bowl, then on a floured surface roll out the pastry to form an oblong (as thin as you can). Cut this oblong into three, then divide the sausage-meat mixture also into three, making three long rolls the same length as the pastry (if it's sticky sprinkle on some flour).

Place one roll of sausage meat onto one strip of pastry. Brush the beaten egg mixture along one edge, then fold the pastry over and seal it as carefully as possible. Lift the whole thing up and turn it, so that when you put it down the sealed edge is underneath. Press lightly, then cut into individual rolls each about 2 inches long. Snip three V-shapes in the top of each roll with scissors, and brush with beaten egg. Then repeat all this with the other portions of pastry and meat. Place all the rolls on a baking-sheet and bake high in the oven for 20–25 minutes. Store the sausage rolls in a tin, and warm them slightly before serving.

Bœuf en croute
(serves 6 people)

Fillet steak is overwhelmingly expensive, but for a very special occasion it does make a most attractive and delicious main course, wrapped in pastry with a mushroom stuffing.

For the quick flaky pastry:
6 oz plain flour (175 g)
4 oz margarine (110 g)
Cold water

The rest of the ingredients:
1¾ lb thick end fillet steak (800 g)
1 Spanish onion
¾ lb mushrooms (350 g)
2 oz butter (50 g)
A little brandy
Beaten egg
Salt, freshly-milled pepper, and nutmeg

Pre-heat the oven to gas mark 5, 375°F (190°C)

First of all make up the pastry, pop it into a polythene bag and chill it in the body of the fridge for half an hour. Meanwhile you can be trimming the meat, removing any excess fat and bits of sinew. Brush it all over with some brandy, rub ½ oz (10 g) of butter over it, place it in a roasting tin and cook for 40 minutes (basting it now and then with the juices). Then remove from the oven and leave to get quite cold.

Chop the onion and mushroom as finely as possible, then melt the remaining 1½ oz (40 g) of butter in a small saucepan. Stir the onion into it, allow it to cook for 5 minutes, then stir in the mushroom and continue to cook the mixture over a gentle heat (without a lid) for about 20–25 minutes, so that the juices will be drawn out of the mushrooms and onion and evaporate, leaving you with a concentrated mixture. The final mixture *mustn't* be too liquid.

Season it then with salt, pepper and a grating of nutmeg. When both the meat and mushroom mixture are ready, pre-heat the oven to gas mark 8, 450°F (230°C). Take the pastry from the fridge and roll it out to a rectangle approx. 14 × 10 inch (35·5 × 25·5 cm). Trim the edges (keep the trimmings for decoration), then spread half the mushrooms over the centre. Place the fillet on top and the rest of the mushroom on top of that: pat it down into a good shape. Now brush the edges of the pastry with beaten egg, and wrap the pastry like a parcel round the meat—if necessary brush the edges at each end and fold them over again.

Place the whole lot on a baking sheet, brush all over with beaten egg (including any decorations you have added), and bake in the oven for a further 30 minutes. This should be served cut into thick slices, together with some gravy made with the meat juices left in the roasting tin and some red wine.

Eccles cakes
(makes about 18–20)

These spicy currant pastries are, predictably, a northern delicacy—which are never better than when homemade.

For the quick flaky pastry:
8 oz plain flour (225 g)
6 oz margarine (175 g)
A good pinch of salt
Cold water to mix

For the filling:
3 oz butter (75 g)
5 oz soft brown sugar (150 g)
5 oz currants (150 g)
1 teaspoon cinnamon
$\frac{1}{2}$ teaspoon freshly-grated nutmeg
The grated rind of 1 large orange
2 oz finely-chopped peel (50 g)

To finish off:
Milk and caster sugar

A greased baking sheet.

To make the pastry, weigh the margarine (hard from the refrigerator), then wrap it in a piece of foil and place it in the freezing compartment of the fridge for half an hour.

Meanwhile sift the flour and salt into a bowl, then when you take the margarine out of the freezer hold it with the foil, dip it into the flour, then grate it on a coarse grater placed in the bowl over the flour. Carry on dipping the margarine down into the flour to make it easier to grate. When you have finished you will have a lump of grated margarine sitting in the middle of the flour. Then take a palette knife and start to cut the fat into the flour (don't use your hands) until the mixture is crumbly. Now add enough water so that it forms a dough that leaves the bowl clean (you *can* use your hands for the dough), then place it in a polythene bag and chill it in the main part of the refrigerator for half an hour.

Meanwhile, prepare the filling by first melting the butter in a small saucepan. Then take it off the heat and stir in all the filling ingredients quite thoroughly and leave it to cool.

Next turn the dough out into a lightly-floured surface. Roll it out to about $\frac{1}{8}$ inch (3 mm) thick, then using a plain $3\frac{1}{2}$ inch (8 cm) cutter, cut the pastry into rounds. Put a teaspoon of filling onto each round, then brush the edge of half the circle of pastry with water, and bring the other side up to seal it. Then bring the corners up to the centre and pinch to seal well. Now turn your sealed pastry parcel over, so that the seam is underneath, then gently roll it flat to about $\frac{1}{4}$ inch thick ($\frac{1}{2}$ cm) and pat it into a round shape.

Place them all onto the greased baking sheet and gash each cake diagonally across three times, using a sharp knife. Now brush them with milk and sprinkle with caster sugar and bake them in the oven pre-heated to gas mark 7, 425°F (220°C), for about 15 minutes or until golden-brown. Then transfer them to a wire rack to cool.

Suet crust pastry

If you've never tried this pastry, then it's a must next time you make steak and kidney pie. Because it is made with shredded beef suet, it has the best possible flavour for a beefsteak pie. But more than that—it is beautifully easy to make since there is no rubbing-in. It is resilient and easy to roll out, and it is deliciously light and crusty.

Important note: Suet crust is always made with self-raising flour, because suet being a heavy fat the pastry needs a raising agent to aerate it and make it lighter. And as it is made with self-raising flour, it follows that suet crust should always be rolled out and used *immediately*—because once the raising agent in the flour becomes damp it will begin to lose its raising power. This pastry can't be made in advance, but it is easy to make so this should not be a problem.

Butcher's suet

Butcher's suet can be used, but it's a very tedious job separating
the suet from all the skin and membrane and then grating it
finely. Packet suet is quite pure, with just a fine coating of flour
(or rice flour) to keep the grains separate.

Basic suet crust pastry

These quantities will be enough to top
a 1½ pint rimmed pie-dish. (For a 2½
pint pie-dish use 12 oz of self-raising
flour and 6 oz of shredded suet.)

8 oz self-raising flour (225 g)
4 oz shredded suet (110 g)
Cold water
Salt and freshly-milled pepper (for a savoury crust)

Sift the flour into a bowl, then sprinkle the suet in and just mix
it in lightly with your hands to distribute it evenly. Now sprinkle
in some cold water (you'll find you need more for this pastry
than for shortcrust). Begin mixing with a round-bladed knife,
and then use your hands at the end to bring it all together to a
smooth elastic dough that leaves the bowl clean.

Suet crust should be left for 5 minutes, then rolled out
immediately. Remember, too, that you always roll it out rather
more thickly than shortcrust (approximately ½ inch thick).

Beefsteak and kidney pie

(serves 4 people)

Once you've eaten this, I'm sure you
will never want to make it with
anything but suet crust again.

Suet crust pastry made with 8 oz flour and 4 oz suet as above
For the filling:
1½ lb chuck steak (700 g) cut into 1 inch cubes
6 oz ox kidney (175 g), chopped
½ lb dark-gilled mushrooms (225 g)
2 medium onions, roughly chopped
1½ tablespoons flour

1 tablespoon beef dripping
$\frac{3}{4}$ pint beef stock (425 ml)
$\frac{1}{2}$ teaspoon Worcestershire sauce
2 teaspoons mushroom ketchup
$\frac{1}{2}$ teaspoon dried mixed herbs
Salt and freshly-milled black pepper

In a large saucepan fry the chopped onion in the dripping for a few minutes, then add the cubes of steak and the kidney. Continue to cook (stirring now and then) till the meat is nicely browned, then add the flour and stir it in well. Add the herbs next, followed by the Worcestershire sauce and the ketchup: season with salt and pepper and gradually stir in the stock. Finally add the mushrooms (sliced), bring the whole lot to simmering point, and simmer gently for about 2 hours or until the meat is tender. When cooked, check the seasoning and pour everything into an oval pie-dish (see below). Then pre-heat the oven to gas mark 7, 425°F (220°C).

Mix the pastry to a smooth elastic dough, and roll it out on a lightly-floured surface to a shape about 1 inch (2·5 cm) larger than the rim of the pie-dish. Now cut a 1 inch (2·5 cm) strip all round, dampen the edge of the pie-dish and press this pastry strip on. Then dampen the strip and lay the pastry lid on top, pressing it down and sealing it around the edge. Flute the edge, make a small steam-hole in the centre, and bake in the oven for 30–40 minutes, until the pastry is golden-brown.

Note: For this recipe you need a 2 pint (1 litre) pie-dish. To make a pie for 6 people, use a 3 pint (1·5 litre) dish (and the ingredients will be 2$\frac{1}{2}$ lb (1 kg) chuck steak, $\frac{3}{4}$ lb (350 g) ox kidney, $\frac{1}{2}$ lb (225 g) mushrooms, 2 tablespoon flour, 1 pint (570 ml) stock; and for the pastry: 12 oz (350 g) self-raising flour, 6 oz shredded suet.

Beefsteak and kidney pudding

(serves 4 people)

Properly made, I think this is one of the glories of real British cooking! For notes on steaming see page 236.

For the suet crust pastry:
12 oz self-raising flour (350 g)
6 oz shredded suet (175 g)
Salt, pepper and cold water

For the filling:
1 lb chuck steak (450 g)
½ lb ox kidney (225 g)
1 medium onion, sliced
2 level tablespoons well-seasoned flour
Some Worcestershire sauce
Cold water
Salt and freshly-milled pepper

Make up the pastry to form an elastic dough that leaves the bowl clean, keep a quarter of it (for a lid), roll the rest out and line a well-buttered 2 pint (1 litre) pudding basin with it. Next chop the steak and the kidney into fairly small cubes, toss them in the seasoned flour, then add them to the pastry-lined basin. Pop the slices of onion in here and there, then add enough cold water to reach almost to the top of the meat and sprinkle in a few drops of Worcestershire sauce and season.

Roll out the pastry lid, dampen its edges and put it in position on the pudding. Seal well and cover with a double sheet of foil—pleated in the centre to allow room for expansion while cooking—secure with string, and place it in a steamer over boiling water. Steam for 5 hours—you may find you need to add more boiling water halfway through.

Old English rabbit pie

(serves 4–6 people)

This is a really delicious pie, good for a dinner party—and if you can get hold of a wild rabbit for it so much the better.

For the suet crust pastry:
12 oz self-raising flour (350 g)
6 oz shredded suet (175 g)
Cold water, to mix
½ teaspoon salt
Freshly-milled black pepper

For the filling:
1 rabbit approx. 3 lb (1 kg 350 g), cut into joints
2 medium onions, chopped fairly small
½ lb unsmoked streaky bacon (225 g), in one piece

1 medium cooking apple, peeled and sliced
¼ lb pitted prunes (110 g) (weighed after the stones have been removed), chopped
½ pint dry cider (275 ml)
¾ pint stock (or water) (425 ml)
½ whole nutmeg, grated
1 bayleaf
1½ oz plain flour (40 g) *and* 1½ oz butter (40 g) mixed together to a smooth paste
Salt and freshly-milled black pepper

Pre-heat the oven to gas mark 7, 425°F (220°C)

A 2½ pint (1·5 l) pie-dish.

Wash the rabbit joints first of all, and place them (apart from the ribs, which don't carry much meat) in a large saucepan. Tuck in the onion and apple amongst the meat. Now remove the rind from the bacon, chop the meat up into 1 inch (2·5 cm) cubes and add that to the saucepan along with the bayleaf, a little salt and some freshly-milled pepper. Pour in the cider and the stock, bring to simmering point, skim off any bits of scum, then put a lid on and leave to simmer gently for about an hour or until tender.

When it's cooked remove the rabbit pieces together with the bacon, apple and onion (with a draining spoon) and transfer them to the pie-dish, sprinkling in the chopped prunes as well. Now add the butter-and-flour mixture to the stock in the saucepan, adding it in tiny (peanut-size) pieces, stir them round over a medium heat to melt and thicken the sauce. Sprinkle in the nutmeg and when the sauce reaches simmering point pour it over the rabbit.

Now make up the suet crust pastry. Mix the flour, salt, pepper and suet together, then add enough cold water to form a fairly soft, elastic dough that leaves the bowl cleanly. Roll the dough out to a shape 1 inch (2·5 cm) wider than the top of the pie-dish, and cut a 1 inch (2·5 cm) wide strip all round. Dampen the edge of the dish and press this strip around the rim of the dish. Now dampen the rim of the pastry, and place the pastry lid in position on top, pressing well all round to seal the edges, which can be decorated with fluting if you like. Make a small hole for steam to escape, then bake for 30 minutes or until golden-brown.

Fish

Including recipes for:

Unfortunately one of the really essential ingredients in fish cookery is the one that so often is missing, namely a good fishmonger. In many parts of the country fishmongers of any description have become rather thin on the ground, and to find a really reliable one has grown increasingly difficult. This is partly offset by the ready and regular supply of commercially-frozen fish (which is probably the root cause of our vanishing fishmongers in the first place). However, unlike other types of frozen food, frozen fish has much to commend it: only the best quality is frozen and sub-zero temperatures do not materially affect the flavour—indeed very often rather more fresh flavour is retained by freezing (since it is generally carried out immediately or soon after the fish is caught).

Having said that though, there is nothing to compensate for a trustworthy and friendly fishmonger, who is willing to help and advise. There are two ways to tell a good one: firstly if his shop is busy and attracting a lot of regular custom, and secondly by how much fish there is left on the slab towards the end of the afternoon. If there is a lot then beware, because it's all going to be put away and brought out again the next day. (One of the best fishmongers I ever knew was virtually sold out by two o'clock every day.)

In spite of our proud fish 'n' chip shop tradition and the dreaded, breaded fish fingers, as a nation we don't eat nearly enough fish. I suspect this is because, unlike some other countries, we have always had an over-plentiful supply of meat. Yet fish contains as much protein as meat, is easier to digest, and has one crucial advantage: it can be cooked so quickly. If you don't have a lot of time for cooking, think of fish. It can be grilled, fried, poached or baked to provide a nutritious meal in hardly any time at all.

Buying fresh fish
There is no mistaking really fresh fish. It has a plumpness and firmness about it that proclaims it to be fresh straight away. Scaled fish should have a sequin-like iridescence, and all fishes' eyes look sparkling, almost alert (and in the case of herrings, red). In general the thing to look for is overall brightness: stale fish, however often they are hosed down, look grey, dull and droopy with blurred eyes and flabby flesh.

Preparing fish
All fish, with the exception of sprats and other tiny species, should be gutted by the fishmonger, and all fish, apart from mackerel and

herrings (see pages 114–115), should be skinned and filleted—if that's what is needed—by him. Why struggle at home with diagrams and blunt filleting knives, when you can have the job done for you at no extra cost? In fact fish is now so expensive it's all the more reason to have it prepared for you.

If you want to cook fish on the bone, then just ask to have it gutted and, where appropriate, scaled (if the fishmonger doesn't make a proper job of this, you can do it yourself by simply scraping along the skin with the blunt side of a knife in the opposite direction to the way the scales are, i.e. from head to tail). If you are lucky enough to buy your fish straight off a boat or even catch it yourself, then gutting at home isn't too complicated. You can either remove the insides through the gill-slits (if the heads are to be left on) by squeezing and scraping with a teaspoon, or by making a slit along the belly, opening the fish out and then scraping. If you are cutting off the heads some of the entrails will come out attached to the gills (which are bright red flaps underneath openings on each side of the head, and should also be cut away before cooking). Always wash away any traces of blood and slime, and then dry the fish as thoroughly as possible with kitchen paper or a clean cloth.

Storing fish
Like anything else, fish that has been frozen should not be allowed to thaw out and then be re-frozen—so if you want to freeze some yourself, check that it is very fresh. The safest rule obviously is to eat fresh fish as soon as possible, though a day's storage in the refrigerator isn't going to hurt. One exception to this, and a curious one, is the Dover sole, which because of a chemical that develops after death actually improves in flavour a couple of days after it is caught. How kind of nature to give us at least one variety of fish that can cope with the time taken up by its journey inland.

The methods of cooking fish
Shallow-frying To shallow-fry a whole, or part of a fish to the best degree of crispness, use olive oil. If on the other hand you'd like to get a buttery flavour, then use half oil and half butter (on its own butter burns too easily and can spoil the flavour). Solid fat is not very good for fish—except perhaps bacon fat or pure lard for frying herrings. Have enough oil or fat in the pan to give a depth of $\frac{1}{8}$ inch (3 mm) and make sure it is really hot before the fish goes in. I think it best to thaw frozen fish before frying, whatever it says on the packet: the coldness of the fish brings the temperature of the fat down dramatically (and that is what makes food oily). Times for

shallow-frying fish are approximately the same as for grilling
(see below).

Deep-frying Olive oil or groundnut oil is to be preferred for this—
both can be stored and used several times over, but be careful to
label the jar 'fish oil'. Ideally a cooking thermometer should be
used to check the correct temperature of the oil (370°F, 187·5°C for
fillets, goujons and fish in batter; 375°F, 190·5°C for whitebait,
croquettes and fishcakes), and always warm the thermometer in
hot water first to prevent the glass cracking. If you have no cooking
thermometer, the best way of testing if the oil is hot enough is to
thaw a small cube of bread into it and if it turns golden-brown in
60 seconds you can go ahead. Do not, however, allow the oil to
overheat or the flavour will be spoiled.

The pan needs to be only one-third full of oil—any more than
that and there is a danger of it bubbling over when the food goes
in. A frying basket isn't necessary—the fish or the batter has a
habit of getting stuck in the mesh—just use a draining-spoon with a
long handle to get the fish in and out.

Fish destined for the deep-fryer ought to be at room
temperature: chilled or frozen fish lowers the oil heat and the food
will taste soggy and oily (and in any event try, if you can, to raise
the heat under the pan as you lower the fish in, then turn it down
again). To tell if the fish is cooked, the batter or coating turning a
golden-brown is a good indication. Small fish or pieces of fish rise
to the surface when they are cooked. But if in doubt, the best way
of all is to try a bit. Always drain fried fish on crumpled greaseproof
paper before serving.

Grilling The first tip here is to line the grill pan or grid with foil
before you start—this will prevent a fishy flavour lingering in the
pan. Pre-heat the grill to high, before placing the fish under it.
White fish need to be brushed generously with melted butter before
grilling and basted with the buttery juices when you turn them.

Type and size of fish	Grilling time
Whole Dover sole and plaice	4–6 minutes each side
Fillets of sole or plaice	2–3 minutes each side
Fish steaks (salmon, halibut, cod, turbot, etc.) weighing approx. 6–8 oz	Allow 5–6 minutes each side, and have extra butter ready for basting during cooking to prevent dryness

Whole mackerel	Make 3 diagonal scores on each side and for 8 oz (225 g) fish brush with melted butter. Grill for approx. 6–7 minutes each side
Herring	For 6–8 oz (225 g) fish, score as above and allow 4–5 minutes grilling on each side

Poaching For poaching you need some form of liquid, though not too much of it: a mixture of white wine (or dry cider) and water with a few herbs, a bayleaf, peppercorns, sliced onion, sliced carrot and a piece of lemon peel is a very suitable poaching liquid. Or for some white fish a mixture of milk and water with flavourings is used. The operative word here is gentle—the liquid should barely simmer, in order not to overcook or break up the fish. Rolled-up fillets of sole or plaice will only need 4–5 minutes poaching: larger whole fish or pieces weighing $1\frac{1}{2}$–2 lb (700–900 g) will need 7–10 minutes. I have to admit that, on the whole, I think it preferable to cook fish in the oven in foil rather than poach it, as this retains more of the flavour.

Steaming A useful method to know, which offers gentle cooking that safeguards the flavour and juices of the fish. Again foil is useful: just butter a piece of foil generously, lay the fish in it with some seasoning and a squeeze of lemon juice, then wrap it up into a parcel and place in a steamer over boiling water. Depending on thickness it will take 10–15 minutes to cook. (You can save on fuel with this method, by placing the steaming fish over the potatoes as they're boiling.)

Baking This way the fish is brushed with melted butter or with oil (maybe with a stuffing added) and then baked in the oven— sometimes open, sometimes lightly covered with a piece of buttered foil for protection. At other times a small quantity of poaching liquid is used, or extra butter for basting: methods of baking vary quite a lot, so see instructions in individual recipes.

In foil or en papillote This is an excellent way to cook fish, because all the essential flavour and juices are retained inside a sealed parcel (which when opened will give off a beautiful, fragrant and appetising aroma). For fish like salmon and salmon trout, which are sometimes served cold, the parcels can be left unopened until just before serving. Various flavourings can be added: lemon juice, wine, butter, slivers of onion, garlic, fresh herbs. In Italy I have eaten sole cooked like this surrounded by fresh mint leaves. For timings, see individual recipes.

Popular varieties of fish

In the British Isles there are five main groups of fish available to us; white fish, oily fish, freshwater fish, smoked fish and shellfish. These last two groups will be dealt with in a later book. Of the others let's look first at some of the most popular varieties of the group known as white fish.

Sole

First—because it is said to have the finest flavour of all—is the *Dover sole*. This is a flat fish, weighing anything from 8 oz up to 2 lb (225–900 g), white on the under-side with its speckled grey camouflage on the upper-side, with a rounded not pointed head. Its flavour is best preserved by serving it simply: brushed with melted butter, grilled in its own juices and served with some parsley butter and lemon juice. I also believe that any fish (like meat) benefits in taste from being cooked on the bone instead of filleted.

Grilled Dover sole on the bone Ask the fishmonger to skin it for you. Then brush it with melted butter, and give it from about 4 to 6 minutes on each side under the hot grill, depending on thickness.

Lemon soles (and *Witch soles*) are similar fish, but look rather more pointed. They are certainly cheaper but don't compare in flavour.

Goujons of sole

(serves 2 as a main course or 4 as a first course)

Goujons are small strips of fish coated in egg and breadcrumbs.

To make this more economical you could use plaice fillets but, either way, ask the fishmonger to skin them for you.

8 small fillets of sole or plaice
3 level tablespoons of well-seasoned flour
1 large egg, beaten
4 oz fresh white breadcrumbs (110 g)
Some oil for deep frying

To garnish:
Chopped parsley and slices of raw onion

First wipe the fillets and cut them into thinnish strips diagonally across the grain. Roll the strips in the seasoned flour, then dip them first in the beaten egg and then in the breadcrumbs. (Have the breadcrumbs on a flat working surface so that you can roll the strips under the palm of your hand to get them well and evenly coated.)

Next heat the oil in a deep pan to 350°F (180°C)—test the temperature either with a thermometer or drop in a small cube of bread and if it turns golden and crisp in one minute it's hot enough. Then deep fry the fish for 2–3 minutes until golden-brown. You'll probably need to do the frying in 2 or 3 separate lots. When cooked, drain on crumpled greaseproof paper. Serve garnished with chopped parsley and slices of raw onion.

Skate

Swimming in the sea, a skate looks like a cross between Concorde and a space-craft, with its huge wings. The wings are what we buy at the fishmonger, triangular in shape with a pinky flesh (if they are from a small fish they weigh about 8 oz (225 g) each, if from a large fish they are bought cut into pieces). It is a delicious fish: the flesh parts so conveniently from the soft bones, which themselves stay intact, so there is little likelihood of finding any unwelcome, spiky bits of bone. It is hard to beat just washed, well dried, given a light coating of flour, then fried in a mixture of butter and oil till crisp and golden: or else served with browned butter, which adds a lovely buttery flavour as in the next recipe.

A group of white fish belonging to the skate family—and often referred to rather misleadingly as rock salmon—are the *dogfish*, *huss* or *flake*. In fact they have nothing at all in common with salmon, actually are rather dull (if cheap) and need to be jazzed up a bit with other ingredients.

Skate with black butter

(serves 4 people)

The important thing to remember here is not to overcook the butter—a split second too much and it can be burnt rather than browned.

4 skate wings
3 tablespoons white wine vinegar
1 bayleaf
1 blade mace
A couple of sprigs of parsley

| 1 level tablespoon chopped capers |
| Salt and freshly-milled black pepper |
| 3 oz butter |

| *To garnish:* |
| Lemon slices |

First of all place the skate wings side by side in a wide pan or a roasting tin. Sprinkle with salt and pepper, then add 2 tablespoons of the wine vinegar, bayleaf, mace and parsley sprigs. Add merely sufficient water to cover, bring slowly to the boil and simmer over a low heat for 10–15 minutes, but be sure not to overcook the fish.

Meantime, slowly melt the butter in a small saucepan, then pour the clear golden butter into another saucepan, leaving the white sediment behind. Heat the butter until it's a rich warm brown, then remove at once from the heat, stir in the remaining vinegar and the capers and season with salt and pepper. Drain the fish well—discard the herbs—and arrange it on a warmed serving dish. Finally pour the butter over and garnish with slices of lemon.

The cod family

There are several branches to this family, varying amongst themselves more in size than in texture or flavour. *Cod* itself is a very firm, flaky fish that can weigh up to 14 lb (6·5 g) (*codling* is simply a small cod, by the way), but sadly it loses much of its flavour if not eaten very fresh. It is available all through the year. So too is *hake* (except sometimes in the early autumn), which is a similar if elongated version of cod. *Haddock* is another relation, smaller and more finely textured, much of which goes to be smoked. *Coley* is a rather dull cousin, *whiting* a much more succulent one, and Norwegian *red fish* a somewhat ferocious-looking one that surprisingly tastes as good as cod and is in need of more promotion. All these fleshy, firm fish lend themselves to a wide spectrum of seasonings, flavourings and sauces.

Turbot and halibut

These are usually large flat fish, although turbot can be as small as 2 or 3 lb when it can be cooked whole with a stuffing. Halibut on the other hand can weigh up to 40 lb. Both are available all through the year, have a fine flavour, are quite expensive, but are easy to grill, fry, poach or bake in long cutlets on the bone.

Plaice

A fish that does need, I think, some extra flavourings added. It is a flat white fish, easily recognisable by the bright orange spots on the upper side. A whole plaice can weigh up to 5 lb or be as small as 8 oz. It is available in this country all the year round. You can grill it just like Dover sole, but you might want to consider a sauce or flavoured butter to go with it. Deep-fried in a light crisp batter, it goes well with tartare sauce. Filleted, it can be used in any sole recipe and I think the smaller frozen fillets are particularly good. *Dabs* and *flounders* are smaller, less interesting, versions of plaice.

Italian baked fish

(serves 4 people)

Four pieces of any white fish can be used for this dish in which the fish is baked in a thick tomato sauce.

4 thick pieces of white fish
1 medium onion, finely chopped
1 fat clove garlic, crushed
14-oz (400-g) tin Italian tomatoes
1 teaspoon dried basil
2 tablespoons olive oil
$\frac{1}{4}$ lb mushrooms (110 g), thinly sliced
1 dessertspoon black olives
Juice of half a lemon
Salt and freshly-milled black pepper.

Pre-heat the oven to gas mark 5, 375°F (190°C)

Start by making a good thick tomato sauce. Heat the olive oil in a saucepan and fry the onion for about 5 minutes. Now add the garlic and tomatoes. Season with salt and pepper and stir in the dried basil. Bring to simmering point and cook gently—uncovered—for 15 minutes, stirring occasionally. Next add the sliced mushrooms, making sure that they are well stirred in. Simmer for a further 10 minutes until it looks like a thick purée

Now place the fish in a shallow baking dish or tin, season with salt and pepper and sprinkle a little lemon juice on each piece. Next spoon an equal quantity of the purée onto each piece of fish and arrange a few olives on top. Cover the dish with foil and bake on a high shelf for about 25 minutes, depending on the thickness of the fish. Serve this with brown rice and a tossed green salad.

Flaky fish pie
(serves 4 people)

Any white fish can be used for this—whiting, coley, etc.—and even if using the more expensive haddock or cod, $\frac{3}{4}$ lb (350 g) will feed 4 easily.

12 oz any white fish (350 g)
Milk
1 oz butter (25 g)
2 tablespoons flour
1 teaspoon capers, chopped
1 small gherkin, chopped
2 tablespoons chopped parsley
2 hard-boiled eggs, chopped
1 tablespoon of Lemon juice
Salt and freshly-milled black pepper

For the quick flaky pastry:
8 oz flour (225 g)
6 oz margarine (175 g)
For method see page 90

To glaze:
Beaten egg

First place the fish in a medium-sized saucepan with just enough milk to cover, bring to the boil, cover and simmer gently for about 5–10 minutes. Now strain off the milk into a measuring jug and, when the fish is cool enough to handle, flake it into large pieces (discarding all the bones, skin, etc).

Next, melt the butter in the same saucepan and stir in the flour. Cook for about 2 minutes over a medium heat, then gradually add $\frac{1}{2}$ pint (275 ml) of the milk the fish was cooked in, stirring all the time. Bring the sauce to the boil, simmer gently for 6 minutes, then take the pan off the heat and add the flaked fish, chopped capers, gherkin, parsley and eggs. Season with salt and pepper and lemon juice. Cover and leave until the mixture is quite cold.

When you're ready to cook the pie, pre-heat the oven to gas mark 7, 425°F (220°C). Roll out the pastry to a 12-in. (30-cm) square, trimming if necessary. Lift the square onto a greased baking sheet, then place the cold fish mixture in the centre. Glaze around the edge of the pastry with beaten egg, then pull the opposite corners of the pastry to the centre and pinch all the edges together firmly, so you have a square with pinched edges in the shape of a cross. Glaze all over with beaten egg and decorate with any pastry trimming. Glaze these and then bake the pie for about 30 minutes or until the pastry is well risen and golden.

Fisherman's pie
(serves 4 people)

Whatever white fish is available can be used for this delicious family recipe.

1½ lb white fish
4 oz butter
1 pint milk
2 oz plain flour
4 oz peeled prawns
2 hardboiled eggs (roughly chopped)
1 level tablespoon capers (drained)
3 tablespoons fresh chopped parsley
1 tablespoon lemon juice
Salt and freshly-milled pepper

For the topping:
2 lb freshly-cooked potatoes
1 oz butter
¼ pint soured cream
A little freshly-grated nutmeg

Preheat oven to gas mark 6, 400°F (200°C)

Start by arranging the fish in a baking tin and seasoning it well with salt and pepper. Then pour over ½ pint of the milk, dot with a few flecks of butter, then bake in the oven for 15 to 20 minutes. Pour off (and reserve) the cooking liquid, and remove the skin from the fish, flaking the flesh into fairly large pieces.

Now make the sauce: melt the remaining 3 oz of butter in a saucepan, then stir in the flour and gradually add the fish cooking liquid—stirring well after each addition. When all the liquid is in, finish off the sauce by slowly adding the remaining ½ pint of milk and seasoning with salt and pepper.

Next mix the fish into the sauce, along with the prawns, hardboiled eggs, capers and parsley (taste at this stage to see if it needs any more salt and pepper) and stir in the lemon juice. Now pour the whole mixture into a 2½ pint baking dish (well buttered).

Next cream the cooked potatoes with the butter and soured cream, add some freshly-grated nutmeg, then spread it evenly all over the fish. Bake on a high shelf (same temperature) for about half an hour, or until heated through and browned.

Fish kebabs
(serves 2 people)

This is an unusual and delicious way of serving fish—any white fish, like the thick end of a cod fillet or haddock.

1 lb white fish (450 g)
3 tablespoons olive oil
1½ tablespoons lemon juice
1 tablespoon dry white wine
2 tablespoons parsley, finely chopped
1 medium green pepper, chopped
1 medium onion, quartered
Salt and freshly-milled black pepper
Lemon quarters

First remove the skin from the fish and cut it into 1-in. (2·5 cm) cubes. Next, put in a bowl the olive oil, lemon juice, wine and chopped parsley and seasoning and mix well with a fork to amalgamate thoroughly, then plunge the cubes of fish into it. Now separate the layers of the onion quarters and arrange them evenly over the fish. Put aside in a cool place to marinade for at least an hour.

When you're ready to cook the fish, pre-heat the grill to high and line the grill pan with foil. Then thread the pieces of fish onto skewers, alternating with pieces of onion and green pepper. Place the skewers on the grill pan, brush with the marinade and grill for a minute or two under the high heat. Then turn the heat to medium and cook for a further 4–5 minutes on each side, brushing on more of the marinade before turning.

Serve with a savoury rice, the juices from the pan poured over, and lemon quarters. Brown rice looks nice, if you can get it.

Halibut with bacon

(serves 4 people)

This is nicest served with creamy potatoes mashed with soured cream and flavoured with a little nutmeg.

4 halibut steaks (single-portion-sized steaks)
2 carrots, very thinly sliced
1 stick celery, very thinly sliced
4 oz mushrooms (110 g) thinly sliced
4 slices back bacon, rinds removed
1 large onion, finely chopped
2 tablespoons chopped parsley
½ teaspoon dried thyme
4 slices lemon
2 oz butter (50 g)
½ pint dry white wine (275 ml)
Salt and freshly-milled black pepper

Pre-heat the oven to gas mark 7, 425°F (220°C)

Start by laying the bacon slices in a well-buttered baking dish, which is large enough to take the fish steaks. Then sprinkle over the prepared carrots, mushrooms, celery and onion followed by the wine. Cover tightly with foil and bake for 30 minutes.

Next, remove the dish from the oven and arrange the fish steaks on top of the vegetables. Then sprinkle with parsley, thyme, salt and freshly-milled black pepper; place a lemon slice on each steak and dot with flecks of butter. Cover the dish again with foil and bake for a further 15–20 minutes, then serve.

Baked fish with soured cream and capers

(serves 2 people)

This would be suitable for some thick fish cutlets—cod, halibut or turbot or some thick pieces of fresh haddock.

1 lb fish (450 g)
2 fl. oz dry white wine or dry cider (55 ml)
1½ oz butter (40 g)
½ teaspoon dried tarragon leaves
1 chopped white of leek
¼ pint soured cream (150 ml)

1 teaspoon flour
2 teaspoons drained chopped capers
1 tablespoon finely-chopped watercress leaves
Salt and freshly-milled pepper

To garnish:
Sprigs of watercress
Lemon quarters

Pre-heat the oven to gas mark 5, 375°F (190°C)

Place the pieces of fish in a buttered baking dish just large enough to accommodate them. Add the cider and dot with half the butter. Season with salt and pepper, sprinkle in the tarragon, then cover the dish with foil and bake near the top of the oven for 20 minutes.

Meantime, melt the rest of the butter in a saucepan, add the chopped leek and let it soften gently. Then sprinkle in the flour and, stirring all the time, cook over a low heat for a couple of minutes.

When the fish is ready, lift up a corner of the foil and pour the liquid into a jug. Now add this liquid, a little at a time, to the mixture in the saucepan, stirring after each addition. When it's all added, bring to boiling point and cook for at least a minute. Then turn the heat low and stir in the cream, capers and chopped watercress. When it's heated through, pour it over the fish and garnish with sprigs of watercress and lemon quarters.

Baked fish with mushrooms

(serves 3–4 people)

For this you need 2 large whole plaice or Dover sole, boned, cut into fillets and skinned.

4 large plaice fillets, skinned
$\frac{1}{2}$ lb dark mushrooms (225 g), finely chopped
1 oz butter (25 g)
1 tablespoon oil
1 small onion, finely chopped
Freshly-grated nutmeg
Lemon juice
1 tablespoon finely-chopped parsley

$\frac{1}{4}$ **pint milk (150 ml)**
2 level tablespoons flour
1 tablespoon thick cream
Salt and freshly-milled black pepper

To garnish:
Chopped parsley

Pre-heat the oven to gas mark 4, 350°F (180°C)

First of all melt half the butter and all the oil together in a pan and fry the onion gently until soft and golden. Add the mushrooms and cook until all the juices have evaporated and the remaining mixture is a dryish, spreadable paste—this will probably take about 20 minutes. Remove from the heat, season with salt, pepper and nutmeg, then transfer all but 2 tablespoons of the mixture to a basin and mix with the parsley.

Next cut the fish fillets in half lengthways and spread an equal quantity of the mushroom mixture on the skinned side of each piece of fish. Roll up the fillets from the head to the tail end and place them closely together in a baking dish. Now pour in $\frac{1}{4}$ pint (150 ml) water, place a piece of buttered paper directly on top of the fish and bake in the oven for 20 minutes.

Meantime, melt the remaining butter in a saucepan, blend in the flour and cook for 2 minutes, stirring continuously. When the fish is ready transfer it to a warmed serving dish, using a draining spoon; cover and keep warm. Now add the cooking liquid to the butter and flour mixture, beating all the time to get a smooth sauce, and also blend in the milk. Then bring to boiling point, stirring all the time, add the remaining mushroom mixture, season with salt, pepper and a squeeze of lemon juice and stir in a tablespoon of cream. Pour over the fish and sprinkle with parsley before serving.

Plaice fillets with garlic and herbs

(serves 2 people)

For this ask the fishmonger for 2 plaice boned and filleted into 2 flat fillets each, or use frozen fillets (thawed first).

4 plaice fillets
2 tablespoons fresh breadcrumbs
1 clove garlic, chopped very small

1 teaspoon dried thyme
1 tablespoon fresh chopped parsley
1 egg
2 oz butter (50 g)
1 tablespoon olive oil
1 small lemon
Salt and freshly-milled black pepper

Melt the butter and oil in your largest frying-pan and, while it's melting, combine the breadcrumbs, garlic, thyme, parsley and the grated peel of the lemon in a shallow dish. Then beat the egg and season it with coarsely-milled pepper and salt. Pat the fillets dry with some kitchen paper and dip them first in the beaten egg, then in the breadcrumbs, making sure they get a good even coating.

Now fry the fillets in the hot butter and oil till golden-brown—about 3 minutes each side or more if they're thick.

Drain on crumpled greaseproof paper and serve with the lemon, quartered, to squeeze over.

These go very well with sauté potatoes and a crisp green salad.

Oily fish

Under this heading come a group of fish which are rich in flavour, but because of their slight oiliness do need to be eaten fresh.

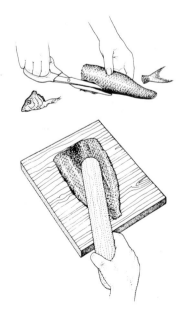

Herrings

A prince of fish, in my opinion, a true delicacy when freshly caught. Yet until recently herring were amongst the cheapest and most abundant of our native fish, and little thought of in consequence. The irony is that present-day intensive fishing (for animal-feed products among other things) has contrived to put the species in jeopardy. It has therefore become scarcer and more expensive—and probably, like the oyster, will become more highly regarded.

It is quite possible you might find yourself faced at some time or another with the prospect of having to bone a

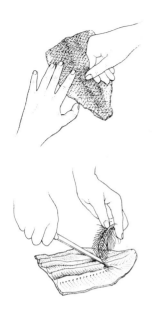

herring. It is actually quite easy—more formidable in the anticipation than in practice. First of all ask the fishmonger to clean, scale and trim the fish—that much he must do. Then when you get home, take a pair of scissors and cut each fish along the tummy, turn it over (flesh-side down) on a board, then bash (with a rolling-pin if you like) the fish out to flatten it completely. Now press hard with your fingers all along the backbone, to loosen it from the flesh. Then, turning the fish over, get hold of the backbone at the head and ease it away—it will bring all the little bones with it. If it proves a bit stubborn, use a sharp knife to prompt it a little. Remove any reluctant small bones left behind—and you have now boned a herring.

Soused herrings

These are delicious served with home-made wholewheat bread and a salad, but they do need to be made a couple of days in advance. For 6 pickled herrings you'll need:

1 pint white wine vinegar (425 ml)
1 teaspoon whole allspice berries
1 teaspoon whole coriander seeds
$\frac{1}{2}$ teaspoon mustard seeds
1 dried chilli
2 bayleaves
1–2 teaspoons brown sugar
6 freshly filleted herrings (frozen ones are not so good)
1$\frac{1}{2}$ tablespoons salt
2 dill pickles
1 Spanish onion, thinly sliced
Some made-up mustard
6 cocktail sticks

First of all make the marinade in a saucepan by combining the vinegar, spices, bayleaves and sugar with $\frac{1}{4}$ pint (150 ml) water. Bring to boiling point, then simmer very gently for 5 minutes. Remove from the heat and leave until cold.

Next sprinkle the herrings with the salt and let them drain in a colander for about 3 hours. After that rinse off the salt and dry off any excess moisture with kitchen paper. Now cut each dill pickle in three lengthways, spread the filleted side of each fish thinly with mustard and place a piece of dill pickle and some slices of onion horizontally at what was the head end of each fillet. Then roll up the fillets from the head to the tail end—the skin being on the outside—and secure each roll with a cocktail stick. Pack them into an oval casserole and sprinkle the remaining onion on top. Pour over the marinade, cover with a lid, and put them in the lowest part of the refrigerator. They will not be ready for serving for at least 48 hours and, in fact, they will keep well for at least a week.

Stuffed baked herrings
(serves 4 people)

For this you need 4 medium herrings. Ask for the soft herring roes to go in the stuffing.

4 herrings with roes
1 tablespoon butter
1 small onion, finely chopped
2 hard-boiled eggs, chopped
1 clove garlic, crushed
3 tablespoons chopped parsley
1 teaspoon dried thyme
2 slices white bread (crusts removed)
Milk
1 teaspoon lemon juice
Salt and freshly-milled black pepper
A little butter

Pre-heat the oven to gas mark 5, 375°F (190°C)

You'll need a shallow, buttered baking dish.

When buying the fish ask the fishmonger to remove the heads and to gut and fillet them, if you're not sure how to do this; and make sure you get the roes.

First wash the fish and dry them on kitchen paper. Then heat the butter in a small saucepan and gently fry the onion for about 10 minutes or until soft. Transfer the onion to a bowl and add the chopped hard-boiled eggs, garlic, parsley and thyme. Then soak the bread in milk, squeeze out the excess and shred it into the bowl. Chop the herring roes and stir this into the mixture together with the lemon juice and seasoning.

Next, fill each herring with some of the stuffing, then re-shape them to their original form and lay them in the prepared baking dish. Dot each fish with a generous knob of butter and bake on a high shelf for 30–40 minutes, basting occasionally with the buttery juices.

Mackerel
An under-estimated fish if ever there was one. It has a bad reputation with older generations, who were suspicious of its career as a scavenger (it is all right for humans to eat the flesh of other creatures, but wrong apparently for the poor mackerel). It is a sobering thought, in these days of high prices, to read of Cornish fishermen having to dump mackerel catches back in the sea because nobody will buy them, and a saddening one, because mackerel eaten fresh (which they usually are) are a treat. If they look floppy, grey and dull they should be avoided of course: a fresh mackerel will be stiff and rigid, with a sparkling, positively beautiful rainbow hue.

The smaller mackerel are the best size to buy—working out at one fish per person. Bone them in exactly the same way as herrings (see above). They are excellent plainly grilled: make diagonal cuts across the body, season on both sides with salt and pepper, and give them about 5 minutes under a high grill on both sides. They are traditionally—and rightly—served with a sharp purée of gooseberries flavoured with a little nutmeg, or with a purée of rhubarb flavoured with a spot of ginger.

Marinaded mackerel
(serves 3 people)

If you can get your fishmonger to fillet the mackerel for you, so much the better. If not, follow the instructions for boning herring on page 115.

3 large mackerel, filleted
¾ pint dry white wine (425 ml)

1 onion, thinly sliced
1 carrot, thinly sliced
2 tablespoons olive oil
A large bouquet garni*
1 teaspoon brown sugar
Salt

* Bouquet garni—consisting of celery leaves, strips of lemon zest, bayleaf, parsley sprigs, sprigs of thyme, a whole clove of garlic, 10 black peppercorns and 1 seeded chilli—all tied together in a piece of gauze.

Begin by heating the oil in a thick-based saucepan, then add the carrot and onion and stir around. Cover and cook gently for 10 minutes. Next add the white wine, also ¼ pint (150 ml) water and the bouquet garni. Bring to simmering point, cover and cook gently for approximately 30 minutes.

Towards the end of the cooking time arrange the fillets in a single layer, in a roasting tin, then empty the contents of the saucepan over the fillets. Bring up to simmering point and simmer for a minute.

Next, using a draining spoon, transfer the fillets to an oval earthenware casserole or dish which accommodates them neatly. Return the pan to the heat and boil the juices for 2–3 minutes or until reduced sufficiently to just cover the fish. Season to taste with salt, add the sugar, remove the bouquet garni, then strain the liquid over the fillets.

Put aside to cool, then cover and chill for at least 12 hours before serving. (They will keep quite well for 3–4 days.)

Whitebait

Whitebait are tiny baby herring, rarely more than an inch long. At one time—more than a hundred years ago—they were caught at the mouth of the Thames, and consumed by Members of Parliament at 'whitebait feasts' in Greenwich at the end of the parliamentary session. Alas, they are almost never sold fresh nowadays—at least I've never seen them—but it doesn't matter too much, because frozen whitebait are perfectly good. They are eaten whole, deep-fried and crisp enough to rustle as they're served on the plate. Let them de-frost first, dry them thoroughly, then coat them with a dusting of flour and deep-fry them for about 3 minutes.

Sprats

Cousins to the herring, only smaller—yet larger than whitebait. Usually they are 2½–3 inches long (6·5–7·5 cm). They are delicious fried or baked, and always a bargain price-wise.

Deep-fried sprats in mustard sauce

(serves 2 people)

Fresh silvery sprats are always an economical fish, and deep-fried and crisp they really are a delicacy.

1 lb sprats (450 g)
Some seasoned flour
Groundnut oil for frying

For the mustard sauce:
1 oz butter (25 g)
½ oz flour (10 g)
½ pint milk (275 ml)
½ small onion, peeled and chopped
2 teaspoons dry mustard
Salt and freshly-milled black pepper
2 teaspoons lemon juice
A generous pinch sugar
2 pinches cayenne pepper

Make the mustard sauce first. Melt the butter in a saucepan and gently soften the onion in it for about 10 minutes. Now blend in the flour and cook very gently for a minute or two before adding the mustard powder. Now add the milk a little at a time, stirring after each addition, and when it's all added, bring the sauce to boiling point and let it simmer very gently for about 3 minutes. Season to taste with salt, pepper, lemon juice and a pinch of sugar, then keep the sauce warm whilst you prepare the sprats.

First make a small incision behind a gill of each fish and gently squeeze the belly up towards the head to eject the gut, but try to keep the head intact. Rinse the fish well and dry off any excess moisture with kitchen paper before tossing in the seasoned flour. Heat the oil in a deep pan to 350°F (180°C)—to test, either use a thermometer or throw in a small cube of bread and if it turns golden in about a minute it's hot enough. Now deep-fry the sprats for about 3 minutes—you'll probably need to do them in 2 or 3 separate lots. When cooked, drain on crumpled greaseproof paper, keep hot and serve as soon as possible sprinkled with a little cayenne pepper and with the mustard sauce poured over.

Freshwater fish
Trout
There are two kinds of trout, the *brown* and the *rainbow trout*: the latter is actually becoming more widely available and less expensive because of notable successes up and down the country with commercial fish-farming. These farming methods can produce small trout weighing 6–10 oz each (175–275 g), which from frozen will poach in about 10 minutes (6 minutes if fresh). Put some parsley, lemon slices, bayleaf, peppercorns, onion rings and a few herbs in the poaching water, along with a glass of white wine. When cooked, drain the fish and serve with parsley butter. Alternatively they can be fried, dipped first in flour and with a few capers and lemon juice or white wine added to the pan at the end. Trout also bakes and grills well: it is in fact an excellent all-round fish. *Note:* it is normal to leave the heads on, though the gills should be removed as usual.

Trout with caper sauce
(serves 2 people)

A couple of frozen trout would be all right for this—only let them thaw first.

2 trout, gutted
5 tablespoons oil
1 large clove garlic, crushed
4 oz capers (110 g), drained and coarsely crushed
The juice of a large lemon
Salt and freshly-milled black pepper

A few hours before cooking time, put the oil in a bowl with the crushed garlic and beat in the lemon juice followed by the capers and some salt and pepper. Then leave it aside for the flavour to develop.

When you're ready to cook the fish, remove the grill rack and line the grill pan with foil. Pre-heat the grill and arrange the fish over the foil, after gashing each side of the fish twice in the thickest part of their bodies, and brushing a little oil on both sides. Sprinkle with salt and pepper and pour on the caper sauce. Grill under a high heat so that the skins turn crisply brown—they will need 3–4 minutes on each side. Then serve with all the pan juices poured over and you'll need lots of crusty bread to mop up the liquid.

Salmon
The salmon has a fascinating career. Once matured—that is anything between 2 and 7 years old—it will always return to the river to spawn, sometimes to the exact spot where it was itself hatched. Unfortunately once a salmon enters the river it stops feeding and starts to deteriorate in quality. So commercially-sold salmon are always caught in the estuary just as they leave the sea. Their season starts in February and goes on till mid-September: prices (never cheap, regrettably) begin to descend from June when there are more salmon available. One can never afford to buy any but the freshest, and these will have a bright silver belly and flank, an iridescent purple-black back, with peach-coloured flesh that's firm to the touch.

   The very best way to cook it is wrapped in buttered foil in the oven. If you are serving it cold, it can stay in the foil to cool and the skin taken off just before serving. A whole, 8-lb (3·5 k) salmon can feed an entire party, but for a smaller number of people ask the fishmonger for a middle cut.

Fresh salmon

(serves 4 people)

1½ lb middle-cut salmon (675 g)
2 oz butter (50 g)
2 bayleaves
Salt and freshly-milled black pepper

Pre-heat the oven to gas mark ½, 250°F (130°C)

Start by wiping the fish with some damp kitchen paper, then place it in the centre of a large double sheet of foil. Half the butter and both bayleaves should be placed in the centre cavity of the fish, and the rest of the butter smeared on top. Season well with salt and pepper, then wrap the foil over the salmon to make a loose but tightly-sealed parcel. Put the foil parcel on a heatproof plate and bake in the oven for 1 hour and 10 minutes. The skin will come off very easily once the fish is cooked.

For larger pieces of salmon the cooking times are: for 2 lb (900 g), 1½ hours; for 3 lb (1 kg 350 g), 2 hours; for 4 lb (1 kg 800 g), 2½ hours; for 5 lb (2 kg 250 g), 3 hours. Salmon steaks weighing up to 8 oz each, cooked in this way, need 20–25 minutes.

Salmon trout

Also called sea trout, though it is not exactly salmon, trout or sea-going. With its firm but delicate pink flesh, it is said to combine all the virtues of trout and salmon. It weighs anything from 1½ to 4 lb (675 g to 2 kg), and can be cooked in exactly the same way as salmon (see above).

Basic fish batter

I have found this very simple flour-and-water batter the best of all for deep-frying fish, as it really turns out crisp. These quantities should be enough for 4 pieces.

4 oz self-raising flour (110g)
½ **teaspoon salt**
¼ **pint (plus 1 scant tablespoon) water (150 ml)**

Just sift the flour and salt into a bowl, then gradually whisk in the water till smooth and free from lumps.

Meat: roasting and pot-roasting

Including recipes for :
Yorkshire pudding
Bœuf en daube
English pot roast
Boiled beef and dumplings
Roast pork with green butter
Stuffed pork tenderloin

Loin of pork Dijonnaise
Bacon pot roast
Sugar-glazed gammon
Stuffed breast of lamb
Shoulder of lamb with rice and kidney stuffing
Baked lamb with coriander

Never you mind about the pieces of needlework, the maps of the world made by her needle. Get to see her at work on a mutton chop. . . .
Cobbett's Advice to a Young Man Getting Married

I think that if we all had to pass an examination in meat cookery before getting married nowadays, there would be rather a surplus of spinsters in this country. And the reason would be that the whole subject of meat cookery—not to mention meat butchery—is daunting for anyone. Even the cuts of meat vary from region to region, sometimes from butcher to butcher, and however skilled you are as a cook you have to have an ally in a helpful local butcher. I fear my own experience of butchers is that really helpful ones are few and far between—but then maybe we get what we deserve, by not asking to see what gets whisked into those plastic bags before we have time to blink. There is an alternative, of course, and that is the meat counter at a good supermarket (some of which have a resident butcher, who *will* cut you anything you need that's not on display). The advantage of supermarket meat is that you can examine what you're buying, and the weight and price are both clearly displayed.

Pot roasting

The trouble with a straightforward roast, quite apart from requiring the more expensive cuts of meat, is that the meal as a whole (including Yorkshire pudding and roast potatoes) can take up a great deal of your time and attention. Pot roasts on the other hand leave you in peace. You still get a reasonably-sized joint to carve and at a cheaper price.

The principle of pot roasting is long, slow cooking of the meat in a fairly heavy cooking-pot (with a tight-fitting lid) in a small amount of liquid which can be stock, wine or cider. This creates a steamy atmosphere inside the closed pot, which keeps the joint moist as it cooks. Herbs and vegetables may be added too, and sometimes the meat is marinaded first. The finished dish should be very tender and succulent.

The medium-priced and cheaper cuts are usually the most suitable for pot roasts: *silverside* and *top rump* are both good, and so is *chuck* and *blade* boned and rolled. My own favourite is *brisket* (economical and with lots of flavour), but you do need a reliable butcher to roll it for you, because a lot of excess fat and gristle can be lurking unseen inside.

Principles of roasting meat

Strictly speaking, roasting means exposing a piece of meat to an open fire, turning it (usually on a spit) so the air circulates around it and each part comes near to the source of the heat and the whole is cooked evenly. True roasting in fact is more like grilling as we know it: the nearest equivalent is the modern spit-roast, which is fitted to some domestic ovens or sold as a separate unit. Still, for most of us, in practical terms roasting means cooking a joint inside an ordinary oven.

Oven roasting

It is best to begin roasting with a very high oven setting (gas mark 9, 475°F, 245°C) and then lower the heat to continue cooking. This initial blast of heat at the beginning, produces a more attractive joint with a tasty outside crust. In order to approximate some circulation of air in an enclosed oven, setting the joint on a roasting rack is often advised. It doesn't make a great deal of difference though, unless you object to the very crusty, well-cooked bit of the meat that sits on the base of the roasting tin. With something like a piece of sirloin or a rib joint on the bone, the bone itself provides a form of built-in rack.

Beef

Scotch beef, bred in the Highlands, grass-fed, mature and well hung, is the best in the world. And in the last couple of years I have also had some very good Irish beef, but I cannot reconcile myself to the immature, barley-fed beef (which is widely sold in my neighbourhood at any rate): an insipid imitation of what good beef should be, it seems to me. I even feel it would be better to have less meat—make a really good piece of beef a treat—so that we would not have to rear it so intensively.

I have heard breeders say that this mass-produced beef is what the housewife wants, that is, lots of it, tender and almost fat-less. But what people so often fail to realise is that fat means flavour: tender lean meat that is lacking the one essential, flavour, is no pleasure at all. Nature has so arranged things that when a good piece of meat with its proper percentage of fat is placed near a fire or in an oven, the heat draws out some of the juices while the fat melts and bastes the meat within as well as outside, keeping the meat succulent (which is why wise old cooks, and wise new ones too, take care to baste the meat as it is roasting). If you can't eat the fat at the end, that doesn't matter, its presence during cooking is essential.

Roasting beef

The cardinal rule here is to buy the right cut in the first place. It's no wonder that letters pour in from people who are unsuccessful in roasting beef when you consider some of the so-called roasting joints on offer—all manner of things get tied up with string and labelled 'roasting'. My advice is to buy an unequivocal, decent-sized piece of *sirloin* for a special occasion, and otherwise a *double rib joint* (which as it happens is next door, anatomically).

Do buy, and cook, your joint *on the bone*. You won't be paying any extra, since meat bought on the bone costs less per pound. The bone provides a good conductor of heat inside the joint, thus cooking the meat more evenly with less loss of juices; it also helps to stop the meat disintegrating, which you will appreciate when you come to carve. If you are worried that your family is too small to cope with a large joint, bear in mind that good roast beef is delicious cold with chutney and jacket potatoes, and minced it makes lovely rissoles. However, if you prefer it, both the above joints can be boned and rolled. When you buy a piece of sirloin, make sure it contains the 'eye' or undercut, which some butchers take out and sell as fillet steak (which it is). A decent joint of sirloin on the bone will weigh 4–5 lb (2·0–2·5 kg). If you choose a wing rib for roasting, then ask for a 'double rib' as a single one is too thin—it looks the same as a sirloin but without the undercut. A more economical roasting joint—which unhappily is not always available unless you order it—is a cut called the *aitchbone*. A whole one is very large, but some butchers will sell part of one. It comes from the pelvic region of the animal, just behind the rump, and as it needs slower roasting it isn't really suitable for eating rare, but its flavour is excellent.

To prepare a joint for roasting Dust the fat-surface with a mixture of flour and dry mustard, and sprinkle with freshly-milled pepper (but no salt, since this encourages the juices to escape). Add a knob of beef dripping to the tin, just to moisten the base, before placing the joint in it. Start by giving it 20 minutes at gas mark 9, 475°F (245°C), then lower the heat to gas mark 5, 375°F (190°C), and cook for 15 minutes per pound (for rare), plus 15 extra minutes (for medium-rare), plus 30 minutes extra (for well-done), and baste the meat by spooning the pan juices over it during the cooking.

Try to plan the meal so that the joint is allowed to 'relax' for about 30 minutes before carving. Keep it in a warm place but don't worry that it will become cold—it will hold its heat for this time. Removing it from direct heat will firm up the texture, making it easier to carve. This will also permit you to increase the heat in the oven for the roast potatoes and Yorkshire pudding. As the meat relaxes, some of the juices will exude onto the plate: these should be added to the gravy. And while on carving, may I refer you back to my comments on knives on page 16. Carving is only difficult and dangerous when the carving-knife is blunt.

Accompaniments to beef

Grating fresh *horseradish* is a tiresome job: the fumes cause tears and discomfort. It is possible, though, to buy preserved grated horseradish, which you can combine with cream to make your own sauce—or else stir in a little grated horseradish to some commercially bottled horseradish sauce to give it an extra kick. Whether it is on its own or mixed with cream, horseradish is very strong—so be warned. *Mustard* is the other traditional accompaniment, and should be made up ten minutes, at least, before it is needed. *Yorkshire pudding* was originally served as a first course, to temper the appetite and make the meat go further. But crisply-made Yorkshire pud is now—and with every reason— something of a delicacy. There are just a few rules: for a successful pudding you must (i) have the oven very hot, (ii) use a metal container, and (iii) always use plain flour rather than self-raising.

Yorkshire pudding (for 4 people)	
	3 oz plain flour (75 g)
	1 egg
	3 fl. oz milk (75 ml)
	2 fl. oz water (50 ml)
	Salt and freshly-milled pepper
	2 tablespoons beef dripping (for the roasting-tin)

Pre-heat the oven to gas mark 7, 425°F (220°C)

To make the batter, sift the flour into a bowl, make a well in the centre, break an egg into it and beat it gradually incorporating the flour, milk, water, and seasoning (an electric hand-whisk will do this in seconds). You don't have to leave batter to stand, so make it when you're ready. About 15 minutes before the beef is due to come out of the oven, increase the heat to gas mark 7, 425°F (220°C), and place an oblong tin (11 × 7 inches) on a baking-sheet on a free shelf, adding the dripping to the tin. After 15 minutes remove the meat and leave on one side to rest, then place the tin over direct heat while you pour the batter into the sizzling hot fat. Then return the tin to the baking sheet on the highest shelf (or second highest, if you have roast potatoes on that one). The pudding will take about 25–30 minutes to rise and become crisp and golden. It is important to serve a Yorkshire pudding as soon as possible, as it loses its crunchiness if it has to wait around too long.

Bœuf en daube

(serves 6 people)

3–3½ lb top rump of beef (1 kg 350 g to 1 kg 750 g), tightly rolled and tied
About 4 tablespoons beef dripping
1 tablespoon flour
½ pint stock (275 ml)
4 tomatoes, peeled and quartered
2 oz dark grilled mushrooms (50 g), sliced
1 rounded tablespoon flour, worked to a paste with a tablespoon of butter
freshly-milled black pepper
For the marinade:
½ pint of red wine (275 ml)
2 tablespoons olive oil
2 tablespoons red wine vinegar
2 onions, halved and sliced
2 carrots, sliced in rounds
A bouquet garni*
2 teaspoons salt

* Bouquet garni—consisting of a bayleaf, a strip of orange zest, ½ teaspoon dried thyme, ½ teaspoon black peppercorns, 6 allspice berries, 2 large unpeeled cloves, garlic, halved lengthways—all these tied together in a little piece of gauze.

First prepare the marinade by combining all the ingredients in a bowl, then put in the meat. Cover with a cloth, then put in a cold place for at least 12 hours, and during that time, turn the meat over occasionally.

When you wish to begin cooking, pre-heat the oven to gas mark 1, 275°F (140°C) Remove the meat from the marinade and dry it thoroughly on kitchen paper.

Now heat the dripping in a thick cooking pot which will take the meat neatly and, when the fat is hot, add the meat and sear it all over—it should be a nutty brown colour—then transfer to a plate, and pour off all but about 1 tablespoon of the fat from the pan.

Next, remove the vegetables from the marinade with a draining-spoon, reserving the liquid. Dry them on kitchen paper, then tip them into the cooking-pot and fry them until they are lightly browned. Then stir in the flour and brown this slowly, but be careful it doesn't burn. Now stir in the reserved marinade liquid, the bouquet garni, stock, tomatoes and mushrooms, add the meat and season with freshly-milled black pepper.

Bring to simmering point, cover with a piece of foil and a tight-fitting lid, then place the pot in the centre of the oven and let it cook slowly for about 3 hours. To test if the meat is fully cooked a skewer should go into the meat easily.

When ready, remove the meat and keep warm. Tip the contents of the pot into a sieve placed over a bowl and press the vegetables against the side of the sieve to extract all the juices. Return the liquid to the pan and boil quickly to reduce and concentrate the flavour. Now add the butter and flour mixture and whisk, with a balloon whisk, until the sauce thickens.

Season to taste with salt and pepper. Carve the meat, pour over some of the sauce and pour the rest into a warmed sauce boat.

English pot roast

(serves 4–6 people)

The root vegetables in this seem to absorb the meat flavour, which makes them extra good.

2½ lb rolled brisket (1 kg)
4 small whole onions, peeled
4 smallish carrots, peeled
4 sticks celery cut in three
½ large swede, peeled and cut in chunks
Some beef dripping
¼ lb dark grilled mushrooms (110 g)

$\frac{1}{2}$ pint hot stock (or hot water enriched with $\frac{1}{2}$ teaspoon Worcester sauce and 2 teaspoons mushroom ketchup)
A sprig of thyme
A bayleaf
1 tablespoon flour and 1 tablespoon butter worked to a paste
Salt and freshly-milled black pepper

Pre-heat the oven to gas mark 1, 275°F (140°C)

First melt the dripping in a thick cooking-pot and, when it's hot, put in the meat and sear and brown it all over, then transfer it to a plate. Next lightly brown the onions, carrots, celery and swede, then remove them temporarily to the plate too.

Next, empty all the fat from the pot, then replace the brisket and arrange the vegetables and mushrooms around the meat. Add the hot stock, bayleaf and thyme and a little salt and pepper. Cover with foil and a tightly-fitting lid and as soon as you hear the sound of simmering place in the centre of the oven and leave to cook for about 3 hours.

When ready, place the meat and vegetables on a warmed serving dish, then bring the liquid to the boil and boil briskly until reduced slightly. Add the butter and flour paste and whisk until the sauce thickens. Serve with the meat and some sharp English mustard.

Boiled beef and dumplings

(serves 6 people)

Salted silverside would do for this, but salted brisket is even better.

3 lb joint boned, rolled brisket (1 kg 350 g), salted (ask your butcher if it needs soaking or not)
1 sprig thyme
1 bayleaf
A few parsley stalks
5 medium carrots
5 small onions
2 turnips, quartered
2 celery stalks, cut into 1 inch (2·5-cm) lengths
Salt and pepper

For the dumplings:
4 oz self-raising flour (110 g)
¼ teaspoon salt
2 oz suet (50 g)
¼ teaspoon dried mixed herbs
Salt and pepper

Place the meat in a deep saucepan and cover it with cold water. Add the herbs, some salt and pepper, and bring slowly to the boil. Cover and simmer for about an hour, skimming the surface to remove any scum halfway through. Then add the vegetables, cover and simmer gently for another hour or until tender.

To make the dumplings, mix the flour, salt and pepper in a bowl. Stir in the suet and herbs and add just enough water to make a soft but not too sticky dough. Shape it into 8 small dumplings.

Next, remove the meat from the pan and keep warm. Pop the dumplings into the pan, cover, and cook for 20–25 minutes.

Slice the beef and serve it surrounded by the vegetables and dumplings with a little of the broth as gravy and plenty of mustard.

Pork

The pig has long played an honourable part in the British diet. Every part of him can be consumed, even his skin translates into crisp, crunchy crackling and his fat is rendered down into pure lard. Before the Enclosure Acts and the industrial revolution, almost every cottage kept its pig which was consumed by the family in the seasons when there was an R in the month (this was before the days of refrigeration). Winter sealed the fate of the cottage pig; the dressed boar's head was a festive Christmas dish, and the salting, lard-making and preserving of the pork were all done in the coldest weather. Even the pig-sty was cleansed by the sharp January frosts, ready for the young porker to be moved in in the spring and be fattened up for the next winter. By a happy coincidence a cottage would often have a small orchard attached, where in autumn the windfall apples provided a succulent addition to the pig's diet (so apple sauce became a natural environmental accompaniment for him when he got served up on the plate).

Today pork is reared fairly intensively. Again our modern preoccupation with leanness has taken its toll on character and flavour. Still, pork is now plentiful and, with imaginative cooking (and plenty of crackling), a pleasure all the year round.

Pork cuts for roasting

Leg of pork is the most popular roasting joint, but because of its size it mostly has to be sold in two or else boned and rolled without the knuckle. This cut promises the most lean meat but not, I think, such a sweet flavour as others.

Loin of pork is also a prime roasting joint, equivalent in the anatomy of the animal to the sirloin and ribs of beef. This is best bought on the bone, but the butcher *must* chine it for you—that is, loosen the bone yet leave it attached so it can easily be cut away before carving.

Blade bone This comes at the top of the foreleg, so could be more accurately described as a piece of the shoulder. The meat has an excellent flavour cooked on the bone. Alternatively it can be boned for you and stuffed before roasting.

Spare rib Like loin, this is sometimes sold as individual chops. It is actually the collar of the animal and, when roasted, full of flavour.

Hand and spring This is the curious name for the upper part of the foreleg of the pig, which happens to be well endowed with crackling and can be boned, stuffed and then roasted.

Belly of pork Sometimes sold in rashers as streaky pork, but the thick end (i.e. the leanest end) can be bought as a roasting joint. It has much to recommend it, good crackling, a sweet flavour, and not least it is the most economical joint.

Fillet or tenderloin These on the other hand are among the most expensive, but they are lean cuts without any wastage. In my opinion they need other flavours and ingredients with them to create interest.

Roasting pork

If you want to serve genuinely crisp crackling, ask the butcher to score the skin well (if you have to do it yourself, use the tip of a sharp knife and cut down the skin with quick, jerky movements). Then sprinkle the scored surface quite generously with salt to give it a thin coating—on no account put any fat near the crackling.

For a touch of extra flavour you can insert a few slivers of garlic into the flesh (make a small incision first) and sprinkle some thyme or rosemary over the joint. Place it on its own in a roasting tin—there is fat enough in the meat to lubricate it while it's cooking—

and give it 20 minutes in the oven at gas mark 9, 475°F (245°C), then lower the heat to gas mark 5, 375°F (190°C), and continue roasting for 35 minutes to the pound for leg or loin of pork. For other joints mentioned above lower the heat to gas mark 4, 350°F (180°C), and allow 45 minutes per pound.

What goes wrong with crackling Several things can turn the skin into tough old leather instead of crackling. One is using too deep a roasting tin, where that part of the crackling inside does not get proper exposure to the heat. Another reason could be that the skin was wet and soggy (especially if the meat has been frozen) : to get good crackling it has to be dried thoroughly before salting and cooking. Another mistake is to plaster fat on the surface before cooking.

Roast pork with green butter

(serves 6 people)

Ask the butcher—giving him a bit of notice—to bone out a hand and spring of pork for this recipe.

5–5½ lb hand and spring of pork (2·25–2·5 kg)
Salt

For the butter:
1 tablespoon chopped parsley
1 tablespoon chopped watercress
1 teaspoon rock salt
1 teaspoon black peppercorns
1 teaspoon juniper berries
1 clove garlic
The grated rind of 1 lemon
The juice of ½ lemon
1½ oz butter (40 g)
Some white wine

Pre-heat the oven to gas mark 8, 450°F (230°C)

First of all, using a pestle and mortar or a bowl and the end of a rolling-pin, grind down the rock salt, peppercorns, juniper berries and garlic. Then add them to the butter with the rind and lemon juice, the chopped parsley and watercress, and mix thoroughly. Next, lay the boned joint, rind side down, on a flat working surface, wipe it with kitchen paper, then spread the butter mixture carefully all over it. Now tie it with string in several places so that it has the appearance of a long, roundish sausage, then transfer it to a roasting tin and sprinkle with salt.

Roast the joint in the top half of the oven for 20 minutes, then move it down to the centre of the oven and bake for a further 2 hours. To make sure that the meat is cooked, test with a skewer— the juices should be yellowy without any trace of pinkness.

Remove the string before carving and use the pan juices and a dash of white wine to make a gravy to serve with it.

Stuffed pork tenderloin
(serves 4 people)

This is a good recipe for a dinner party, as it's easy to carve and serve. To serve 8 just double the ingredients and use 2 tenderloins.

1 pork tenderloin (weighing about 1 lb (450 g))
3–4 rashers streaky bacon, rind removed
$\frac{1}{2}$–$\frac{3}{4}$ oz butter (10–15 g)
For the stuffing:
1 oz butter (25 g)
1 medium onion, finely chopped
$\frac{1}{4}$ teaspoon thyme
$\frac{1}{4}$ teaspoon sage
3 oz mushrooms (75 g), finely chopped
4 oz fresh breadcrumbs (110 g)
4 tablespoons chopped parsley
The grated rind of a lemon
2 teaspoons lemon juice
1 egg, beaten with 2 tablespoons cream or top of the milk
For the gravy:
1 tablespoon brown flour
About $\frac{1}{2}$ pint dry white wine or dry cider (275 ml)
salt and freshly-milled black pepper

Pre-heat the oven to gas mark 4, 350°F (180°C)

Leave the fat on the tenderloin, as this will help to keep it moist. With a sharp knife, split it in half lengthways and, using a rolling-pin, batter the two halves to flatten and widen them slightly. Season with salt and freshly-milled black pepper.

To make the stuffing, melt the butter in a pan and fry the onion and herbs gently for about 10 minutes, then add the mushrooms and raise the heat slightly. Cook for a further 3–4 minutes or until the juices from the mushrooms have almost evaporated, then empty the contents of the pan into a bowl and add the rest of the stuffing ingredients. Fork the mixture together lightly, then season to taste.

Next spoon the stuffing onto one half of the tenderloin, patting it down to firm it slightly, then place the other half on top. Smear with some butter and season with freshly-milled black pepper. Cover the top of the fillet with the rinded bacon and tie with string at about 2 in. (5 cm) intervals to keep it neat and tidy, then transfer, carefully, to a buttered roasting tin. Bake near the top of the oven for 1 hour, then place on a serving dish and keep warm.

To make the gravy, stir the flour into the pan juices, add the wine and some seasoning and let it bubble until syrupy.

To serve, carve the meat into thick slices, pour over the gravy. A garnish of fried apple rings would go well with it.

Loin of pork Dijonnaise
(serves 6 people)

This has a lovely golden crust and the crackling is cooked separately to go with it.

1 piece loin of pork with crackling approximately 3 lb (1 kg 350 g) in weight
3 level tablespoons breadcrumbs
3 level teaspoons Dijon mustard
1 heaped teaspoon whole peppercorns
1 heaped teaspoon dried sage
Salt
3 small Cox's apples
Some butter
$\frac{1}{2}$ pint dry cider (275 ml)

Pre-heat the oven to gas mark 7, 425°F (220°C)

Start by scoring the skin of the pork with the tip of a sharp knife. Then take off the skin, together with about half the layer of fat underneath—in one piece if possible. Place this on a shallow baking tray and put it on the highest shelf of the oven for 15–20 minutes. At the end of this time it will be a very crisp and crunchy piece of crackling to accompany the meat. When you remove it from the oven, pour the fat into a bowl to use later for frying, etc.

Meantime, place the breadcrumbs in a mixing bowl, crush the peppercorns with a pestle and mortar or using the back of a tablespoon, and add them to the breadcrumbs together with the sage and about $\frac{1}{2}$ teaspoon salt.

Next spread the mustard all over the layer of fat left on the pork, then press the breadcrumb mixture firmly all over, making sure that it is well coated. Transfer the joint to a roasting tin and place a square of foil lightly on top. Place the meat on a high shelf in the oven, reduce the heat to gas mark 5, 375°F (190°C), and roast the pork for about 2 hours, basting occasionally, and removing the foil for the last 30 minutes. When the pork is cooked, leave it in a warm place to relax, then spoon off the fat from the roasting tin, sprinkle a little flour into the juices and make some gravy with the cider.

Core the apples and cut into rings—but do not peel—and fry gently in butter till tender.

Serve the pork cut in slices with the gravy and garnished with the fried apple rings.

Ham, gammon and bacon

Each of these are terms used to describe meat from the pig that has been cured, i.e. preserved and flavoured in several different ways, either by salting, smoking or being steeped in brine (or molasses or honey). There are hundreds of refinements of the curing process used throughout the world: the wafer-thin Parma ham or *prosciutto* is a great delicacy in Italy, and in France the raw ham from the Bayonne district in the Pyrenees is smoked with aromatic herbs. In this country we have our own specialities:

York ham is the most famous. It is dry salt-cured and lightly smoked with a mild flavour. A similarly mild cure is the *Wiltshire cured ham*. For those who like a stronger, smokier flavour there is the *Suffolk cure*, which is prepared in molasses which adds a sweetness to the flavour. *Braddenham ham*, very expensive, is also steeped in molasses, which turn the skin completely black.

Soaking Whole hams need long soaking, not just to remove the saltiness from them but also to replace some of the moisture lost during the curing. Whole hams should always carry the specific curer's soaking and cooking instructions. For smaller gammon and bacon joints the modern curing methods are far less salty than they used to be, and soaking is not so essential. The ideal would be to cover them with water overnight, but, failing that, a joint can be immersed in cold water and brought up to the boil. This water should then be thrown out and the cooking started with fresh water.

Cuts The best cuts for boiling, braising or half-braising/half-roasting are *middle-cut gammon* (the leanest and best), *bacon collars*, *corner gammon* or *gammon slipper*. If you want to eat a joint of gammon or bacon cold, it is a good idea to give it 15 minutes less cooking time and leave it to cool in its cooking water, which will keep it extra moist. Or if you're serving it hot, keep it in the water for 15 minutes after it comes off the heat. In general the cooking times for joints are: 25 minutes per pound (450 g). For whole hams: 15–20 minutes per lb.

Bacon pot roast
(serves 6–8 people)

In this recipe the bacon is half simmered then finished off as a pot roast on a bed of vegetables.

3 lb collar of bacon (1 kg 350 g)
1 small potato, peeled
1 small onion (stuck with a few cloves)
1 bayleaf
6 black peppercorns
½ pint dry cider (275 ml)
For the pot-roasting:
1 small swede, cut into chunks
2 carrots, sliced
1 onion, sliced
3 sticks of celery, cut into chunks
2 oz butter (50 g)
Freshly-milled black pepper

Begin by placing the joint in a suitably-sized saucepan along with the potato (to take care of any saltiness), the onion, bayleaf and peppercorns. Pour in the cider and top up with enough cold water to just cover the bacon. Then cover with a lid and simmer the joint for 45 minutes. Towards the end of that cooking time, pre-heat the oven to gas mark 4, 350°F (180°C).

Meanwhile fry the prepared vegetables in the butter to tinge them with colour, then arrange them in the bottom of a casserole. Season with some pepper, and when the 45 minutes are up, remove the bacon from its liquid, cut off the skin with a sharp knife, and place the joint on top of the vegetables in the casserole. Pour in enough of the cooking liquid to just cover the vegetables, season only with pepper, put a lid on and place the casserole in the oven for a further 45 minutes. Serve the bacon cut in slices, with the vegetables and some of the juice spooned over.

Sugar-glazed gammon
(serves 6 people)

I think this is one of the nicest ways to cook gammon—half in liquid and then finished off in the oven with a mustard and sugar glaze.

1 piece of middle-cut gammon, rolled approx. 3½ lb (1 k 75 g)
1 onion peeled and stuck with a few cloves
A bayleaf
1 pint of dry cider (570 ml)
2 dozen cloves
½ teaspoon of black peppercorns
2 tablespoons dark brown sugar
1 tablespoon made-up English mustard

Place the gammon joint in a saucepan that will take it comfortably, cover it with cold water, bring it up to the boil, then throw out the water. Now add the bayleaf, peppercorns and onion, and pour in ¾ pint (425 ml) of cider and enough water to cover. Bring this to the boil and simmer gently for an hour. Then remove the gammon, let it cool a little, then with a sharp knife cut off the string and remove the skin.

Now stand the gammon up (fat side uppermost) and score the fat diagonally first in one direction, then the other, so that it stands out in a diamond-shaped pattern. Into each diamond insert a clove, then spread the mustard all over the joint and press the brown sugar all over too (it is easiest to do this with your hands). Put the joint into a roasting tin with the remaining $\frac{1}{4}$ pint (150 ml) of cider in the bottom, place in the oven (pre-heated to gas mark 6, 400°F, 200°C) and bake for 45 minutes, basting it now and then with the cider and juices. Serve this cut into slices with some Cumberland sauce (see page 156).

Lamb

If Scotland has the finest beef, then I think Wales has the best lamb—even the sheep in the hills seem to look more attractive, whiter and woollier than elsewhere. Even so, all lamb in Britain is extremely good, since it has the advantage of living happily in its natural habitat—in other words being completely free-range. It therefore has a natural seasonal cycle, which is at its peak in June, July and August (in fact it progresses from West Country lamb which is available by April to Scottish lamb which reaches the shops in August). New Zealand lamb starts to arrive in this country in December. I believe there is nothing to beat fresh lamb in June, when all the young spring vegetables are in season too, tiny melt-in-the-mouth peas, baby carrots tossed in herb butter and fresh Jersey potatoes.

Roasting cuts

Leg and shoulder of lamb are the commonest, most popular cuts. Shoulder is more economical and has the sweetest meat of the two, because it is interlaced with layers of fat which melt and keep it moist during the cooking. Some people are averse to shoulder because they think it is hard to carve, though I feel a really sharp knife solves most problems.

Best end of neck is another joint that can be roasted. But it is extremely fatty and as the inside should conventionally be slightly pink and underdone, the result is that the layers of fat don't have time to melt. So often have I eaten this in a restaurant where it has arrived surrounded by an unappetising layer of undercooked fat. My own preference would be to cut it into cutlets and grill them to crisp up the fat.

Breast of lamb when rolled and stuffed makes an economical roast.

To roast a shoulder or leg of lamb, pre-heat the oven to gas mark 8, 450°F (230°C), give it 30 minutes, then turn down the heat to gas mark 4, 350°F (180°C), and time it for 30 minutes to the pound thereafter. (If you like the flavour of garlic, a few slivers inserted here and there won't go amiss.)

Accompaniments to lamb

In the summer *mint sauce* is a favourite accompaniment. Be careful—strong malt vinegar can mask all the flavour of the meat. Better, I think, to use a milder wine vinegar and even dilute it with water. Some very finely-shredded lettuce and one spring onion, also very finely chopped, are nice additions. So use: 3 tablespoons of chopped mint, 1 tablespoon of wine vinegar and about 3 tablespoons of water.

Redcurrant jelly goes equally well with lamb. But do make sure it's a really authentic one that is actually based on redcurrants.

My own favourite accompaniment, however, is a combination of both these. *Redcurrant, orange and mint sauce* (see page 157).

Stuffed breast of lamb
(serves 2 people)

This needs a large breast of lamb. Ask the butcher to remove the bones for you, but if you don't have this done by him, you'll find them quite easy to remove provided you have a sharp knife.

A large breast of lamb
2 oz of fresh breadcrumbs (50 g)
Grated rind of $\frac{1}{2}$ lemon
$\frac{1}{4}$ whole nutmeg, grated
1 tablespoon freshly-chopped mint
1 tablespoon freshly-chopped parsley
1 medium onion, very finely chopped
1 teaspoon finely-crushed rosemary
1 small egg, beaten
Salt and freshly-milled black pepper

Pre-heat the oven to gas mark 4, 350°F (180°C)

First of all, in a mixing bowl put the breadcrumbs, onion, parsley, mint, grated nutmeg, rosemary and lemon rind, and season well with pepper and salt. Mix thoroughly, then stir in the beaten egg to bind the mixture together.

Now spread the stuffing evenly over the breast of lamb. Roll it up gently but not too tightly, tuck the flap end over, then tie securely with string in three places—again not too tightly. Tuck in any bits of stuffing that fall out. Wrap the meat in foil, set in a roasting tin and cook for 1½ hours. At the end of this time unwrap the foil, baste with the juices and let it brown for a further half hour.

Serve the meat cut into thick slices with a thin gravy made with the pan juices and some redcurrant jelly.

Shoulder of lamb with rice and kidney stuffing

This, again, is an excellent dinner-party recipe. It's easy to carve and serve, doesn't mind waiting around and tastes absolutely delicious.

(serves 4–6 people)

3½–4 lb shoulder of lamb (boned but not rolled) (1·75–2 kg)
½–1 oz butter (10–25 g), softened
Salt and freshly milled black pepper

For the stuffing:
1 onion, finely chopped
2 oz butter (50 g)
1 clove garlic, crushed
2 oz long grain rice (50 g)
¼ pint stock (150 ml)
½ teaspoon dried thyme
4 lamb's kidneys

First prepare the stuffing. Heat 1 oz (25 g) butter in a small saucepan and gently fry the onion in it until softened and golden. Then stir in the garlic, the rice and thyme and cook for a further 2 minutes before pouring in the stock. Now bring it all up to simmering point, cover and cook gently for about 15–20 minutes (by which time the rice should have absorbed all the liquid and be just tender).

Meanwhile, heat the rest of the butter in another saucepan. Core and slice the kidneys and toss them in the hot fat for a minute over a fairly high heat, then stir the kidneys into the cooked rice. Now, lay the meat, skin-side down, on a board and pack the stuffing into all the pockets and crevices left after boning. Roll the joint up and tie it into a neat shape with string. Place it in a meat-roasting tin, smear it with softened butter and season with salt and pepper, then bake in the oven at gas mark 5, 375°F (190°C), for 1½–2 hours.

Make a thick gravy from the pan juices to go with the lamb.

Baked lamb with coriander
(serves 4 people)

If you don't want to spend too much time but would like to cook lamb a little differently, then this is a good recipe.

½ **leg of lamb—fillet end**
2 cloves garlic
1 heaped tablespoon coriander seeds, crushed
Dripping
A little wine

Pre-heat the oven to gas mark 5, 375°F (190°C)

First, with the point of a sharp knife, make 6–8 evenly-placed incisions in the meat, and put slivers of garlic and the crushed coriander seeds in these cuts. (If you haven't a pestle and mortar to crush the seeds, use the back of a tablespoon.) Double these quantities if you are cooking a whole leg or shoulder. Personal taste will dictate the amount of garlic you use—I suggest either 1 large clove or 2 small ones.

Place the meat in a roasting tin together with a knob of dripping and cook in the pre-heated oven for 30 minutes to the pound. When the lamb is cooked, transfer to a warmed serving dish, tip off fat from the roasting tin and if possible add a little wine to the remaining juice to make a gravy.

To serve, carve it in thick slices. Redcurrant jelly goes well with it.

Sauces

It's the one subject that strictly divides us from our cousins on the other side of the English Channel, *sauces*. In France there are literally hundreds: over here (according to the French) we have only one, and that's custard. Of course we do have more than one, but the chauvinists are for ever arguing that the quality of our meat, fish and game is so superior that it has no need of clever sauces to enhance the flavour! Be that as it may, every honest cook will have to admit that—superior meat or not—the British are tireless consumers of bottled commercial ketchup, salad creams, gravy powders, instant packet sauces and even tinned custard.

It seems to me it's not so much that we despise sauces, but rather that as a nation we have never properly acquired the techniques of making them. So, when a housewife hurries out to the supermarket to buy her packet cheese sauce or gravy mix, what is it she's afraid of making at home? There may be an understandable fear of the unknown (for without experience how can anyone *know* anything), but usually there are more practical barriers—like the age-old problem of:

Lumps

The very first thing to know, if you're going to master the art of sauce-making, is that lumps simply *don't matter*. If a sauce goes lumpy all you do is whisk the lumps out of it or pass it through a sieve—that's precisely what sieves are for. You can even pop the offending sauce into a liquidiser, if there's one handy. This is not to say that a lump-free sauce isn't preferable in the first place: but don't let the problem cause you a moment's concern.

Curdling

Another headache, when it comes to the more advanced butter- and-egg based sauces, is curdling. But again it needn't be a problem. In the first place a beginner (or indeed anyone who's not an absolute purist) can use a little stabiliser—such as cornflour—to help things along. Or, if the sauce has curdled, it *can* be remedied. With egg yolk sauces such as hollandaise the remedy is to use a fresh egg yolk and start again, adding the curdled ingredients to it. With proper custard a teaspoon of cornflour will prevent curdling happening in the first place. Let's begin by examining the basic ingredients of a sauce and what they are doing in it.

Flour

Flour—in a basic white sauce and all the others that are derived from it—is what thickens the liquid. As we have already seen (page 43), little granules of starch are present in wheat flour, and when these become wet and hot they burst as boiling point is reached: the granules collapse and spread, becoming gelatinous. Whisking then distributes this throughout and the sauce is thus thickened. (In this context I have found that self-raising flour is more inclined to go lumpy than plain flour, so I don't use it for sauces.)

Cornflour

This is pure starch separated from the rest of the flour, which does the thickening job very efficiently. But unfortunately it does not make a sauce with either the character or creamy texture that comes from white flour. Although I never make sauces with cornflour, I find it very useful for adding to egg-based sauces (especially 'proper' custard) to prevent the eggs from curdling— but only in a *small* amount so as not to affect the flavour.

Arrowroot

This is an edible starch which comes not from corn but from a plant root grown in the West Indies, which is ground down to a fine powder. As a thickening it is excellent for making a glaze for, say, a fruit flan because, unlike cornflour, it will thicken fruit juices and keep them clear and transparent at the same time. To use it, you need about 1 rounded teaspoon for every ¼ pint (150 ml) of liquid, and it has to be added to a little cold water first before being mixed with your liquid and being brought up to boiling point (at that stage remove it from the heat straight away, as over-boiling can cause it to liquify and lose its thickening power).

Liquid

The liquid base for a sauce can be almost anything: light home-made chicken or bone stock, the stock from boiling vegetables (especially if the sauce is to be served with those vegetables), sometimes milk, other times a mixture of milk and stock. Both wine and cider are particularly good for gravies or sauces to accompany meat or fish.

Whenever expert cooks continually disagree on a finer point of cookery, it usually means it's not that important. So it is with the question of the temperature of liquid being added to a sauce. There are those who swear it must be hot, and those who insist it should be cold: in my humble opinion it doesn't matter one scrap. If it happens that the liquid you're adding is hot from the stock-pot, fine. On the other hand, if it's cold milk from the fridge, that's fine too. But one exception I must state now—and this is when you are making an *all-in-one sauce* (see page 148): for this the liquid you start off with should be cold.

Butter and fats

Butter is what makes a sauce creamy and rich, and as a rule is added in the same proportion as the flour. For extra creaminess the amount of butter can be increased, or else cream or soured cream added. Soured cream needs careful attention, though, because boiling can cause it to curdle: whereas ordinary cream *won't* hurt if it comes to the boil. Dripping, pork fat and lard are sometimes used in place of butter to make a brown roux.

What is a roux?

To make a classic béchamel 'white' sauce, the first process is to combine melted butter with an equal quantity of flour. The result is called a *roux*: the basis into which the required amount of liquid is worked to make the finished sauce.

In this cookery course we need never actually bother with the word roux, because when a recipe requires an equal quantity of butter and flour mixed together, it will say that. However, roux is the term used in French classic cookery to describe the base of three different types of sauce: *roux blanc* (white base), *roux blond* (pale-cream roux), and *roux brun* or brown roux where the fat and flour are allowed to go on cooking longer—up to 30 minutes—to brown and give the finished sauce a nutty flavour. It is quite a tricky operation to perfect, rarely needed except in advanced cooking.

You may have heard that it is possible to make up a batch of butter-and-flour and store it in the refrigerator ready for use. But it will only keep for about 4 weeks (and anyway only takes a few seconds to mix) so I don't really see the point. I know I can never tell how much I might need in the space of 4 weeks—if any.

How long should a sauce be cooked?

White sauces, when they're first made, can have a rather 'raw' flavour—which means that not all the starch granules have burst and disintegrated into the sauce. For that reason they have to be 'cooked', that is to say left over the gentlest possible heat for about

6–10 minutes. During this cooking process a thin layer of skin may form on the surface. I find this can usually be whisked back into the sauce quite happily, but you can actually prevent this skin forming by keeping back 1 or 2 tablespoons of liquid and 'floating' it on top at the end, without stirring it in. Then whisk it in normally after the sauce has cooked.

Keeping a sauce warm

The only acceptable way to keep a sauce warm, or re-heat it, is to place the saucepan in another larger saucepan or pot of gently simmering water (to provide heat all round and not just underneath).

Basic white sauce: traditional method

We've considered the basic ingredients: now they have to be combined correctly. Here are the standard proportions for a pouring sauce—badly-made sauces are often too thick and pasty, so do measure quantities carefully.

For 1 pint:
1½ oz plain flour (sifted) (40 g)
2 oz butter (50 g)
1 pint milk or half milk, half stock (570 ml)
Salt and pepper

For ¾ pint:
1 oz sifted plain flour (25 g)
1½ oz butter (40 g)
¾ pint milk or half milk, half stock (425 ml)
Salt and pepper

The basic procedure is to (a) melt the butter over a medium heat, (b) stir in the flour off the heat, and (c) back on the heat, add the liquid bit by bit until it has all been incorporated and the sauce is smooth and glossy.

Have the liquid ready in a measuring jug, then melt the butter in a small saucepan very gently—it must not brown or it will affect the flavour and colour of the finished sauce. Take it off the heat as soon as the butter has melted and stir in the sifted flour. Stir to form a smooth glossy paste, then return the saucepan to a medium heat and start to add the milk—about 1 fl. oz (25 ml) at a time—stirring quite vigorously with a wooden spoon as you pour, to incorporate each bit of liquid thoroughly before adding the next. If you're conscientious about the stirring you won't get any lumps: if you do, then either whisk them away with a wire- or rotary-whisk or sieve the finished sauce.

When all the milk has been incorporated, turn the heat to its lowest possible setting and let the sauce cook for 6–10 minutes. Then taste and season as required. *Note:* I always use freshly-ground black pepper because I don't mind the little dark speckles, but if you do then use freshly-ground white. For extra creaminess beat in an extra knob of butter at the end or else a couple of tablespoons of thick cream.

Béchamel sauce

When a plain white sauce is called for, you can give it extra flavour by *infusing* the milk beforehand for about 30 minutes. For this you need:

For ¾ pint of milk:
1 small piece of carrot
½ smallish onion
2-in. piece of celery
6 whole peppercorns
1 blade of mace
½ bayleaf.

Place the above ingredients in a saucepan with the ¾ pint (425 ml) of milk, and then bring it to the boil very slowly. After that, remove from the heat and allow it to infuse for 20 minutes. Then strain the milk into a jug and proceed to make the sauce following the method described above. Alternatively you can let it cool for 45 minutes, and carry on with the all-in-one method below.

Basic white sauce: all-in-one method

This speeded-up version is even easier than using a packet! All you need is a balloon whisk (or a coiled wire- or rotary-whisk) and a wooden spoon. It is suitable for all sauces except those where a vegetable has to be 'sweated' in butter first. *But* the liquid you add to this one must be cold: the dreaded lumps will form if the flour goes straight into hot liquid.

1½ oz butter (40 g)
1 oz plain flour (25 g)
¾ pint of cold milk (or half milk, half stock) (425 ml)
Salt and pepper

Simply place all the ingredients in a saucepan, put the saucepan on a medium heat and whisk until the sauce starts to bubble and thicken. Then stir with a wooden spoon, to get right into the corners of the pan, and whisk again thoroughly. Turn the heat down as low as possible and cook the sauce gently for 6 minutes.

These first three recipes are the basis for a whole range of sauces; on their own they would be rather dull of course, but so many other ingredients can be used for flavouring. Here first are three variations on the all-in-one method, bearing in mind that the infused milk or stock must be cooled for a minimum of 45 minutes (if you're in a hurry, use the traditional method). Cream is used here to add a touch of luxury, but if not available it can be replaced by the same quantity of milk.

Mustard sauce   This is a good sauce which is often served with herring.

½ pint of milk (275 ml)
1 small onion, halved
1½ oz butter (40 g)
1 oz plain flour (25 g)
2 rounded teaspoons mustard powder
¼ pint single cream (150 ml)
1 teaspoon lemon juice
Salt and cayenne pepper

Bring the halved onion and the milk slowly to the boil, then remove from the heat and let it infuse until cooled. Now place the strained infused milk together with the butter, flour, mustard powder and cream in a saucepan, and bring to the boil, whisking continuously. Then cook the sauce gently for 5 minutes. Taste and season with salt, cayenne and lemon juice.

Cheese sauce

This is a basic cheese sauce which can be used in a wide variety of dishes. Grated Gruyère cheese could be used instead of Cheddar here, for a spot of refinement.

$\frac{1}{2}$ **pint milk (275 ml)**
$\frac{1}{2}$ **pint single cream (275 ml)**
1 level teaspoon mustard
1 oz plain flour (25g)
1$\frac{1}{2}$ oz butter (40 g)
2 oz strong Cheddar cheese, grated (50 g)
1 oz grated Parmesan cheese (25 g)
A pinch of cayenne pepper
$\frac{1}{2}$ teaspoon lemon juice
Salt and freshly-milled black pepper

Place the first five ingredients in a saucepan and whisk over the heat till smooth and thickened. Now add the cheeses, stir to melt them in, then cook the sauce *gently* for 5 minutes. Season to taste with salt, pepper, cayenne and lemon juice.

Parsley sauce

I like parsley sauce best with baked fish cutlets of various kinds: it's also very good with boiled gammon.

$\frac{1}{2}$ **pint milk (275 ml)**
$\frac{1}{4}$ **pint single cream (150 ml)**
1$\frac{1}{2}$ oz butter (40 g)
1 oz flour (25 g)
3 tablespoons finely-chopped parsley
1 teaspoon lemon juice
Salt and freshly-milled black pepper

Place the first four ingredients in a saucepan, and whisk them over the heat till smooth and thickened. Then cook for 5 minutes, add the parsley and lemon juice, and season to taste. *Note:* For extra flavour you can infuse the milk with the parsley stalks first—but let it get absolutely cold before using it for the all-in-one method.

Hollandaise sauce*

This adaptation of one of the famous French butter sauces goes particularly well with vegetables, like fresh artichokes or new season's asparagus.

For the reduction:
2 tablespoons white wine vinegar
3 tablespoons water
1 slice of onion
1 blade of mace
$\frac{1}{2}$ small bayleaf
6 black peppercorns

For the sauce:
1 tablespoon water
3 egg yolks
6 oz unsalted butter (room temperature) (160 g)
Lemon juice to taste
Salt and freshly-milled black pepper

Place the first six ingredients together in a small saucepan and simmer gently (uncovered) until the mixture is reduced to about 1 tablespoon—keep your eye on it because it can boil away before you know it! Then strain the reduced mixture into a bowl, add a further tablespoon of water and a little seasoning. Whisk in the egg yolks.

Next place the bowl over a pan of *barely* simmering water, and add $\frac{1}{2}$ oz (10 g) of the butter, whisking until it has melted and the mixture has thickened slightly. Carry on adding lumps of butter— approx. $\frac{1}{2}$ oz (10 g) at a time—and allow the butter to melt and the mixture to thicken before adding any more.

When all the butter is in, carry on whisking and cooking gently for a further 2 minutes. Then remove the bowl from over the water, taste, and add lemon juice and seasoning as required. If the mixture curdles (which it will only do if overheated) place a fresh egg yolk in a clean bowl and gradually whisk in the curdled mixture to bring it back.

* See page 39 for a simpler version of this sauce.

Buttery onion sauce

(serves 4 people)

A lovely sauce, this one, to serve with lamb in the late autumn.

1½ oz butter (40 g)
1 oz flour (25 g)
½ pint milk (275 ml)
¼ pint single cream (150 ml)
1 large onion, chopped small
Salt, pepper and a scraping of nutmeg
An extra ½ oz butter to stir in at the end (10 g)

Since the onion needs to 'sweat' in the butter first to release its juices, it is best to use the traditional white sauce method for this recipe.

Start off by melting the butter in a saucepan, then keeping the heat very low allow the onion to cook for about 10 minutes without colouring. Stir it around from time to time. Then add the flour and stir to a smooth paste.

Now gradually incorporate the milk and cream, a little at a time, whisking or stirring vigorously after each addition till you have a smooth sauce. Turn the heat down to its absolute minimum setting, and let the sauce cook for 6 minutes. Season with salt, pepper and a scraping of nutmeg—and finish off by stirring a lump of butter in just before serving.

Leek cream sauce

A delicious sauce to serve with a boiled bacon joint; this can be made by using the above recipe, replacing the onion with 2 medium leeks, cleaned and chopped.

Celery sauce

For serving with chicken or boiled bacon, this sauce is ideal.

6 oz celery stalks (160 g), cut into ¼ inch (½ cm) pieces
1½ oz butter (40 g)
1 oz flour (25 g)
¼ pint chicken stock (150 ml)
¼ pint milk (150 ml)

1 teaspoon lemon juice
Salt, pepper, nutmeg

First place the celery in a saucepan and pour boiling water on it, add some salt and simmer for 10 minutes. Then drain the celery and, in the same saucepan, melt the butter and fry the celery in it for a further 10 minutes with the lid on. Then uncover, stir in the flour till smooth, and gradually beat in the milk and chicken stock, a little bit at a time. Cook for 2 minutes, then liquidise the sauce to a purée: return it to the saucepan to re-heat, and season with salt, pepper, lemon juice and a sprinkling of nutmeg.

Cucumber sauce

This is the sauce to serve with fish, say fillets of brill or even salmon if the season (and the price) is right.

1 firm young cucumber
2 fl. oz dry white wine (50 ml)
1½ oz butter (40 g)
1 oz flour (25 g)
¼ pint single cream (150 ml)
½ teaspoon lemon juice
Salt and freshly-milled black pepper

Pare off the peel of the cucumber, preferably with a potato peeler as it is important (for the colour of the sauce) to leave some of the green. Then divide the cucumber in half and liquidise one half together with the white wine (this should yield about ½ pint (275 ml) of liquid). Now chop the other half of the cucumber into small dice and sweat them gently with the butter in a covered saucepan for 10 minutes. Next stir in the flour, beat till smooth, then add the cucumber liquid and cream—bit by bit—whisking all the time until you have a smooth sauce. Cook gently for about 5 minutes, taste, and season with salt, pepper and lemon juice.

Sauce béarnaise

This is one of the great French butter sauces. It is tricky to make because it can curdle or—if you really overheat it—even scramble! However, if you're careful, and add a little mustard powder to help stabilise it, you should have no problems. It is delicious with any plain meat or fish, and especially with *Bœuf en croute* (page 92).

1 tablespoon coarsely-chopped fresh tarragon (or $\frac{1}{2}$ teaspoon of dried)
1 tablespoon coarsely-chopped parsley
1 tablespoon chopped shallot (or spring onion)
6 black peppercorns crushed
2 tablespoons white wine vinegar
$\frac{1}{4}$ pint dry white wine (150 ml)
3 egg yolks
1 teaspoon mustard powder
1 oz butter (room temperature) (25 g)
6 oz melted butter (175 g)
Salt

Start off in a small saucepan by boiling the herbs, shallot, peppercorns, wine vinegar and white wine together until the mixture has reduced by about a third—in other words there should be about 3 tablespoons of slightly syrupy liquid left in the pan. Now whisk the egg yolks and mustard together in the top of a double saucepan.

Strain the vinegar mixture through a fine sieve onto the egg yolks, add a tablespoon of water and beat over hot (but not boiling) water, using a wire whisk. Next beat in the solid butter, about $\frac{1}{2}$ oz (10 g) at a time, then gradually add the melted butter, a drop at a time—still whisking after each addition until all the butter is in and the sauce has thickened. Taste and season with salt and keep warm over the hot water till needed.

Spiced apple and onion sauce

(serves 4 people)

An apple sauce—with a little onion added—goes well with most pork dishes. If you don't like cloves, you can leave them out of this recipe.

$\frac{1}{2}$ medium onion, finely chopped
1 tablespoon lard or butter
1 dessertspoon sugar
2 cloves

2 medium cooking apples, peeled and thinly sliced
2 tablespoons water or dry cider
A little freshly-grated nutmeg

Begin by melting the fat in a thick-based saucepan, soften the chopped onion in it for 5 or six minutes, then add the slices of apple. Give them a good stir before adding the cloves and the water (or cider) and sugar. Stir again, cover the saucepan and leave the apples to cook down to a fluff (about 10 minutes). When they're cooked remove the cloves, beat the apples down to a smooth sauce, grate in a little nutmeg and pour into a jug to serve.

Traditional bread sauce

(serves 5–6 people)

This is my favourite sauce for serving with roast turkey, chicken or pheasant. Don't be put off by some of the restaurant or packet varieties because home-made it is deliciously light and creamy.

3 oz freshly-made white breadcrumbs (75 g) (a 2-day-old white loaf with the crusts removed will be stale enough to grate, but the best way to do this is in a liquidiser, if you have one)
$\frac{3}{4}$ pint milk (425 ml)
1 medium onion
1 bayleaf
15 whole cloves
6 black peppercorns
2 oz butter (50 g)
2 tablespoons double cream
Salt and freshly-milled black pepper

A couple of hours before you need the sauce, cut the onion in half and stick the cloves in it. How many cloves you actually use depends on you, but I, personally, like a pronounced flavour; if you really don't like cloves, you can use some freshly-grated nutmeg instead.

Place the onion, bayleaf and the 6 black peppercorns in a saucepan with the milk and put this to infuse in a warm place for about 2 hours. Then, over a very low heat, bring the milk slowly to the boil, which should take about 15 minutes. Next, remove the onion, bayleaf and peppercorns and keep on one side.

Stir the breadcrumbs into the milk and add 1 oz (25 g) of the butter and some salt. Leave the saucepan on a very low heat (stirring now and then) until the crumbs have swollen and thickened the sauce. Now replace the clove-studded onion and again leave the saucepan in a warm place until the sauce is needed.

Just before serving, remove the onion and spices, beat in the remaining butter and the cream, and taste to check the seasoning.

Cumberland sauce

This is, perhaps, my favourite English sauce—delicious at Christmas with hot or cold gammon or tongue and it stores in a screw-top jar for several weeks in a cool place.

4 large tablespoons authentic redcurrant jelly*
4 tablespoons port
1 medium orange
1 medium lemon
1 heaped teaspoon dried mustard powder
1 heaped teaspoon powdered ginger

* I suspect some commercially-made redcurrant jellies are not exactly authentic, so read the labels carefully and go for a make that guarantees a high fruit content

First, thinly pare off the rinds of both the lemon and the orange (either with a very sharp paring knife or a potato peeler) then cut them into very small strips, about ½ inch (1 cm) in length and as thin as possible. Boil the rinds in water for 5 minutes or so to extract any bitterness, then drain well in a sieve.

Now place the redcurrant jelly in a saucepan with the port and melt them together over a low heat for about 5 or 10 minutes. The redcurrant jelly won't melt completely, so it's best to sieve it afterwards to get rid of any obstinate little globules.

In a serving bowl mix the mustard and ginger with the juice of half a lemon till smooth, then add the juice of a whole orange, the port and redcurrant mixture and finally the little strips of orange and lemon peel. Mix well—and it's ready for use. Cumberland sauce is always served cold.

Redcurrant orange and mint sauce

(serves 6 people)

I think the vinegar in mint sauce is far too strong for the delicate flavour of lamb in the peak of summer and that this sauce is a far nicer one.

4 tablespoons authentic redcurrant jelly (one with a high fruit content)
The grated zest of 1 orange
1½ tablespoons fresh chopped mint

Place the jelly in a small basin, break it up with a fork, then mix in the orange zest and the mint—and that's it. It must be one of the quickest sauces in the world, and it's absolutely delicious.

Spiced green tomato sauce

(serves 4 people)

If you're likely to have a crop of tomatoes that will never ripen, fear not, because this sauce is a real winner and really delicious with good pork sausages.

½ onion, chopped
½ green pepper, chopped
½ fresh green chilli, deseeded and chopped
1 tablespoon oil
1 lb green tomatoes (450 g), coarsely minced or very finely chopped (you needn't skin them)
1 large clove garlic, crushed
½ teaspoon whole cumin seeds, crushed
Salt and freshly-milled black pepper

Using a thick-based saucepan, fry the onion, pepper and chilli in the oil over a low heat for about 10 minutes. Now add the tomatoes, garlic, crushed cumin seeds and seasoning, and bring to simmering point. Cover and simmer for 15 minutes with the lid on and for a further 10 minutes without the lid, which will allow some of the excess liquid to reduce.

This sauce also goes very well with some fleshy fish, such as turbot or mackerel.

Tomato sauce provençale

(serves 2 people)

This is one of life's simple luxuries—the fragrant flavour of ripened tomatoes takes a lot of beating. Serve it with fish, plain grilled meat or simply with a dish of pasta.

¾ lb ripe tomatoes (350 g)
1 small onion, finely chopped
1 clove garlic, crushed
1 dessertspoon fresh chopped basil (or 1 teaspoon dried)
1 tablespoon olive oil
4 tablespoons red wine
Salt and freshly-milled black pepper

Begin by pouring some boiling water onto the tomatoes, then leave them for a minute or so, and cool them in a colander under cold running water. Then slip the skins off and chop the flesh roughly.

Now heat the olive oil in a thick-based saucepan and gently soften the onion in it for 5 minutes, then add the crushed garlic and the chopped tomatoes, basil and wine, stir and bring it up to simmering point. Now let the sauce simmer very gently (without a lid) for about 25 minutes, by which time a lot of the excess liquid will have evaporated and the sauce will have a good concentrated flavour.

Now either pass it through a sieve or liquidise it, if you want a smooth sauce, otherwise you can leave it as it is. Season with salt and pepper, then re-heat gently and serve.

For tomato chilli sauce
Make the sauce as above but add ¼ teaspoon chilli powder, in which case it would be a good accompaniment to sausages, rissoles or hamburgers.

Bolognese sauce

(serves 4 people)

Frozen chicken livers seem now to be fairly widely available and they make all the difference if you want to make a really authentic Bolognese sauce.

6 oz lean minced beef (175 g)
3 oz chicken livers, chopped small (75 g)

2 rashers unsmoked streaky bacon, finely chopped
1 teaspoon dried basil
1 small onion, very finely chopped
1 fat clove garlic, crushed
8-oz (225-g) tin Italian tomatoes
4 tablespoons red wine
2 heaped tablespoons tomato purée
1½ tablespoons olive oil
Salt and freshly-milled black pepper

Heat the oil in a thick-based saucepan, then gently soften the onion, bacon and garlic in it for 5 minutes. Now turn up the heat, add the chicken livers and meat, and brown it, keeping it on the move with a wooden spoon. When the meat has browned, pour in the contents of the tin of tomatoes, plus the tomato purée, wine, basil and some seasoning. Put a lid on and simmer gently for 20 minutes, then take the lid off and continue to simmer gently for a further 20–25 minutes to get a nice thick concentrated sauce.

Italian green sauce (salsa verde)

(serves 2 people)

This is a strong-flavoured, quite garlicky, sauce, which does wonders for plain mackerel fillets or some grilled trout.

2 tablespoons fresh parsley, chopped
1 tablespoon fresh basil, chopped (or 1 teaspoon dried)
4 anchovy fillets, drained
1 tablespoon capers
1 small clove garlic, crushed
1 level teaspoon English mustard powder
1½ tablespoons lemon juice
6 tablespoons olive oil
Salt and freshly-milled black pepper

To start with chop the anchovy fillets as small as possible and crush them to a paste in a mortar (if you haven't a mortar a small bowl and the end of a rolling-pin will do).

Put the capers in a small sieve and rinse them under cold running water to remove the vinegar they were preserved in. Dry them on kitchen paper and chop them as minutely as you can and add them to the anchovies.

Next add the mustard, garlic, lemon juice and some freshly-milled black pepper and mix well. Now add the oil, mix again and check the taste to see how much salt to add.

Just before serving, sprinkle in the chopped herbs and again mix thoroughly so that all the ingredients are properly combined.

Note: This behaves rather like a very thick vinaigrette and, before each serving, always needs to have another mix.

Avocado sauce
(serves 4 people)

This pale-green pistachio-coloured sauce is delicious with cold salmon in the summer or for use as a dip with lots of thin slivers of raw vegetables.

1 small or $\frac{1}{2}$ fairly large avocado pear
5 oz carton soured cream (150 g)
1 tablespoon fresh lemon juice
$\frac{1}{2}$ clove garlic, crushed
Salt and freshly-milled black pepper

Scrape the avocado flesh away from the skin into a bowl, making sure you scrape away the very green bit next to the skin as this is important for the colour of the sauce. Then mash it to a purée together with the lemon juice, garlic and seasoning, and combine it with the soured cream, mixing thoroughly until you have a smooth, pale-green, creamy sauce. Cover the basin tightly with cellophane wrap to stop the avocado discolouring and chill in the refrigerator till needed. Do make this sauce the same day as it's required, since it does tend to discolour if left too long.

Sauce sabayon
(serves 4 people)

This is a sweet sauce for serving with hot puddings like a Spotted Dick or light lemony sponge. It's also very good with a bread and butter pudding.

3 large egg yolks
2 oz caster sugar (50 g)
$\frac{1}{4}$ pint dry white wine (150 ml)

Start by placing a small saucepan of water on a low heat, and heat the water to just below simmering point.

Now put the egg yolks and sugar into a pudding basin and whisk until the mixture starts to thicken. Next sit the basin over the saucepan of simmering water and, keeping the heat low and continuing to whisk, add the wine slowly, a little at a time. When you've added all the wine, continue whisking until the egg yolk has cooked and thickened to a fairly thick fluffy sauce.

Serve the sauce warm from a warmed jug or serving bowl.

This could be made with dry cider instead of wine, in which case it would go very well with an apple pudding.

Butterscotch sauce

People never fail to drool over this lovely, thick, butterscotch sauce—delicious poured over ice-cream just by itself, or with chopped bananas or fresh sliced peaches.

2 oz butter (50 g)
3 oz soft brown sugar (75 g)
2 oz granulated sugar (50 g)
5 oz golden syrup (150 g) (that's approximately one-third of a 1-lb (450-g) tin)
4 fl. oz double cream (110 ml)
A few drops vanilla essence

First of all, place the butter and both the soft brown and granulated sugars in a medium-sized, thick-based saucepan together with the syrup. Heat slowly, and once the ingredients have completely melted and the sugar dissolved and formed a liquid, continue to heat gently for about another 5 minutes. Then turn off the heat underneath the saucepan.

Now gradually stir the double cream into the sauce, followed by a few drops of vanilla essence. Stir for a further 2 or 3 minutes, or until the sauce is absolutely smooth.

That's it; serve it hot or cold. If you want to keep it, it will store well for several weeks in a cool place in a screw-top jar.

Port wine sauce

This puts a steamed pudding into the dinner-party class and is especially good with the raisin pudding on page 239.

5 fl. oz ruby or tawny port (150 ml)
Grated zest of 1 Seville orange (but an ordinary orange will do)
2 oz caster sugar (50 g)
5 fl. oz water (150 ml)
½ nutmeg, freshly grated
1 tablespoon Seville orange juice
1 oz unsalted butter (25 g)
1 teaspoon flour

Begin by gently boiling the orange zest, water and sugar in a thick-bottomed saucepan for 15 minutes.

Meanwhile, mix the butter into the flour and divide it up into about 6 pieces, adding them to the syrup at the end of the cooking time, followed by the port, nutmeg and orange juice. Boil the mixture for 1 minute over a gentle heat, stirring continuously, then serve immediately.

Note: The sauce can be prepared in advance, except for the butter and flour part, which should be added just before serving.

Rum or brandy sauce
(serves 4 people)

I always think a pouring sauce is best with a rich Christmas pudding—I happen to prefer it with rum, but if you prefer brandy the quantities you use are the same.

1½ oz butter (40 g)
2 level tablespoons plain flour
1½ tablespoons caster sugar
¾ pint milk (425 ml)
2–3 tablespoons rum (or brandy)

First of all slowly melt the butter in a small saucepan.

Now work the flour into the melted butter, using a wooden spoon, until the mixture is fairly smooth. Then gradually add the milk and stir well after each addition to keep the mixture free from any lumps. When all the milk is added and you have a smooth creamy sauce, stir in the sugar, and let it cook over a very low heat for 10 minutes, stirring it slowly all the time to prevent it sticking. Then add the rum, and taste to check if more sugar or rum is needed before serving.

Flavoured butters

These can be used instead of sauces for all sorts of dishes. They are a lot quicker to make and add interest to something plain.

Herb butter
(serves 6 people)

You can serve this with chops, steaks or fish or simply swirl it around some hot cooked vegetables such as carrots, new potatoes, courgettes or cauliflower. You could also stir some into a vegetable soup or a sauce at the last minute.

6 oz butter (room temperature) (175 g)
4 tablespoons chopped parsley
1½ tablespoons snipped chives
1 teaspoon chopped tarragon or thyme
1 large clove garlic, crushed
1 dessertspoon lemon juice
Salt and freshly-milled black pepper

Combine all the above ingredients together. Store, covered with foil, in the refrigerator in small 2 oz (50 g) portions.

This can also be a good way of storing fresh herbs if you have a freezer (or a 4-star freezing compartment).

Anchovy butter

This can be served spread on wholemeal toast sprinkled with cayenne pepper or melted over plain grilled fish fillets.

5 oz unsalted butter (room temperature) (150 g)
2-oz (50-g) tin anchovy fillets in oil
1 teaspoon lemon juice
¼ teaspoon anchovy essence
Some cayenne pepper

| ½ teaspoon grated onion |
| 1 clove garlic, crushed |

First drain the anchovy fillets, then pat them as dry as possible with some kitchen paper. Then place the butter in a bowl and beat it with a wooden spoon till it's light and creamy—then add the anchovies after pounding them to a pulp. Stir in the garlic, anchovy essence, onion and lemon juice, then taste it and season with cayenne pepper (it should be fairly piquant). Now pile the butter into a bowl, cover and chill for an hour or two before serving.

Note: If you like, you can make this by just placing everything in a liquidiser and blending until smooth—only if you do, use fewer anchovies (about three-quarters of the above) as liquidising them seems to make them taste stronger.

Hot lemon butter

This can be served as a quick accompaniment to asparagus, globe artichokes or fish.

| 4 oz (110 g) salted butter |
| 1 tablespoon lemon juice |
| Grated zest of ½ lemon |
| Salt |
| Freshly-milled black pepper |

Heat the butter, lemon juice and zest in a small saucepan. As soon as the butter melts and starts to sizzle, season with the salt and pepper and serve it very hot.

Gravy

I see from the *Oxford Dictionary* that gravy is supposed to be 'the fat and juices which exude from flesh in cooking' or a dressing for meat and vegetables made from these. Well, if you were roasting a baron of beef in the 18th century no doubt enough juices would exude from it to provide sufficient gravy. Nowadays our more modest joints need a little help with the gravy, if there's to be enough to go around.

First of all I would like to say quite emphatically that commercially-produced gravy mixes, highly-flavoured beef

Right: Eccles cakes, page 93; Wholewheat treacle tart, page 86; Fresh cherry pie, page 80.

extracts, meat cubes or stock cubes are *not* needed. Their chemical flavours will not enhance the meat at all: on the contrary they only compete with it. So what is needed? Quite simply the meat roasting tin containing its fat and juices—or the pan in which the meat has been browned. The additional liquid can be wine, dry cider, stock or even water. There are two ways to make gravy:

Deglazing method

This is useful when just a little thin gravy is required. Most of the fat (if any) is spooned out of the pan, then with a wooden spoon you scrape all the crusty bits that cling to the base and sides of the pan (this is deglazing). Then to these and the juices, add either wine, stock or water: boil briskly for a few seconds to form a sauce.

Good old-fashioned gravy

For this—the familiar thicker gravy that goes with a roast joint—the principles are as follows. First make sure you're using a good thick-based roasting tin, then when the meat comes out of the oven, lift it onto a plate and leave it to 'relax' before carving (see page 126). Now tilt the roasting tin, and you will see quite clearly the actual meat juices down in the corner and the fat, separately, settling on top of the juices. Take a large tablespoon and spoon most of the fat off into a bowl—leaving behind 2–3 tablespoons, depending on how much gravy you need.

Now place the roasting tin over direct heat (turned fairly low), and when the juices start to sizzle sprinkle in some flour—about 1 level tablespoon to each ½ pint (275 ml) of liquid to be used. Next, with a wooden spoon quickly work the flour into the fat, using circular movements all over the base of the tin. Then when you have a smooth paste, begin to add the liquid gradually, keeping up the vigorous stirring all over the base of the tin. Carry on like this until all the liquid has been added and you have a smooth sauce (if it's too thick, add a bit more liquid). If you have already added too much liquid by mistake, just boil briskly for a minute or two and the sauce will reduce and thicken again. Taste and season the sauce, and add a few drops of gravy browning if it needs it. Before serving, pour the gravy into a warm jug.

Instant gravy

There will be times when you want to make some gravy from scratch, without the benefit of any meat juices. All you need do for

Left: Bœuf en croute, page 92.

this is melt 1 oz (25 g) of dripping or lard in a small saucepan and fry ½ finely-chopped onion in it. Keep the heat high and let the onion turn really brown. Then stir in 1 oz (25 g) of flour and gradually whisk in ¾ pint (425 ml) of stock (or hot water flavoured with ½ teaspoon of Worcestershire sauce and 1 dessertspoon of mushroom ketchup). Simmer for 5 minutes and season to taste, adding a few drops of gravy browning if it needs it.

Notes on gravy ingredients

Stock can be meat or chicken giblet stock or some sort of vegetable stock—potato water and so on. If you are just using boiling water you can enrich it with a few drops of Worcestershire sauce and a dessertspoon of mushroom ketchup.

Wine can be useful for gravies if there's some around. Just a couple of tablespoons can really enrich the flavour. Dry cider is a good alternative, and much more economical.

Gravy browning Commercial gravy browning is simply a concentrated caramel (burnt sugar). It doesn't have the chemical flavours of gravy-mixes and is invaluable for enhancing the colour of gravy. If you don't have, or don't want to use gravy browning, then slice ½ onion and place it in the meat roasting tin along with the meat: it will turn jet black and caramelise during the roasting, and colour the gravy for you.

Flour I always use plain flour for gravy, having found in the past that self-raising tends to go lumpy.

Spices and flavourings

Including recipes for:
Steak au poivre
Braised steak with green peppercorn sauce
Indian kebabs
Beef curry with whole spices
Spiced chicken
Chicken paprika
Marinaded pork with coriander
Moussaka
Guacamole
Sautéed cauliflour with coriander
Spiced pears in cider

Countries have grown rich, gone to war, built empires on spice. It was the trading currency of the medieval world, its value greater than gold and precious metals. So it is curious to find, in medieval cookery books, so many different spices competing (and in such prolific amounts) in a single recipe. In one I have in front of me a humble pike is treated to no less than eight different flavourings. Such abandon with precious spices was commonly supposed to disguise the taste of not-very-fresh food. And no doubt it was in many cases, but I also think there was an element of status-seeking in it as well. The cookery-books that have survived, after all, were those compiled by master-chefs for grand households. When—in the 17th century—spices became more widely available and cheaper in England, they began to be used with much more discretion and English cooking improved in consequence (the 'best in the world' according to Defoe at the time).

With our conquest of India, the British became even more spice-conscious as exotic curry flavourings were added to the repertoire, along with the already traditional taste for pickles, relishes and preserves. The Victorians in particular were very partial to a whole range of weird and wonderful compounds of spices, which were commercially produced under names like Harvey's Sauce: some of the better ones have survived to the present day (like Worcestershire sauce and tomato ketchup). I have the feeling that we are still suffering a bit from the legacy of the Victorians in this: there is a tendency to prefer to add flavourings to our food in the form of bottled sauces at the table, rather than incorporate them more discriminatingly in the cooking.

However, the range of spices available, even in local supermarkets, is now most impressive. They open up a whole world of recipes, and there is no excuse for our cooking horizons to be bounded by plain fried fish or grilled lamb chops (excellent though they are). All that is required is the confidence to go out and buy them and to experiment—not like a medieval alchemist throwing anything and everything together in a hotch-potch of flavours, but with restraint allowing the flavour of the spices to enhance and complement the flavour of the food. The recipes in this section (and elsewhere in the book) are designed to demonstrate the balanced use of individual spices in recipes, and the combinations that have been shown to work through experience.

It is impossible to describe the flavour of each spice with any meaning—only testing them for yourself can be any guide—but the list below offers some explanation of their origin and possible uses. I have included in this section those equally important seasonings and flavourings which are normally lumped together under the ungainly title of condiments, and whose proper use is vital to good cooking.

Salt

It's amazing the difference salt makes to food, almost magically bringing out the flavour of a soup or sauce that may have seemed quite bland. Just how much salt you should or should not use has always been a subject for debate: some 'connoisseurs' even suggest that to add additional salt at the table is an insult to the chef. I believe that's nonsense. Each individual's capacity for salt is different, and what may be enough for the chef may not be enough for his diners. At the same time it could be true that adding more salt to food is a matter of acquired habit rather than need (as with sugar), which is why tinned baby foods now do not contain any salt—so at least our babies are not forming the habit! Others argue the health aspect, maintaining that salt—although a mineral essential to life—can in too high quantities exacerbate (not cause) hypertension and high blood pressure, which are themselves contributory factors to heart disease. This, I think, is an argument only for discretion, which is fundamental to all cooking anyway. If you discover that you *have* oversalted a dish with liquid ingredients, you can rescue it by putting in a peeled potato or two, which will absorb some of the salty flavour.

Types of salt

First of all it's as well to discount the snob element. Since the vogue for kitchen shops there's a lot of rock/sea/Mediterranean/crystal salt around. My advice is never to buy it from fancy packets. It is true that pure, unrefined salt is better than refined because it's saltier and you need less, but you can buy it from chemists, delicatessens and health food stores without paying for the packaging.

Basically there are two kinds of salt. For cooking and the table there is common salt mined from rocks or extracted from sea water. The other kind is saltpetre, which comes out of the earth and is used for curing and pickling. The sea salt I use comes from Maldon; it is packaged in ordinary boxes and, although it is too expensive to use exclusively for cooking, there are certain things I invariably serve it with: chips, sautéed potatoes, fritters and other deep-fried foods taste so much better with crushed Maldon salt and coarse pepper over them. Unlike other unrefined salts—such as crystal salt which needs to be crushed first with a pestle and mortar—Maldon comes in tiny flakes and at table can easily be crushed between the fingers. Beware of salt mills, by the way. For grinding salt crystals I have found them quite useless: it is never fine enough and the salt either descends in a rush or not at all.

For everyday use the bulk of our salt comes from rock-deposits in Cheshire. Our so-called 'table salt' is very finely grained and has a chemical (magnesium carbonate) added to make it free-running. Personally I use what is termed 'cooking salt', which has fractionally larger grains, is cheaper and available at supermarkets. Even for the table I can't see the point of paying more for finer grains, particularly using a salt-cellar and spoon rather than a sprinkler.

Pepper

Pepper in my opinion is the most important spice in the kitchen. The one way in which beginners can instantly improve the character and flavour of their cooking and eating is to invest in a pepper-mill. *Freshly-ground* pepper has a fragrance and flavour that the dusty ready-ground stuff cannot approach. This is partly due to the fact that any spice once ground immediately starts to lose its essential flavour, and partly to the fact that most pepper-pots find their way to the table containing ready-ground 'white' pepper. Both black and white pepper come from the berries of the same tree, called *piper nigrum*, but let us see where the difference lies.

Black pepper Black peppercorns are the whole immature berries. The berries themselves are made up of a white inner kernel and a black outer husk. The white is the hottest part of the berry and when used on its own is distinctly fiery. It is the black outer part that has the aromatic fragrance that really enhances the flavour of food. And this part is included in black pepper, where the berries are gathered while still green, then dried whole in the sun until they turn black.

White pepper For this the berries are allowed to mature fully before they are harvested. The husks are then split and discarded, and the white kernels are dried to become white peppercorns.

Stored whole, the dried berries will retain their taste and aroma almost indefinitely. But by the time they have been powdered to dust in a factory, stored in a shop and lain about in a pepper-pot it is not surprising the result bears no comparison to the fresh and delicate flavour you can keep locked up in your pepper-mill (and unlike salt-mills, pepper-mills do work).

Black pepper I always use this, freshly milled, in my cooking. There is a school of thought that objects, aesthetically at any rate, to finding black speckles in a white sauce. I can only say that knowing what they are all my family and friends have grown quite used to them and don't give it a second thought. (Curious, isn't it, that everyone expects grated nutmeg to look brown and speckled on food and raises no objection, perhaps because there is no such thing as white nutmeg?)

Green peppercorns This variety of pepper has only reached us in the last few years. These are the young, soft berries harvested before they have even developed separate husks and kernels. They are not dried, but retain their moisture and are preserved in small tins. Deliciously aromatic—but still with a peppery fragrance—so far they are only available in specialised food shops. So it is worth keeping a few tins in hand, if you can find them.

Capsicums
Under this heading come a bewildering variety of the pepper family—red, green, chilli, sweet, paprika, cayenne. Not least are they bewildering because at times their power (i.e. lethal or mild) can only be identified by one means, and that is by tasting.

Fresh chillies These look like small fresh green peppers: sometimes they are long, finger-thin and somewhat crooked and at other times they are shiny-smooth like small rounded carrots. Treat them with respect for the reason above. If they are hot, take the precaution of discarding the really hot seeds and core, and use just the chopped flesh, which is less ferocious (a little chilli powder can always be added to increase the hotness, but there is little that can be done to subdue it afterwards). However, provided this warning is observed, fresh chillies—plentiful where there are immigrant communities—really give an authentic taste to Indian dishes and curries.

Whole or crushed dried chillies: chilli powder Whole dried chillies are useful when there are no fresh ones available. Again, exercise caution. A good compromise is to remove the seeds and use only the outer paper-like casing. Crushed dried chillies (skins and seeds) are good for a dish like chilli con carne, but should be used more

sparingly than powdered ones, being definitely more pungent.
Chilli powder is the most widely available chilli for the kitchen,
if stored too long it will lose some of its character, if not heat.
All the above are used mostly in curries and chilli sauces.
Sometimes, however, you will find a spice labelled 'chilli con carne
seasoning': this is usually a blend of half chilli and half ground
cummin, so is 50 per cent less powerful. I think chilli con carne
tastes better with pure chilli.

Cayenne pepper The difference between this and chilli powder is not
always clear, because both can be made from varieties of the same
capsicum family. Cayenne is finer and more suitable for sprinkling
on food. It is also a very fiery spice, so caution is needed, but it
certainly adds zest to smoked fish pâtés in particular and cheese
dishes, cheese scones and biscuits (for a cheese topping on any
baked dish, mix some grated cheese with breadcrumbs and a
couple of good pinches of cayenne pepper).

Tabasco sauce This is a commercially-prepared chilli sauce: very
hot, only the merest drop or two is needed at any one time. It is
used in much the same way, and in the same dishes, as cayenne
pepper.

Paprika A spice made from the ground seeds of sweet peppers
(pimentoes as they are sometimes called). It has the flavour of
sweet pepper too, and none of the penetrating hotness of chilli. Of
all ground spices paprika seems to lose flavour the fastest, so buy in
small quantities, and if you haven't used it all after a few months,
start again. I actually only use paprika for Hungarian goulash and
chicken paprika (see below), and always buy Hungarian in
preference to Spanish. If you see the words 'hot' or 'mild' on a jar,
don't take too much notice because it is never a hot spice (to give
an edge to it in a goulash I add just a pinch of chilli).

Garlic
Although garlic is a herb and not a spice, in my repertoire I think it
belongs with the seasonings and it is as such that I tend to use it. It
has its opponents, but in my experience even its strongest critics
can enthuse like anyone else about, say, a salad dressing with garlic
in it—provided no-one tells them it's there!
  Garlic is pungent, though, and a certain amount of care is
needed with it. It's onion-shaped when you buy it, but it separates
out into individual tooth-like sections (referred to as 'cloves'). If

you have a patch of ground to spare, garlic actually grows very easily, and the results are tender and moist.

To use garlic it is usually best to peel off the papery skin, then to crush it to a paste. This can be done with a pestle and mortar, using about $\frac{1}{2}$ teaspoon of salt with each clove, which reduces it to a pulp very quickly. Garlic presses can be used, though I find them difficult to clean afterwards. Another way to crush garlic is to place the peeled clove on a flat surface or chopping board, then press down firmly with your thumb on the flat blade of a knife.

Mustard

Commercially speaking mustard has run riot recently. Where once the supermarket stocked only the familiar canary-yellow English mustard powder, nowadays the shelves display at least half a dozen—often more—imported varieties or at least home-made imitations of them. They are even turning up in tourist gift shops in pretty pottery jars. Wider choice is always to be welcomed of course, but personally I have always preferred my mustard to be pungent and, well, mustardy, which is why I still think our own home-grown mustard from East Anglia qualifies as the best. But what are its rivals, and how do they differ from it?

English mustard is made basically—as it has been for over two hundred years—by the milling and blending of two different mustard seeds, the brown (confusingly sometimes called black) and the white (sometimes known as yellow). It is the brown seed that provides the pungency, the white, flavour: but both only come to life when the resulting powder is mixed with water (see below). It is now possible also to buy English mustard ready made-up—which is fine if the lid is replaced firmly and quickly each time, as mustard exposed to the air loses its kick very rapidly.

Dijon mustard is the main mustard of France. It is the nearest to our own, though less ferocious. As the name implies it is made in and around Dijon in Burgundy, and there are any number of local variations. In some the mustard seed is mixed with spices and the acid juice of unripe grapes (verjuice), in others with diluted vinegar; yet others are blended with various white wines of the region. Like nearly all foreign mustards it comes not in powder form but already made-up, since it contains liquid.

Bordeaux mustard This is what we tend to call French mustard over here. It is much darker, and because it also contains the husk of the mustard seed, it is milder and distinctly aromatic. Packed as it is with vinegar, sugar, spices and tarragon it can tend to compete with rather than enhance the flavour of some food, and it should be used very selectively.

Among the other mustards that adorn our shelves, one might take note of the sweet-sour *German mustard*, dark and not dissimilar to the Bordeaux: it goes admirably with German sausage but otherwise should be used with discretion. *American mustard* is much the same colour as ours, but is positively sweet and strictly for hot dogs. For most requirements in cooking (as opposed to using it as a condiment) our English mustard, and Dijon, are more than adequate.

How to make mustard
It's amazing, but even a simple little task like mixing mustard needs a bit of thought. It is the essential oils in mustard that give it its power and pungency, but these are not developed in the whole mustard seed or in the dry milled powder. What is needed for the flavour to emerge is a chemical reaction brought on by the addition of a little water, and even then it needs a good 10–15 minutes for the flavour to develop fully (so always make up mustard well in advance of using it). The water, too, must be cold—hot water can cause a rather different reaction, which may provide a bitter flavour. Mixing vinegar or salt with dry mustard can also cause bitterness (once the mustard is made up they can be added without any ill-effect). So when making mayonnaise add the vinegar at the end, and with vinaigrette dressing it is best to use mustard that has been made up for at least 10 minutes. Mustard is a very good emulsifier. Apart from the flavour it can add, it does a good stabilising job in something like mayonnaise, and can provide a slight thickening to vinaigrette or to Cumberland sauce (see recipe, page 156).

Vinegar
Originally sour wine (which is the precise meaning of the French 'vin aigre'), but now the name embraces all similar sour liquids: wine vinegar, cider vinegar, malt vinegar and so on. It is created by an entirely natural process in which alcohol is turned into acetic acid. The bacteriological processes need not concern us overmuch, but the differences between the various vinegars—and the uses they can be put to—are most important.

Wine vinegar, like the wine it is made from, can be either red or white. The best comes from Orleans in France, where it is produced slowly and in oak casks—so look out for that name on the label when you're buying. This is the vinegar to use where it is important that the flavour does not dominate or overwhelm other ingredients, for instance in salad dressings or sauces.

Malt vinegar In England vinegar has traditionally been made from beer rather than wine. The resulting malt vinegar is dark coloured and powerfully flavoured. Indeed in cooking it can only too often be a flavour-killer, masking everything else in the vicinity. It is best confined to pickling and chutneys and those recipes that are intended to have a pronounced vinegary flavour (and *never* used for mint sauce).

Cider vinegar, self-evidently made from cider. Healthy it may be (as some food theorists maintain), but it has its own distinctive taste, and is not an automatic substitute for other vinegars. Use it only where a recipe actually specifies it.

Distilled vinegar is colourless, strong and popular in Scotland. Because it is stronger (up to 12 per cent acetic acid) it has excellent preserving powers, and is used for pickling.

Vinegars flavoured with fruit, herbs or spices can be bought in some shops. Their uses are limited and, anyway, you can quite easily make your own. Tarragon vinegar, for instance, is made simply by steeping a bunch of tarragon in wine vinegar for a time, then straining the liquid if necessary.

Allspice
It is not, as the name would suggest, a combination of spices. Bought whole (which is to be recommended) it looks like a smoother version of peppercorns, but is in fact the dried berry of an evergreen. It got its name because it is supposed to have the flavour of three spices: nutmeg, cloves and cinnamon. However, the flavour is not really like any of these. It is used in pickling quite a lot, also for marinades for dishes like soused herring or mackerel. If a recipe calls for ground allspice, it is best to grind it with a pestle and mortar yourself as and when you need it.

Capers
I have included capers—not strictly a spice—here because I look on them as such important store-cupboard ingredients. A few

capers can jazz up many otherwise ordinary dishes, like plain grilled fish, or sprinkled on pizzas or to add an extra dimension to sauces. I have seen caper bushes, with their very pretty pink flowers, growing out of the rocks along the Amalfi coast in Italy, where they are used extensively in the local cooking—especially Salsa verde (see page 159). What they are in fact are the buds of the plant, picked and pickled. Even once the jar is opened they keep their sweet-sharp flavour for some time, provided they remain covered by the pickling liquid. Ideally this should be white wine vinegar, though unfortunately some British firms subject them to our lethal malt vinegar, from which their flavour never quite recovers even when you rinse them under the cold tap. In Italian shops, particularly in London, capers can be bought loose.

Caraway seeds
These, with their nutty toasted flavour, are not much favoured in our cooking nowadays except in old-fashioned seed cake (loved or hated, depending on one's upbringing—I well remember a schoolfriend trying to pick out all the seeds before eating it!). In Austria and Germany they are used quite a lot in various types of sausage, goulash and cabbage dishes.

Cardomum
An eastern spice, the sun-dried pods are pale green-grey, revealing inside the tiny, black, highly aromatic seeds. It is quite expensive, as spices go, but a little goes a long way. One pod crushed and added (add both pod and seeds) to pilau rice will impart a delicious flavour, recognisable even to those unfamiliar with the look of cardomum. It is used widely in curry dishes, occasionally in sweet recipes, and should never be bought ready-ground.

Cinnamon
This is a spice made from the inner bark of a tree belonging to the laurel family, which is what the pale-brown and hollow cinnamon sticks look like. Break pieces off to add in cooking, then extract them, like bayleaves, at the end. British cooks are familiar with it as a pudding spice and for use in cakes (for this it must be bought ready-ground as it's impossible to grind it at home). It is worth noting that its strength can vary enormously, so shop around for a brand that is reliable and buy in small quantities. One of the best flavour tips I've picked up is from Greek cookery, where a hint of cinnamon is often used in savoury dishes. A little added to the meat

in a Moussaka gives the dish an authentic Greek flavour, and I've even taken to adding it to shepherd's pie.

Cloves

Cloves look like tiny wooden nails, and their aroma is dark, pungent and exotic. Those who were subjected to the highly-concentrated 'oil of cloves' as a toothache remedy understandably find their flavour intolerable, but for others cloves can enhance all sorts of dishes, from mince pies and Christmas pudding to bread sauce and baked gammon. Unlike other spices, ground cloves seem to taste stronger than whole ones (perhaps because so little is needed, one tends to add too much). A little ground cloves always goes into my spiced red cabbage. Others like the flavour of cloves in an apple pie—where I think just two or three whole ones are better than adding ground cloves, although consumers have to be diligent in seeking them out!

Coriander

I'm particularly fond of coriander: the tiny, round seeds crush easily and give off an aromatic, almost scented flavour sometimes said to be reminiscent of roasted orange peel (in fact Margaret Costa in her *Four seasons cookbook* suggests tying the crushed seeds in muslin and adding them to the fruit for marmalade). Coriander turns up in the cooking of countries all over the world. In India it is an important curry spice and the leaves—quite different in flavour—are used a great deal as a herb. Spanish, Portuguese, Arab, Turkish and Greek cuisines all rely on coriander: in fact any recipe 'a la grecque' includes it. A lovely way to serve olives with aperitifs is to toss them first in a mixture of crushed coriander seeds, crushed garlic and a little vinaigrette dressing. It quickly loses flavour once ground. Buy it whole, it's so easy to do yourself.

Cumin

Although this turns up in quite a few Mexican dishes, this is a spice I associate with curries. It looks like—and indeed is—long, tiny seeds, which are very easy to grind with a pestle and mortar. Sometimes whole seeds are added to pilaus and, with their strong piquant flavour, they are an essential curry spice.

Curry powder and garam marsala

Curry powder—that is to say a ready-made blend of powdered Indian spices—is always to hand in my kitchen, though by no means always for curries. I sprinkle it onto cheesy biscuits, into sauces, and even like to add some to kedgeree. Unfortunately there is no uniformity among commercial curry powders, and some are a good deal hotter than others. The secret is to know your brand of curry powder, and to try and use a little of a hot one rather than a lot of a mild one. Sometimes Indian recipes call for garam marsala, which is like special curry powder in being a blend of spices.

Curry paste can be used instead of curry powder and is particularly useful for marinades and kebabs. It is a blend of spices preserved in oil with sometimes a smaller amount of vinegar added. Like curry powder these pastes can be of varying strength—from very hot to fairly mild. They are particularly useful for marinading or coating as in the recipe for *Indian kebabs* (see page 184).

Ginger

One of the most widely-used spices of all, which comes to us to use fresh, dried, powdered, preserved in syrup and crystalised: a very versatile spice. In this country we are partial to ginger in our gingerbread, cakes, puddings and pickles—not forgetting the ginger beer which in its heyday came in those beautiful stoneware bottles, now collectors' items. If you can get hold of fresh root ginger, it really does add a clean fresh taste, as well as spiciness, to curries. It looks just like a knobbly, misshapen root and it can be stored in the freezer wrapped in freezer-foil and unpeeled. (Elizabeth David says that, peeled and sliced, it stores well in a small jar covered with sherry.)

Lumps of dried ginger are used in making up pickling spices for chutneys and pickles. Preserved ginger is expensive, though less so if you buy it in plain jars (some supermarkets have good stocks around Christmas): chopped up it adds a touch of luxury sprinkled with some syrup over ice-cream, or added to rhubarb fool—in fact ginger has a great affinity with rhubarb—or adorning the top and inside of a preserved ginger cake. Ginger is most commonly found, and used, in its powdered form: check that it is spicy and fresh-tasting, and not musty and stale.

Juniper

These are purple-black, rather wrinkled berries, most notorious as a basic ingredient in gin. But juniper is very much a cooking spice as well, especially with game and pork dishes (perhaps because it grows wild in hill-country where animals and birds feed on the autumn-ripened berries). For cooking, the berries are dried and always crushed before using. Their flavour seems to have a special sympathy with garlic, and if you want to try out juniper for the first time, I suggest you try the cabbage recipe on page 206, which is really delicious. Juniper berries are not as widely available as some other spices, sadly. So the more we pester our suppliers for them, the more plentiful they'll become.

Mace and nutmeg
These two spices belong together, because they come from the same source. Mace is part of the outer covering of the nutmeg—resembling a thick-meshed cage—which is removed and dried to become brittle and pale orange in colour. It is sold either in pieces (blades) or ready-ground. With a stronger, much more concentrated flavour than nutmeg it has to be used with care. Ready-ground it can eventually get stale, but that is a built-in handicap because the brittleness of the spice makes it impossible to grind at home. It has been used extensively in English cooking in the past, for such recipes as potted meats and fish pâtés. If not available, nutmeg can always be used instead.

Nutmeg Another favourite of mine: I always keep it within arm's reach in the kitchen, in a special compartment in its own grater. It's always been a popular spice in this country—18th-century gentlemen wore miniature graters containing a nutmeg on a chain round their necks, so they could grate some over their hot mulls and toddies at a moment's notice. It's said to be good for sleep and to increase the potency of alcoholic drinks—but I leave you to judge that for yourselves!

It is an important spice for cakes and puddings: all milk puddings should have a dark, caramelised nutmeg crust, and it gives an attractive freckled effect to egg custards and custard tarts. Although the French rarely use it, the Italians accord it great importance—and rightly so, as it contributes a subtle flavouring to cheese dishes, vegetables like spinach, creamy white sauces, meat fillings for ravioli and so on. If I had the power I would ban the sale of ground nutmeg as it's quite useless. If your local grocer or supermarket does not stock whole nutmegs, try a chemist.

Mixed spice
Usually a made-up combination of nutmeg, cinnamon, cloves and allspice. Most useful for puddings and cakes, but buy it in small

quantities and shop around a little for one you like, as they can vary quite a lot in composition.

Saffron
The most expensive spice of all. It comes from the dried stigmas of a variety of crocus, and is used for its deep yellow colouring as well as for flavour. Being so costly it's as well that very little—just a few strands—is needed to colour and flavour something like a Spanish paella or an Italian risotto. It is also used in the South of France in fish stews and soups, and turns up here in Cornish saffron cake. If a recipe calls for it and you don't have any, a teaspoonful of turmeric will give you the authentic colour (though obviously a different flavour). To use saffron, you can crush it and mix it with a small amount of water or stock before adding it to the other ingredients.

Turmeric
This is a spice originating from a plant of the ginger family, and it is a bright orange-yellow colour. For all its flamboyance it's a mild spice, and is used freely in curries where its colour is more robust than its flavour (I also add turmeric to rice for the same reason). It can only be bought ready-ground (be careful with it: it can stain hands and clothes rather badly).

Vanilla
There is a marked difference between pure vanilla essence and vanilla flavour essence. The former is extracted from vanilla pods (from a species of climbing orchid): the latter is made from a substitute.

Whole dried vanilla pods, long, thin, dark and rather wrinkled, are useful to have in the kitchen. I think the flavour they provide is better than from essence: if you have time, warm the milk (for, say, a custard) and allow the vanilla pod to infuse into it for a short while. A single pod will last for ages, and can be wiped and dried after use, then stored in a jar for the next time. Another tip is to keep a pod buried in the jar containing caster sugar—then when you make a custard or a sweet sauce, the sugar will already have its own vanilla flavouring.

Steak au poivre
(serves 2 people)

In restaurants this is sometimes served swimming in a sickly cream and brandy sauce. Personally I think the combined flavours of the peppercorns and the steak need nothing else but a glass of wine to rinse out the pan at the end.

2 entrecôte (sirloin) steaks, or you could use rump steak if you prefer, weighing 6–8 oz each (175–225 g)
2 heaped teaspoons whole black peppercorns
2 tablespoons olive oil
$\frac{1}{4}$ pint red wine (150 ml)
Salt

First crush the peppercorns very coarsely with a pestle and mortar (or use the back of a tablespoon on a flat surface). Pour the olive oil into a shallow dish, then coat each steak with the oil and press the crushed peppercorns onto both sides of each steak. Then leave them to soak up the flavour in the dish for several hours—turning them over once in that time.

When you're ready to cook, pre-heat a thick-based frying-pan (without any fat in it) and when it's very hot sear the steaks quickly on both sides. Then turn down the heat and finish cooking them according to how you like them (a medium-rare entrecôte will take about 6 minutes and should be turned several times during the cooking). One minute before the end of the cooking time pour in the wine, let it bubble, reduce and become syrupy. Then sprinkle a little salt over the steaks and serve immediately with the reduced wine spooned over. These are delicious served with *Gratin dauphinoise* (page 203).

Braised steak with green peppercorn sauce
(serves 2 people)

This has a lovely piquant flavour. If possible try to get two whole slices of braising steak weighing $\frac{1}{2}$ lb each; failing that cubes of steak will do.

1 lb braising steak (450 g)
1 large onion peeled and sliced
1 tablespoon of beef dripping
4 fl. oz dry white wine (or dry cider) (110 ml)

| 3 teaspoons of green peppercorns |
| 1 teaspoon tomato purée |
| 1 heaped teaspoon flour |
| 1 clove of garlic |
| 1 sprig of thyme |
| Salt and freshly-milled black pepper |

Pre-heat the oven to gas mark 2, 300°F (150°C)

Start by melting the dripping in a frying-pan till it is nice and hot, then pop the pieces of steak in and sear them till brown on both sides. Then remove them to a casserole, with the aid of a draining spoon. Now to the fat left in the pan add the sliced onion, and brown these, then spoon them over the meat. Next spoon off any excess fat from the pan—tilting it to one side will help—and to the juices that remain add the wine; bring it up to simmering point, at the same time scraping the base and sides of the pan.

Pour the wine over the meat, and add the thyme and clove of garlic (crushed slightly) and a little seasoning. Cover the casserole, then braise the steak in the oven for 2 hours. After that, pour all the juices and the garlic clove into the goblet of a liquidiser and (keeping the onions and meat warm meantime) add the flour, tomato purée and two teaspoons of the green peppercorns to the juices. Blend at top speed until smooth, then pour the sauce into a saucepan with the remaining teaspoon of peppercorns. Bring up to simmering point, and pour it over the meat before serving. *Note:* This could be braised on top of the stove and a very low heat, provided it is covered with a well-fitting lid closely covered in foil.

Indian kebabs
(serves 4 people)

These spicy kebabs are first marinaded, then coated with a curry paste before being grilled.

| 1½ lb fillet end of leg of lamb (675 g), cut into cubes |
| 2 tablespoons olive oil |
| 1 small green pepper |
| 4 firm tomatoes |
| 1 medium onion |
| 1 large lemon |

$\frac{1}{4}$ **pint natural yoghurt (150 ml)**
1 small piece root ginger
2 teaspoons mild curry powder
2 teaspoons curry paste
Salt and freshly-milled pepper

First of all—4 hours or so before you cook—place the cubes of lamb in a wide shallow dish, season with salt and pepper, then pour in 2 tablespoons of olive oil. Leave the meat to soak up the oil for about 2 hours, turning the pieces over once or twice.

Cut the onion into quarters, split the quarters into pieces and add these to the meat: also cut the tomatoes into quarters and the pepper into 1 inch pieces and add these also to the marinading meat. Now in a small basin mix the curry powder, curry paste, lemon juice and yoghurt together and pour this mixture over the meat, etc. Stir and mix everything around well, then leave for another 2 hours in a cool place.

To cook the kebabs: pre-heat the grill, then peel and slice up a 1 inch piece of ginger. Now onto four long flat (rather than rounded) skewers thread the meat, onion, tomato and pepper alternately with a little slice of ginger here and there. Pack everything up tightly together, and grill the kebabs under the grill for about 15 minutes, turning them frequently and basting occasionally with the marinade. Serve on rice with the juices spooned over.

Beef curry with whole spices
(serves 3 people)

Good as real Indian curries often are in restaurants, it is possible—using the proper spices—to make them as well if not better at home.

$1\frac{1}{2}$ **lb chuck steak (675 g), cut into cubes**
2 large onions, sliced
2 fresh green chillies, de-seeded and chopped
1 piece of fresh root ginger (about $1\frac{1}{2}$ in. long), grated or very finely chopped
2 level teaspoons coriander seeds, crushed
1 teaspoon cumin seeds, crushed
1 level tablespoon turmeric powder
2 cardomum pods, crushed
$\frac{1}{4}$ **pint natural yoghurt (150 ml)**

2 fl. oz water (50 ml)
2 cloves of garlic, crushed
Some groundnut oil
Salt

Start by browning the cubes of meat in oil in a flameproof casserole, then transfer them to a plate. Add the onions to the pan and fry that for about 5 minutes, before adding all the spices and the garlic—continue to cook for a further 5 minutes to draw out the flavours from the spices, before returning the meat to the pan.

Now gradually stir in the yoghurt and water, and add some salt. Cover the casserole and keep the heat at the lowest possible simmer for 2 hours, stirring everything around a few times.

After 2 hours, take the lid off and continue to cook for a further 15 minutes to reduce the sauce slightly. Serve this with pilau rice, Indian pickles and mango chutney. *Note:* If you can't get fresh root ginger, use a dessertspoon of ground ginger.

Spiced chicken
(serves 4 people)

I would definitely put this recipe amongst my top ten: it's easy to prepare, convenient to serve, and always tastes delicious.

1 chicken weighing 3½ lb (1 kg 600 g), (cut into 4 pieces)
2 medium onions, chopped small
1 level dessertspoon ground ginger
1 level dessertspoon turmeric
1 level teaspoon Madras curry powder
1 clove of garlic, crushed
1 tablespoon groundnut oil
1½ oz butter (40 g)
A 5-oz carton of natural yoghurt (150 g)
A 5-oz carton of single cream (150 g)
Salt and freshly-milled black pepper
A few sprigs of watercress, to garnish

A few hours before you eat, arrange the pieces of chicken in a large shallow casserole with a lid (or failing that a meat roasting tin covered with foil—the chicken pieces must be side-by-side in a single layer).

Season the chicken with salt and pepper, then mix the powdered spices together and sprinkle approximately 1 heaped teaspoonful over the chicken. Now put a little piece of crushed garlic onto each section of chicken, then drizzle some oil over and, using your hands, rub the spices, oil and garlic into the chicken flesh. Pierce each portion with a skewer in several places, so that the flavours can penetrate. Leave the chicken in a cool place for several hours.

When you're ready to cook, pre-heat the oven to gas mark 4, 350°F (180°C). Pop a fleck of butter on each chicken joint and place the casserole in the oven (uncovered) for half an hour.

Meanwhile fry the onions in a little butter and oil over a low heat for 10 minutes to soften, and mix the remaining spices together with the yoghurt and cream.

When the 30 minutes are up, take the chicken out of the oven, spoon the onion over them, then pour the yoghurt mixture all over. Put on the lid (or cover with foil) and return the chicken to the oven for another 30–45 minutes—or until the joints are tender— basting with the juices once or twice during the cooking.

Garnish with a few sprigs of watercress, and serve with spiced rice and mango chutney. *Note:* There are always rather a lot of juices left over with this dish, but this is unavoidable—so just spoon a little over the chicken before you serve and discard the rest.

Chicken paprika
(serves 4 people)

This is nice served with some well-buttered noodles and a crisp green salad.

1 chicken weighing about 3 lb (1 kg 350 g), cut into 4 quarters
2 medium onions, chopped
1 medium green pepper, deseeded and cut into small strips
1 lb tomatoes (450 g), skinned and chopped (alternatively a 14-oz (400 g) tin of Italian tomatoes)
$\frac{1}{4}$ pint chicken stock (150 ml)
1 dessertspoon flour
1 heaped tablespoon paprika (preferably Hungarian)
A 5-oz carton of soured cream (150 g)
Oil, for cooking

| Salt and freshly-milled black pepper |
| 2 good pinches of cayenne pepper |

Pre-heat the oven to gas mark 3, 325°F (160°C)

Begin by heating a little oil in a frying-pan and gently frying the chicken joints to a golden colour. Then use a draining spoon to transfer them to a casserole, and season them with salt and pepper.

In the oil left in the pan fry the onions gently for about 10 minutes to soften. Now stir the flour, cayenne and paprika into the pan, with a wooden spoon, to soak up the juices before adding the chopped tomatoes. Stir them around a bit, then add the stock.

Bring everything up to simmering point, then pour over the chicken in the casserole, put a lid on and bake in the oven for 45 minutes. After that stir in the chopped pepper, replace the lid and cook for a further 30 minutes. Just before serving spoon the soured cream all over, mixing it in just to give a marbled effect, then sprinkle on a little more paprika.

Marinaded pork with coriander

(serves 3 people)

The Greeks call this traditional dish Afelia. If you have time to leave the meat to steep overnight and for the flavours to develop, so much the better.

| 1 pork fillet, cut into bite-sized cubes |
| 1 lemon |
| 2 heaped teaspoons of coriander seeds |
| 1 fat clove of garlic, crushed |
| 3 tablespoons olive oil |
| $\frac{1}{2}$ pint dry white wine (or dry cider) (275 ml) |
| Salt and freshly-milled black pepper |

Place the pieces of pork in a shallow dish and season them with salt and freshly-milled pepper. Next, crush the coriander seeds, either with a pestle and mortar or with the end of a rolling-pin in a basin.

Now pour the oil over the pieces of meat, followed by the juice of the lemon and 2 tablespoons of the white wine. Then sprinkle in the crushed coriander seeds and the garlic, and mix everything together. Cover the dish with a cloth and leave it all to marinade overnight—or as long as possible—stirring now and then.

To cook the pork: Melt a little oil in your largest frying-pan and when it's fairly hot add the cubes of pork and cook them over a medium heat, turning them and keeping them on the move. When they have browned a little, pour in the rest of the white wine, let it bubble and reduce to a syrupy consistency. The pork will take approximately 10–15 minutes to cook altogether. Serve with a little rice and a salad.

Moussaka
(serves 4 people)

The small amount of cinnamon gives it a really authentic Greek flavour.

1 lb of minced lamb or beef (450 g)
½ lb onions, peeled and sliced
2 cloves of garlic, chopped
3 medium aubergines, cut into rounds about ½ in. (1 cm) thick
2 tablespoons tomato purée
3 fl. oz wine (red or white) (75 ml)
1 teaspoon ground cinnamon
1 tablespoon fresh chopped parsley
Oil
Salt and freshly-milled black pepper

For the topping:
3 oz plain flour (75 g)
3 oz butter (75 g)
1 pint milk
2 oz Cheddar cheese, grated
2 eggs
Salt, pepper and freshly-grated nutmeg

Pre-heat the oven to gas mark 4, 350°F (180°C)

First of all prepare the aubergines. They should be sliced and packed into a colander, then sprinkled with salt. Then place a plate on top of them and a heavy weight on top of that, and leave them for half an hour. This is to drain off some of their excess moisture. Meanwhile fry the onions and chopped garlic in some oil (preferably olive oil) for about 5 minutes, then add the minced meat to the pan to brown—stirring it to break up any lumps. In a basin mix together the tomato purée, wine, cinnamon and parsley, season it all with salt and pepper, then pour the mixture over the onions and meat when it has browned. Stir well, and leave on a gentle heat to simmer quietly.

Now back to the aubergines: heat some olive oil in another frying-pan, dry the aubergine slices in kitchen paper, then fry each one to a golden-brown on both sides. When they are browned leave them on kitchen paper to drain (aubergines eat up cooking oil!).
When the aubergines are done, take a casserole and arrange some of them in it. Spread part of the meat mixture on top, followed by another layer of aubergines—until everything is incorporated.

Next make up the topping for the moussaka. Melt the butter in a saucepan and stir in the flour until smooth, then add the milk gradually, stirring vigorously with each addition until you have a smooth white sauce. Next stir in the grated cheese, followed by a seasoning of salt, pepper and freshly-grated nutmeg. Allow the sauce to cool, then whisk up the 2 eggs, first on their own and then into the sauce. Pour the sauce over the meat and aubergines, then bake (uncovered) in the oven for an hour—by which time the top will be fluffy-golden.

Guacamole
(serves 4 people)

This recipe is originally from Mexico. If you like spicy food, it makes an ideal first course.

2 medium avocados
1 clove of garlic, crushed
½ medium onion, grated
2 large tomatoes
½ teaspoon chilli powder
A dash of tabasco sauce
The juice of medium lemon
Salt and freshly-milled black pepper

Skin the tomatoes to start with—if you pop them in a basin, pour boiling water over them and leave for a few minutes, you'll find they slip off quite easily. Then cut the tomatoes into quarters, scoop out and discard the seeds, then chop the flesh into fairly small pieces.

Now halve the avocados and remove their stones. Place each half skin-side up) on a wooden board and, with a sharp knife, make an incision down the centre of the skin of each one. Peel the skins off. Chop up the avocado flesh and transfer it to a fairly large mixing bowl, and straightaway pour the lemon juice over it to help stop it discolouring. Now with a teaspoon scrape off from the under-side of the skins all that very green avocado flesh still clinging to them: this is what gives the guacamole a really good green colour. Add this to the bowl, then mash all the avocado with a large fork almost to a purée (it doesn't matter if there are a few little lumps).

Now add the tomatoes, grated onion and garlic to the avocado, season with salt and pepper, and finally stir in the chilli powder and tabasco. Taste it at this stage to check the seasoning (it does need a fair amount of salt to bring out the flavour) and add more chilli if you think it needs it. Cover the bowl with cling-film and keep in a cool place—best in the lowest part of the refrigerator until needed.

Serve in individual dishes with some hot crusty bread or slices of thin toast. *Note:* Don't make this too far ahead, because avocado does tend to discolour. If that happens just give the guacamole a good stir—the taste won't be affected.

Sautéed cauliflower with coriander

(serves 2 people)

Cauliflower florets, just tossed in oil and fried quickly, seem to retain their crunchiness and flavour—which they can so easily lose when cooked with water.

1 smallish cauliflower
$\frac{1}{2}$ onion, finely chopped
1 level teaspoon whole coriander seeds
1 small clove of garlic
2 tablespoons olive oil
1 knob of butter
Salt and freshly-milled black pepper

First prepare the cauliflower, by separating it into fairly small florets (about an inch long, including the stalk). Wipe them but don't wash them—they'll be cooked anyway at a fairly high temperature. Now heat the oil in your largest frying-pan and soften the onion in it for 5 minutes. Meanwhile chop the peeled clove of garlic finely and crush the coriander seeds with a pestle and mortar (or use the end of a rolling-pin and a small bowl).

When the onion is softened, turn the heat right up, and add the cauliflower. After a minute or two toss the pieces over by shaking the pan, then add the coriander seeds and continue to cook the cauliflower for about 5 minutes, seasoning it with a sprinkling of salt and pepper. Finally add the butter and chopped garlic to the pan and cook for a further minute—by which time the cauliflower will have turned an attractive nutty-golden colour, but still retain some bite. Serve straight away.

Spiced pears in cider

(serves 6 people)

For this you need to get hold of really hard pears. After long cooking they will turn a lovely glazed amber colour, most attractive in a glass serving bowl.

6 large hard pears
1 pint dry cider (570 ml)
4 oz sugar (110 g)
1 vanilla pod
2 whole cinnamon sticks
1 level dessertspoon arrowroot
Some toasted flaked almonds
$\frac{3}{4}$ pint double cream (150 ml)

Pre-heat the oven to gas mark $\frac{1}{2}$, 250°F (130°C)

Peel the pears but leave the stalks on them, then lay them whole in a large casserole. Then in a saucepan bring the cider, sugar and cinnamon to the boil, add the vanilla pod to the mixture, and pour the whole lot over the pears. Cover the casserole, and bake very slowly for about three hours, turning the pears over halfway.

After the three hours transfer the pears to a serving bowl to cool, and pour the liquid back into a saucepan (you can discard the vanilla pod and cinnamon sticks now).

In a cup mix the arrowroot with a little cold water till you have a smooth paste, then add this to the saucepan with the liquid. Bring to the boil, stirring till the mixture has thickened slightly to a syrup. Then pour it over the pears, allow to cool a litttle and baste each pear with a good coating of the syrup.

Place in the fridge to chill thoroughly, and serve sprinkled with toasted flaked almonds and thick whipped cream.

Winter vegetables

Including recipes for:
Potatoes boulangère
Gratin dauphinois
Sauté potatoes Lyonnaise
Sauté potatoes Niçoise
Fried cabbage with bacon
Cabbage with garlic and juniper
Braised red cabbage with apples
Punchnep
Creamed parsnips
Mashed swedes with crispy bacon
Baked aubergines with tomatoes
Buttered leeks
Cauliflower with garlic and bacon
Carrot and artichoke soup
Braised celery with cheese and onion sauce

In this country meat-eating has been virtually part of our heritage: apart from periodic shortages during wars or depressions the British have been renowned for their huge consumption of meat and game. And as a nation entirely surrounded by sea, our fish intake has been pretty high too. It's not surprising then that vegetables have not featured largely in the history of our cooking—their role has been to help the meat go down, rather than as things to be enjoyed in their own right.

Now that meat is so expensive, however, I think vegetable eating (and growing) is at last coming into its own. Here education is of paramount importance. I have seen—and it's a sad reflection on our past attitudes—the winner of First Prize for aubergines in a local Horticultural Show giving away his whole crop because his wife had not the faintest idea how to cook them!

There is one important point to make before we discuss the cooking of vegetables. If we want to get the very best out of them, we have to be familiar with their various seasons. In this modern jet-age the natural seasons of our home-grown vegetables have become obscured by the mountains of imports flown in from all round the world; and deep-freezing, which makes it possible to eat in December what was grown in June, has furthered the confusion. I firmly believe that part of the boredom attached to the daily round of wondering what on earth to cook today is caused by the continuous availability of absolutely everything. Nature has provided us with a perfectly varied diet on its own, which Progress has helped us to lose sight of.

Without being extremist about this (in fact I'm delighted we can nowadays literally shop around the world) I do feel that with the disappearing seasons some of the joy of food has been lost. For me looking forward to something is part of the pleasure—those first tiny peas of early June, or the heightened flavour of compact brussels sprouts after a sharp November frost. And there's one other point. Out-of-season vegetables inevitably cost more, so that imported tomatoes in January are not only tasteless but far more expensive. It's true that someone with a large garden can grow and freeze large crops and therefore save quite a bit of money; but then it's also true that smaller crops of a wider variety will also save money *and* provide something fresh in the kitchen garden every single month of the year.

A final note before going on to the preparation of vegetables: an important part of your kitchen equipment is—a plain thin skewer.

Sliding a skewer into a potato or brussels sprout to test for tenderness is still the easiest way to see if vegetables are cooked.

Potatoes

Potatoes are the most important source of vitamin C in our diet—it was only when potatoes became one of our staple foods in the 18th century (we now eat approximately 6 oz (175 g) per head a day) that diseases like scurvy began to die out. The protein value of potatoes is higher than in most other plant foods. Per ounce, of course, an orange will give you more vitamin C, but whereas we don't all eat an orange a day most of us do eat potatoes. Having said that, it is also a fact that careless preparation and cooking can destroy much of their goodness as well as flavour—I'd go so far as to say that learning to cook potatoes so that they really taste like potatoes is one of the most important lessons in cooking.

Buying and storing potatoes

If you have the storage space it's obviously cheaper and more convenient to buy old potatoes in bulk. I buy mine in ½-cwt bags which, provided they are closed properly each time they're opened, protect the potatoes adequately from the light. It is light that causes damage and turns them green (so it is odd that the small supermarket packs should be transparent and expose their contents to the full glare of the light). Nor do potatoes that have been scrubbed keep so well—so for small quantities my advice is to buy them loose with the earth still clinging to them. New potatoes should always be eaten as fresh as possible and not stored: a sign of their freshness, when you're buying them, is that the skin slips off easily when rubbed with the thumb. Also the earth around them should look moist.

Preparation

That part of the potato directly beneath the skin is richest in nutrients, so peeling needs to be done with a certain amount of care. Ideally they should not be peeled at all. New potatoes taste better with their skins left on, and main crop potatoes too are better just scrubbed, then boiled or steamed with the skins on, and peeled afterwards. When the actual skins are eaten (as with jacket potatoes) they provide fibre, another valuable item conspicuously lacking in our modern diet. Where a potato obviously has to be peeled, to preserve the best part beneath the skin it is preferable to use a good potato peeler that pares off the thinnest amount of peel.

Varieties of potato

So far as new potatoes are concerned none can compare for flavour with the kidney-shaped Jerseys that arrive in the shops in June, so delicious I could eat them just on their own, steamed in their skins with chopped mint and melted butter! Now that we can choose which variety of potato we buy (since it has to be described on the packet or counter), my personal choice for an early potato would be Pentland Javelin, and for a good all-round, well-flavoured maincrop variety—Red Desirée, which remains firm during boiling, fluffs easily around the edge for roasting, and makes very good chips. In the garden I have found both these varieties crop fairly well.

Boiling or steaming

First, new potatoes. Here opinion is unanimous that they should be started off in boiling water—so they can be cooked in as short a time as possible and so retain most of their flavour. With maincrop potatoes it is said that putting them in cold water and bringing them up to the boil helps them absorb some of the water and become juicier (new potatoes contain more water and have no need of this), and that this also helps prevent them breaking up.

My own opinion is based on the idea that in general water is the enemy of flavour (with potatoes as with all root vegetables): so I prefer to add boiling water to maincrop also, so they spend less time in contact with the water and breaking is never a problem with a good quality variety like Red Desirée. At all events the heat for boiling, once they have returned to the boil, should be gentle; and to stop the water evaporating too fast a well-fitting lid is essential.

To steam potatoes—which is the best way of preserving nutrients and flavour—place them in a steamer over a saucepanful of boiling water, sprinkle them with salt, cover the steamer with a lid and steam until tender. How much salt? This really depends on who is going to eat them, but a rough guide is 1 rounded teaspoonful to each 1 lb (or 500 g) of potatoes. To serve: once the boiled potatoes have been drained, place a clean cloth over the saucepan instead of the lid. This will absorb some steam and give them a floury edge.

Mashed or creamed potatoes

How you mash or cream potatoes can be a personal thing: my mother won't use anything but a large kitchen fork, while several friends of mine swear by their potato mashers. Inclined to laziness myself, I use my electric hand-whisk. But whichever implement you use, make sure your saucepan is big enough to give you plenty of mashing room. Drain the potatoes first, add a little salt and freshly-milled pepper, a good knob of butter (1 oz (25 g) per 1 lb of potatoes), and preferably cream or top of the milk (2 tablespoons per pound)—failing that, milk will do. Then whisk, beat or mash until the potatoes are soft, creamy and free from lumps. Here are a few variations:

Creamed potatoes with soured cream and chives Soured cream is delicious with potatoes—a ¼ pint (150 ml) carton for 2 or 3 lb of potatoes. Whisk it in with the butter, along with 3 tablespoons of freshly-snipped chives.

Creamed potatoes with nutmeg Again use soured cream or fresh natural yoghurt (if it's not *fresh*, yoghurt will be too acid for this) to whisk into the potatoes, then finish off with about a quarter of a whole nutmeg, freshly grated.

Crunchy roast potatoes

I've deliberately added the word 'crunchy' to this section because I believe properly-cooked roast potatoes are a rare delicacy, and it is crunchiness that is so often missing. The first essential ingredient is a good, solid roasting tin with a really sound base—the cheap, tinny ones that buckle in a hot oven are useless. For the sake of flavour the best sort of fat to use is the same as the meat with which the potatoes will be served (i.e. beef dripping for beef, lamb dripping for lamb, lard for pork), and if you're roasting the joint in the oven you can probably spoon off enough fat from that for the potatoes; the best alternative to these is pure lard.

Because the fat for roasting needs to be *really* hot, it is not a good idea to roast the potatoes around the meat (besides, if you have a large family, there simply won't be room). The oven temperature should be gas mark 7, 425°F (220°C). If the joint is still roasting, remove it to a lower shelf: if it is cooked, take it out of the oven (a joint will hold the heat for about 40 minutes, in a warm place, and is all the better for 'relaxing' before it is carved).

Place the roasting tin with about 2 oz (50 g) of fat per pound of potatoes to pre-heat. Then peel and cut the potatoes into even sizes, pour boiling water over them, add some salt, and simmer for 10 minutes—then drain (reserving the water for gravy). Now put the lid back on the saucepan and shake it vigorously up and down: what this does is roughen the edges of the potatoes and make them floury, giving a crispier surface.

Make sure the fat in the roasting tin is really hot when the potatoes reach it: if it is the outsides of the potatoes will be immediately sealed, if it isn't they will stick or become greasy. As you add the potatoes to the tin, the temperature of the fat will come down—so what you do is remove the tin from the oven (closing the door to keep the heat in) and place it over direct heat, medium should be enough to keep the fat sizzling. Then spoon in the potatoes, and tilt the pan (holding it with a thick oven glove) and baste each one with a complete covering of hot fat. Now transfer them to the highest shelf of the oven, and roast for 45–55 minutes. Turn them over at half-time. *Note:* roast potatoes don't take kindly to being kept warm, so serve them as soon as possible.

Jacket potatoes

One of the nicest and most nutritious ways of eating potatoes (I love the crisp skins dipped in home-made chutney!). Maris Piper, King Edward, and Desirée are all good varieties for serving in their jackets. If you can, scrub and thoroughly dry them in a cloth well in advance as this will help to crisp the skins. Before baking, pre-heat the oven to gas mark 7, 425°F (220°C), prick the potato skins in several places (to prevent splitting), then rub the skins with a smear of olive oil all over and a little bit of salt as well. Large potatoes will take about 1–1½ hours to bake through, but you can cut the cooking time by pushing metal skewers through the centre of each potato. Metal is such a good conductor of heat that it starts the inner potato cooking straight away. To test if they are done, push a skewer into the thickest part of the flesh; then slit them open and serve with a generous knob of butter and some seasoning. And here are a few alternative fillings:

Jacket potatoes with soured cream and chives For 3–4 potatoes, mix ¼ pint (150 ml) of soured cream with a bunch of freshly-chipped chives and a seasoning of salt and freshly-milled pepper. When the potatoes are cooked, hold them with a cloth and make a slit lengthways across the top and then widthways: then lift up the four flaps of skin and make a depression in the potato. Add a good knob of butter to each one, and pour in the cream-and-chive mixture.

Stuffed potatoes with garlic and herbs For 3 large jacket potatoes you'll need: a 5 oz (150 g) packet of Boursin cheese (or any other cream cheese containing garlic and herbs—you can even make up your own combination), 2 oz (50 g) of butter, 2 oz (50 g) of grated Cheddar cheese. When the potatoes are cooked, slice them into

Right: Steamed raisin pudding, page 239; Cider baked apples with toasted muesli, page 248.

halves, then, holding each half in a cloth, scoop out the cooked potato into a bowl. Combine the potato with the cream cheese and butter, and season to taste. Pile the mixture back into the empty potato shells. Sprinkle each half with the grated Cheddar, and pop them under a grill until they're brown and bubbling.

Chips

A perfect chip should be (i) crisp on the outside, (ii) soft, almost melting, in the middle, and (iii) dry, which is to say not greasy, oily or soggy. It is relatively easy to cook soggy chips, but far more difficult to produce a beautifully dry, crisp and melting chip.

To start with you need the right kind of potato. New potatoes—apart from being too small to chip—ought only to be cooked in their skins. Of the maincrop potatoes the best are the mealy-textured varieties like King Edward and Desirée (both reds), or Majestic and Maris Piper (whites). Once peeled you could slice up the potatoes with a chip-cutter, though that always seems to require a great deal of strength. I prefer to use a small sharp knife, slicing the potatoes first across, at intervals of just less than $\frac{1}{2}$ in. (1 cm), then slice into chips the size of my little finger.

If you have time at this stage to soak the chips for half an hour—to reduce their starch content and swell them with water—all well and good: if not, make sure you rinse them well under cold water. Most important of all, dry them *thoroughly* in a clean tea-towel.

To fry them you can use either lard or oil, but if it is oil I do advise a good-quality groundnut oil (because there are so many nasty cooking oils on the market which will impregnate your chips with their unwelcome flavour). Fill the chip-pan, or at least a wide, thick-based saucepan, only one-third full of oil or lard—any more than that and it will very likely bubble over the top when the chips go in. The temperature of the oil/lard is all-important. It should have reached 375°F, 190°C before the chips go in, and the only accurate way to tell is by using a cooking thermometer (and place it in the pan at the beginning, to eliminate any danger of it cracking in the hot fat). In the absence of a thermometer you can test the temperature by dropping in a cube of bread: if it browns within 1 minute, the chips can go in.

The safest way to lower the chips in gently is to use a chip-basket, and be ready to pull it out if the fat erupts too violently (which probably means the chips were not dry enough). Fry the batch for 4–5 minutes and then remove them—you can hang the basket on the lip of the pan in fact. The temperature of the fat will

Left: Spiced chicken, page 186.

now have dropped dramatically, and it must be re-heated to 390°F, 195°C for the final browning—which will take just 1 or at the most 2 minutes. Watch the chips very carefully at this stage and lift them out as soon as they are golden-brown—any longer and they will turn hard.

Now transfer the chips to a warmed serving dish lined with some crumpled greaseproof paper, to remove any vestiges of fat. Then remove the paper, crush some flaky sea salt and some coarsely-ground pepper over them and take them straight to the table. Chips *cannot* be kept hanging round or even kept warm successfully: within no time at all they will start to go soggy, no matter how crisp they were when they came out of the pan.

Potatoes boulangère

(serves 4–6 people)

This French method of cooking potatoes gets its name from the bakeries where villagers, short of fire fuel, would take their pots of potatoes along to cook in the bread ovens. This is a particularly good dish to serve at a dinner party as it needs no last-minute attention and will wait quite happily if you're running late.

2 lb potatoes (900 g)
1 largish onion
¼ pint hot stock (150 ml)
¼ pint milk (150 ml)
2 oz butter (50 g)
Salt and freshly-milled black pepper

Pre-heat the oven to gas mark 4, 350°F (180°C)

The best cooking utensil for this recipe is either an oblong meat-roasting tin or a wide, shallow baking dish. Butter it generously (all over the sides as well), then peel the potatoes and cut them into thinnish slices. Peel the onion and chop it finely.

Now arrange a layer of potatoes over the base of the tin, followed by a sprinkling of onion and a seasoning of salt and freshly-milled black pepper. Continue with another layer of potatoes, and so on until everything is in and you finish up with a layer of potatoes (seasoned) at the top. Pour in the stock and milk, and fleck the surface all over with dots of butter.

Place the tin on the highest shelf of the oven, and leave it there for about 45 minutes or until the potatoes are cooked and the top layer is nicely golden-brown.

Note: For a change, use a chopped leek instead of an onion.

Gratin dauphinois
(serves 3–4 people)

This is one of the greatest potato dishes I've ever tasted. I know it does seem extravagant to use ¼ pint (150 ml) cream for 1 lb (450 g) potatoes, but I would forgo a pudding with cream once in a while in order to justify it.

1 lb good-quality potatoes (Edwards or Desirée) (450 g)
1½ oz butter (40 g)
¼ pint double cream (150 ml)
¼ pint milk (150 ml)
1 small clove garlic, crushed
Whole nutmeg
Salt and freshly-milled black pepper

Pre-heat the oven to gas mark 2, 300°F (150°C)

A *shallow* gratin dish well buttered.

First, peel the potatoes and slice them very, very thinly (a wooden mandoline is excellent for this operation, if you have one, then plunge the potato slices into a bowl of cold water and swill them round and round to get rid of some of the starch. Now dry them very thoroughly in a clean tea-cloth. Then in the gratin dish arrange a layer of potato slices, a sprinkling of crushed garlic, pepper and salt and then another layer of potatoes and seasoning.

Now mix the cream and milk together, pour it over the potatoes, sprinkle with a little freshly-grated whole nutmeg, then add the the butter in flecks over the surface, and bake on the highest shelf in the oven for 1½ hours.

Note: Sometimes cheese is added to this, but I think it masks the potato flavour too much.

Sauté potatoes Lyonnaise
(serves 2 people)

This is the basic method for making sauté potatoes, but if you prefer them plain, simply leave the onion out. The secret of really crisp sauté potatoes is, first of all, to use olive oil if at all possible and, secondly, to use two or three frying-pans so that the potatoes can cook in a single layer and not overlap each other.

2 lb potatoes (Red Desirée) (900 g)
4–5 tablespoons olive oil
1 small onion, finely chopped
Some coarse rock salt and freshly-milled black pepper

Have ready a warm serving dish with some crumpled greaseproof paper placed in it.

First thinly peel the potatoes and cut them into even-sized pieces—but not too small. Put them in a saucepan, cover them with boiling water, add some salt, bring to simmering point and cook for 15 minutes. Then drain them, arrange them on a wooden board and slice them thinly and evenly.

For the next stage you need two medium-sized frying-pans and a small saucepan. Heat a tablespoon of olive oil in the saucepan, add the onion and fry gently. Now heat 2 tablespoons of oil in each frying-pan and when it begins to sizzle add the potatoes, dividing them between the pans so that they don't overlap. Fry them over a high heat, turning them after 5–7 minutes to cook on the other side until they are golden-brown and crisp all over. Then, using a slotted spoon, transfer them to the crumpled paper to drain and scatter on the fried onion. Loosen the top of the pepper-mill a little to get a really coarse grind and sprinkle over the potatoes; crush some rock salt between your finger and thumb and sprinkle on.

Lastly pull out the paper from underneath and serve at once—if you delay the potatoes will go soggy.

For *Sauté potatoes Niçoise* cook half a finely-chopped green pepper and a crushed clove of garlic with the onion, then stir the mixture into the potatoes and sprinkle with freshly-chopped herbs or parsley before serving.

Cabbage

Cabbage, I'm pleased to say, has come on a lot of late. At one time (at least when I was at school) it was a sadly misunderstood vegetable—too much stalk, too much water and far too much cooking. No wonder so many people opted out of cabbage for life.

In a way I think the Chinese cook cabbage best, simply by stir-frying it—tossing shreds of cabbage in oil over a very high heat for the minimum time, and not so much as threatening it with any water. This way it retains its crispness and flavour. If, however, you want to cook plain boiled cabbage (any variety): cut it into quarters, discarding the tough outer leaves and cutting away the ribs, then shred it finely and pack it tightly into a saucepan. Add some salt and enough boiling water (straight from the kettle) to come halfway up, then cover with a tight-fitting lid. Boil it till tender but still retaining some 'bite' (about 10 minutes). Stir it and turn it over halfway through to make sure it cooks evenly. Drain it in a colander, pressing and squeezing out the excess moisture, season with pepper and toss in some butter before serving.

There are many varieties of cabbage available throughout the season, and for the recipe below any variety can be used—including the hard, white drumhead varieties.

Fried cabbage with bacon

(serves 2 or 3 people)

This is good enough for a meal on its own, and excellent with sausages and jacket potatoes.

1 lb shredded cabbage (450 g)
2 streaky bacon rashers, chopped
1 clove garlic, crushed
1 medium onion, chopped small
2 tablespoons olive oil
Salt and freshly-milled black pepper

Take a large frying-pan and begin by frying the onion and bacon together in olive oil for about 5 minutes. Then add the crushed garlic and cook for another 2 or 3 minutes. Now stir in the shredded cabbage (which will seem rather bulky at first, but as the heat gets to it it will start to collapse) and keep stirring it now and then so it cooks evenly. Season with freshly-milled pepper, but taste before adding salt because of the bacon. The cabbage should cook in about 10 minutes and still retain its crispness, but if you prefer it softer put a lid on the frying-pan—which will give it some steam.

Cabbage with garlic and juniper
(serves 2–3 people)

This recipe gleaned from the famous Miller Howe hotel in the English Lakes, is one of my favourite vegetable dishes.

1 lb cabbage (any) (450 g), prepared and shredded
½ medium onion, finely chopped
1 clove of garlic, crushed
6 juniper berries
2 tablespoons olive oil
Salt and freshly-milled black pepper

In a good solid saucepan or flameproof casserole, gently heat the olive oil and soften the onion in it for 5 minutes. Meanwhile crush the juniper berries (either with a pestle and mortar, or by placing them on a flat surface and crushing them with the back of a tablespoon). Then add these to the onion along with the crushed garlic. Fry for about 1 minute longer, then add the shredded cabbage. Stir it around until it's all glistening with oil, season with salt and pepper, then put a lid on and let it cook in its own juice for 10 minutes—stirring once or twice so that it cooks evenly.

Red Cabbage
There was a time when red cabbage was confined to a lethal dose of malt vinegar inside a pickle jar. But now it's becoming much more popular as a delicious vegetable. Braised slowly in the oven with apples and spices, it really is the perfect accompaniment to pork or pork sausages and is very good served with *Cassoulet* (see page 227).

Braised red cabbage with apples
(serves 4 people)

2 lb red cabbage (900 g)
1 lb onions (450 g), chopped small
1 lb cooking apples (450 g), peeled, cored and chopped small
3 tablespoons wine vinegar
3 tablespoons brown sugar
1 garlic clove, chopped very small
¼ whole nutmeg, freshly grated
¼ level teaspoon ground cinnamon
¼ level teaspoon ground cloves
½ oz butter (10 g)
Salt and freshly-milled black pepper

Pre-heat the oven to gas mark 2, 300°F (150°C)

Discard the tough outer leaves of the cabbage, cut it into quarters and remove the hard stalk, then shred the cabbage finely.

In a fairly large casserole, arrange a layer of shredded cabbage seasoned with salt and pepper, then a layer of chopped onions and apples with a sprinkling of garlic, spices and sugar. Continue with these alternate layers until everything is in.

Now pour in the wine vinegar, add a knob of butter, put a lid on the casserole and let it cook very slowly in the oven for about $2\frac{1}{2}$–3 hours, stirring everything around once or twice during the cooking. Red cabbage, once cooked, will keep warm without coming to any harm. It will also re-heat very successfully—so it can be made in advance if necessary. Serve it with sausages, or pork dishes, or Lancashire hotpot.

Root Vegetables
Turnips, carrots, swedes, celeriac and parsnips are all root vegetables that store well, and keep us supplied through the winter months. To cook them the same principles as for potatoes are applied—namely, always pare off the skin as thinly as possible to preserve the nutrients, and cook them in as little boiling water as possible (this water can be used for stock or gravy, with one exception: parsnip water is too strongly flavoured and would mask other flavours). Root vegetables are perfect for long, slow cooking in stews and casseroles, where they can extend the meat considerably as well as add a character of their own. Browning the raw, peeled chunks of vegetable first—so that the edges become almost black and caramelised—adds a distinctive flavour to a rich brown stew.

Carrots
The young carrots of spring and early summer, sold still in bunches, are sweet, tender and delicious. I like them washed, cooked in their skins with very little water, then tossed in a little fresh herb butter (see page 163). Maincrop carrots, I have found, taste better if you can manage to buy them with the earth still clinging to them—scrubbing and packing them in polythene bags may be convenient but not the best thing for them. To cook: scrub and scrape the skins (even older carrots don't need peeling), and if

they are large, tough and woody then cut them in quarters
vertically and excise any of the hard centre core. Cook them in
very little boiling salted water (just enough to cover) with ¼
teaspoon of sugar added. They will take from 8 to 10 minutes to
cook, depending on size. Then drain them and toss in butter or
bacon fat before serving.

Turnips
I think turnips are much under-estimated—probably because they
have been too often badly cooked in the past, boiled to death and
waterlogged. Just cut into chunks, browned in dripping and added
to stews and casseroles they're marvellous, or sliced in a Pasty Pie
(see page 87). A more sophisticated way to serve them would be
Turnips and leeks boulangère. Follow the recipe on page 202 for
Potatoes boulangère, but using instead of potatoes and onions the
equivalent quantities of turnips and leeks.

   In Scotland turnips are whipped to a purée—bashed neeps—and
in Wales they serve punchnep, a delicious combination of creamed
potatoes and turnips whipped to a smooth purée, which Dorothy
Hartley in her excellent book *Food in England* describes as looking
like 'hot alabaster'. To prepare turnips, peel them as thinly as
possible and keep them in cold water till ready to cook, to prevent
them browning.

Punchnep

(serves 4 people)

Although it might seem unnecessary, the
secret of this to get the right flavour is to
boil the vegetables separately.

1 lb turnips (450 g), peeled and cut into chunks
1 lb potatoes (450 g), peeled and cut into chunks
3 oz butter (75 g)
3 fl. oz single cream (75 ml)
Salt and freshly-milled black pepper

Put the potatoes in one saucepan and the turnips in another and
cover both with boiling water. Season with salt and simmer—
covered—until the vegetables are tender. (You'll find the potatoes
will be ready about 5 minutes before the turnips.)

Meanwhile warm a shallow oval serving dish and, when the
vegetables are ready, drain off the water, then combine them in

one saucepan. Next pour the cream into the empty saucepan and warm it over a gentle heat. Add the butter to the vegetables, season well, and mash thoroughly. Now empty the mixture into the warmed dish, then, using a skewer or similar implement and a circular movement, make several holes in the vegetables and pour the hot cream into the holes. Serve immediately.

Creamed parsnips

(serves 4 people)

Even people who think they don't like parsnips usually have to admit that they like this.

1 lb parsnips (450 g)
¾ pint hot water (425 ml)
¼ pint single cream (150 ml)
Freshly-grated nutmeg
Salt and freshly-milled black pepper

Peel the parsnips and cut out the woody centre bits, then cut them up into small cubes. In a saucepan bring the hot water to boiling point, add the cubed parsnips and simmer—covered—for approximately 10 minutes or until tender when tested with a skewer.

When ready, place a colander over a bowl and drain the parsnips, reserving the liquid. Now, either purée them with the cream in a liquidiser or sieve them and beat in the cream a little at a time with a fork. Taste and season with freshly-grated nutmeg, salt and pepper and, if you think the mixture is too dry, mix in 1 or 2 tablespoons of the reserved liquid.

Mashed swedes with crispy bacon

(serves 4–6 people)

2 lb swedes (900 g)
6 rashers bacon, chopped small
2 oz butter (50 g)
2 tablespoons single cream
Salt and freshly-milled black pepper

Start by peeling the swedes and cutting them into smallish cubes. Put them in a saucepan and just cover them with water. Add salt, bring to simmering point and cook gently for 20–30 minutes or until the swedes are tender when tested with a skewer. Then tip them into a colander to drain thoroughly.

Return the saucepan to the heat, add a knob of butter and fry the chopped bacon until it begins to crisp. Now return the swedes to the saucepan, add the remainder of the butter and the cream and mash well to a creamy consistency. Season well with salt and freshly-milled black pepper and pile onto a warmed dish to serve.

Aubergines

Aubergines are extremely beautiful vegetables, dark, shiny, rich maroon. Some are long—rounded at one end and thinner at the other—with a cap of green leaves and a stalk. Others are round and squat-looking. Inside they are all cream-coloured, with a flavour quite unlike that of any other vegetable (the peel itself has a lot of flavour). Because they contain a great deal of water it is always best to sprinkle the insides or the cut slices with salt—which will draw some of the excess water out. Place the salted aubergines in a colander, put a plate on top and weight it down, and in half an hour or so a lot of the surplus moisture will drain out. Then dry them in a cloth and they're ready to be cooked.

Baked aubergines with tomatoes

Cooked like this aubergines can make a good accompaniment to lamb, or even be eaten as a lunch dish on their own.

(serves 4 people)

4 aubergines—approx. 1¾ lb (800 g)
4 tablespoons oil
1 large onion, peeled and finely chopped
6 largish tomatoes, skinned and chopped
2 cloves of garlic, crushed
2 tablespoons of finely-chopped parsley
A good pinch each of ground allspice, cinnamon and caster sugar
Some butter
Salt and freshly-milled black pepper

For the topping:
2–3 tablespoons of dry white breadcrumbs
1 tablespoon grated Cheddar cheese
1 tablespoon butter

First prepare the aubergines: cut each one into smallish pieces, pile them all in a colander, sprinkle with salt (2 heaped teaspoons), then place a plate on top of them. Weight it down with a scale-weight and leave to drain for 1 hour.

When you're ready to cook, pre-heat the oven to gas mark 5, 375°F (190°C), and butter a shallow baking dish generously. Drain the aubergines and dry them thoroughly on kitchen paper, then heat the oil in a frying-pan. Add the aubergines to the pan and fry to a pale-golden colour, then add the chopped onion and carry on cooking until that has softened a bit.

Next add the tomatoes, garlic and parsley, the spices and sugar, and season with salt and pepper. Let everything simmer gently for about 5 minutes, stirring occasionally. Then transfer the mixture to the baking dish, sprinkle the top with a mixture of the cheese and breadcrumbs, and dot the surface with flecks of butter.

Bake near the top of the oven for about 30 minutes, or until browned and bubbling on top.

Brussels sprouts
My advice is to totally ignore those pale (and highly expensive) sprouts that turn up at the end of August in the shops. More than any other vegetable, brussels sprouts need a sharp frost on them to heighten the flavour (and what need of sprouts have we in August, with so many other vegetables and salads in season?). The best-quality brussels are like tight round buttons: take off the damaged outer leaves, make a cross-wise incision at the stalk end (to enable it to cook as evenly and quickly as the leaves), then pour boiling water over, just enough to cover. Simmer gently for 5–8 minutes, depending on their size. Test them with a skewer, and try not to overcook them—they should be still firm and bright green. Then drain, season and serve in butter. Even better, boil them for a little less time, have some melted butter ready in a frying-pan quite hot and frothy, and toss them quickly in that over a gentle heat.

Parsnips
This is another vegetable that needs a good sharp frost to really sharpen up its flavour; and since there are so many other vegetables about in the autumn, it is best to wait till the end of October or into November if you want to eat them at their best. Peel them thinly, quarter them lengthways, and cut out the woody core before cooking. They can be plain boiled in salted water, but are even better baked.

Baked parsnips For these, follow the method for blanching and roasting potatoes (page 197), but place them on a lower shelf in the oven and give them slightly less cooking time.

Leeks

There is a period, from about the end of January to the end of March, when fresh vegetables seem a bit thin on the ground. But nature hasn't let us down: it provides an abundance of leeks throughout the winter and these two months is the time to make the most of them. Having said that, though, leeks are best served in the simplest possible manner—no water, no white sauce, just a little seasoning.

Sometimes leeks can arrive rather dusty, so care is needed when preparing and cleaning them. The best way is to cut off all but about 1½ inch (4 cm) of the green part, and trim off the root end. Then, using a small sharp knife, make a vertical slit down two-thirds of each leek. Now you can hold each leek under a cold running tap, spreading the layers out in a fan shape to wash out any hidden dirt.

Buttered leeks (serves 4 people)	1½ lb leeks (700 g), trimmed and washed
	2 oz butter (50 g)
	Salt and freshly-milled black pepper

Chop the cleaned leeks into roughly 1½ inch (4 cm) pieces. Then melt the butter in a thick-based saucepan, and add the slivers of leek, stirring them around thoroughly. Season with salt and freshly-milled pepper, and let them sweat in their own juices for 6–8 minutes, or until they're cooked to your liking.

Cauliflower

Whatever did cauliflowers do to deserve their overboiled, watery-white-sauce image? They have far more potential than that, as I hope the recipes here show. Since I've been growing them in my garden I've come to the conclusion that bleached whiteness is not necessarily the hallmark of a good cauliflower: my home-grown caulis have all been creamy-yellow and quite delicious. Tightness and fresh-looking leaves are what to look for when buying.

One of the nicest ways to cook a cauliflower is to separate it first into largish florets, then pack them upright (i.e. stalks downward) in a large, wide saucepan. Tuck in a bayleaf, season with salt and pepper and a little freshly-grated nutmeg, then pour in just about 1½ inches (4 cm) of boiling water. Cover with a lid and simmer for about 5–6 minutes—this way the stalks will cook in the water, and the florets in the steam. Afterwards drain them and toss them in butter before serving.

Cauliflower with garlic and bacon
(serves 3–4 people)

In this recipe the sprigs of cauliflower are first blanched and then finished off in the oven.

1 medium cauliflower
2 rashers streaky bacon, chopped
1 clove garlic, crushed
1 small onion, finely chopped
2 oz butter (50 g)
2 tablespoons olive oil
1 tablespoon freshly-chopped parsley
2 tablespoons fresh breadcrumbs
Salt and freshly-milled black pepper

Pre-heat the oven to gas mark 5, 375°F (190°C)

Begin by dividing the cauliflower into walnut-sized florets; place them in a saucepan and just cover them with boiling water. Add salt, bring up to the boil, simmer for 2 minutes, then drain well in a colander.

Next, using the same saucepan, melt half the butter together with the oil and cook the onion and garlic for about 5 minutes to soften them, then add the bacon and cook for another 5 minutes. Now add the rest of the butter and, when it's melted, stir in the breadcrumbs and parsley and cook for a further minute or two. Then place the drained cauliflower either in a meat-roasting tin or a gratin dish and spoon the breadcrumb mixture evenly on top.

Bake in the oven for 10–15 minutes and, after about 5 minutes of the cooking time, baste with the buttery juices. When ready the cauliflower should be tender but still firm. Before serving, sprinkle on some freshly-milled black pepper.

Jerusalem artichokes

These are vegetables with a distinctive flavour and are another neglected delicacy. Although they're cheap and couldn't be easier to grow, they are largely ignored. My guess is that this is because of their ugliness: the tubers do look most misshapen, covered with daunting knobbly bits. There's no need to be daunted. If you're prepared to buy slightly more than you actually need, you can soon cut off (and discard) the knobbles, which makes life a lot easier. They are then easy to peel, but as they discolour quickly pop them straight into cold water as you peel. As a vegetable they can be roasted like potatoes or sautéed, or cooked as in potatoes boulangère with leeks substituted for the onions, or made into a cream purée. Best of all, I think, they make a really delicious soup with a truly creamy texture.

Carrot and artichoke soup

(serves 6–8 people)

This not only has a delicious, very creamy texture and flavour, but you also have an added bonus because of its beautifully rich saffron colour.

1 lb carrots (450 g)
1½ lb Jerusalem artichokes (700 g)
1 medium onion, chopped
3 sticks celery, chopped
3 oz butter (75 g)
2½ pints light stock (1·5 litres)
Salt and freshly-milled black pepper

Start by peeling and de-knobbling the artichokes and, as you peel them, slice them into a bowl of cold water to prevent them discolouring.

Scrape and slice the carrots, then in a cooking pot melt the butter, soften the onion and celery in it for 5 minutes, then stir in the carrots and artichokes. Add some salt and, keeping the heat low, put the lid on and let the vegetables sweat for 10 minutes. Then pour in the stock, stir well, put the lid back on and simmer for a further 20 minutes or until the vegetables are soft.

Now either liquidise the soup or pass it through a sieve. Taste to check the seasoning, re-heat and serve.

Celery

I never buy imported celery out of season because it never tastes anywhere near the same as our own. I think it's at its best after a good November frost, and Fenland celery is particularly delicious when the black earth still clings to it and the stalks are white all the way up to the leaves. If you scrub the stalks under cold running water and dry them with a cloth they'll stay crisp stored in a plastic bag in the lowest part of the fridge for several days, but remember to seal the bag well. Home-made bread, good cheese and crisp celery are one of the nicest instant meals I know. However, it's just as delicious cooked, as in the following recipe.

Braised celery with cheese and onion sauce

(serves 4 people)

1 large or 2 small heads of celery
1 oz butter (25 g)
1 tablespoon oil
1 carrot, thinly sliced
1 onion, thinly sliced
¼ pint chicken stock (150 ml)
¼ teaspoon celery seeds
Salt and freshly-milled black pepper

For the sauce:
Milk
1 oz butter (25 g)
1 smallish onion, finely chopped
½ oz flour (10 g)
3 oz Cheddar cheese, grated (75 g)
1 egg yolk

Pre-heat the oven to gas mark 4, 350°F (180°C)

For this you'll need a large flameproof casserole.

Prepare the celery by breaking off the stalks and, using a bristle brush, clean each one under cold running water. Trim off the leaf and base of each stalk and cut in half.

Next blanch the celery by putting it in boiling salted water for about 5 minutes, then drain well.

Now in a flameproof casserole, heat the butter and oil, add the prepared carrot and onion and cook for about 5 minutes. Add the drained celery and the chicken stock. Sprinkle with the celery seeds and season with a little salt and pepper. Place the casserole in the oven and bake, covered, for 30 minutes or until the celery is tender.

When ready transfer the vegetables to a serving dish, using a slotted spoon. Empty the cooking liquid into a measuring jug and make it up to $\frac{1}{2}$ pint (275 ml) with milk.

To make the sauce, heat the butter in a saucepan and fry the finely-chopped onion until golden, then blend in the flour and cook for a couple of minutes before adding the milk mixture a little at a time, stirring well after each addition. Bring to simmering point, still stirring, and simmer gently for a minute or two, then remove from the heat and beat in the cheese and egg yolk. Pour the sauce over the vegetables and bake in the oven for a further 20 minutes or until you're sure it's all piping hot.

Served with rice this makes a complete and delicious meal for two—even without meat.

Pulses

With our food there seems to be an inexorable process at work: yesterday's poor-man's diet is today's luxury. It's hard to believe you could once buy oysters, fifty of them for a shilling; or that the fish-porters at Billingsgate once went on strike because they were getting too much salmon for lunch! The plain fact is, of course, that over the past century our consumption has far outstripped our resources, except in one rather neglected area—pulses (that is to say, the family of beans, peas and lentils). Pulses for thousands of years have been the staple diet of poor countries all over the world, from China to Mexico.

Sadly, that is still their image. It must be rather humiliating to be a bean: a 'bean-feast' was a meal judged fit only for workmen, and if you 'hadn't got a bean' you really had not got anything at all. Yet ancient peoples were far more respectful than we are: some appointed a god in charge of beans, and others never buried their dead without a supply of beans to take them into the other world.

Doubtless it will be pointed out that we still consume beans in Britain in absolutely vast quantities. I recall a cartoon at the time when de Gaulle was objecting to this country joining the Common Market: it showed the General recoiling from a report on how many million tons of baked beans the British consumed in a year. 'Mon Dieu!' was his reaction. As well it might have been, when you think that out of the great range of beans available (kidney, haricot, butter, lima, broad ... and so on) in this country beans means just one bland, processed variety.

Nutritional value for money

I believe that our attitudes to pulses are gradually changing, in fact. There is no doubt about their nutritional value: according to a recent report by the Consumers Association they took four of the top ten places in the list of vegetable proteins—with dried peas, for instance, you get over 8 g of protein for 1p. (Vegetable proteins are, a bit unfairly, referred to as 'second-class proteins' because they lack the important amino-acids that are found in meat, fish, dairy foods, etc.; but this is not to undermine their value—the missing amino-acids are found in flour or rice or pasta, so a plateful of beans-on-toast will provide you with the same amount of protein as beefsteak.) Soya beans are the most nutritious of all the pulses. Their yield, in the countries where they're grown is so enormous compared with the acreage involved that ecologically the soya bean seems set to figure very largely in the future of this small planet with its ever-growing population.

There cannot be much argument about the need to create a new balance in our present-day way of eating. The meat-based diet we have been used to is rapidly disappearing out of reach of many people's pockets: the need to 'stretch' the meat we can afford is becoming an economic necessity. The food technologists' answer to this problem has been to come up with meat-substitutes, textured vegetable proteins (TVP) masquerading as mince.

I find this quite extraordinary—pretending we've got meat when we haven't. The commercial giants responsible for its manufacture claim it is to extend meat rather than replace it, but then so will beans, peas and the rest of the pulses on their own, without the cost of refining and disguising them, and far more pleasantly. On the Continent, where they have always been less meat-conscious, pulses have long been used with imagination to extend a meat-ration. They are *not* dull or unattractive, and I hope the recipes here will prove my point.

Varieties of pulses

First let us run through the commoner types of pulse—there are so many varieties it would be tedious to include them all. People who live alongside immigrant communities will doubtless find some pulses not mentioned here, but those described below can be found on some supermarket shelves or in specialised food shops.

Butter beans These are large, flat beans, cream in colour. Boiled on their own (as I remember them at school) they do tend to be dull: but they make a good thick soup, and are useful if haricot beans are unavailable as they respond well to a well-flavoured vinaigrette dressing with lots of chopped shallots and parsley strewn over.

Haricot beans There are two main types of haricot bean: the long, thin shiny-ivory one which the Italians call 'fagioli'. These are delicious in salads, stews, and Tuscan bean and pasta soup: they are also the kind used in France, cooked in the Breton way and served with mutton and lamb. The other type of haricot is the small round one of tinned baked bean fame. In my opinion they are inferior to, and lack the flavour of, their handsomer cousins.

Red kidney beans Not surprisingly, these shiny-polished beans are both red and kidney-shaped. They have a delicious flavour, a must for *Chilli con carne* (page 224). They make a good salad and will adapt themselves to any recipe for bean soup.

Soya beans Smallish, round, and a pale yellow/cream colour. They need careful soaking and long cooking, and are rather mealy-textured when cooked. For me their flavour and texture are not up to that of white haricots.

Aduki beans These are tiny, red-brown beans with a little white thread down one side. Because of their size they make perfect partners to brown rice, to give a good protein balance (see recipe page 222).

Chick peas Light brown, nutty-looking peas, which need careful soaking (definitely overnight) and as much as 3 hours' cooking. But they are worth it in my opinion with their lovely nutty flavour. They can be made into cutlets, soups, salads, or puréed with oil and lemon to a paste to make what the Greeks call 'hummus'.

Split peas These halved dried peas can be deep green or golden-yellow. I think the green ones are superior in flavour, but both are suitable for thick, warming pea soups, or for purées or cutlets.

Whole dried peas The ones used to make 'mushy peas'. They are delicious, with more character than tinned or frozen peas. Especially good with pork or boiled bacon, or made into the traditional pease pudding.

Lentils There are in fact over sixty varieties of lentil. But as far as whole lentils are concerned there are three main types that concern us. Most popular are the green-brown variety (as I call them since they're usually a mixture of both colours) that look like little pills. I love their flavour, and if I never had any more meat I'd be content with a plentiful supply of these around. There is a smaller version of these, sometimes called Chinese lentils, which are more red-brown and also rarer and more expensive. The French 'lentils du pays' are a slate-grey colour and, if you can find them, have a very superior flavour.

Split lentils These are literally filleted lentils, with the skins removed and split naturally into two halves. They cook to a mush very quickly and are suitable for thick purées and soups.

Other varieties of pulses are much rarer over here, though they play an important part in the cooking of other countries. The white flat *Lima beans* are used in America for soups and salads, and *black-eyed beans* (cream with a 'black eye') are served with ham. In the Caribbean *black beans* are served spiced or in a sauce as a side-dish, as are *Egyptian beans* (round and brown) in the Middle East. The beautiful pale-green *flageolets* in France are a high-class variation of the haricot, and quite delicious.

Buying and storing pulses

Although British farmers are experimenting with growing different types of pulse, most of them are imported at the moment. The vegetables are harvested annually and dried in the autumn, so the year's crop usually begins to reach us around November. Obviously one of the big advantages of dried vegetable pulses is that they do store easily and—provided suitable soaking time is taken into consideration—can be used fairly spontaneously.

However, it is wrong to think that, for cooking, pulses keep indefinitely. After about a year they start to harden to such an extent that sometimes no amount of cooking will soften them. Therefore it is important to buy them from somewhere reliable (and if you do get landed with a batch that is more ancient than it should be, take them back and complain). Also if your memory is as bad as mine, place a little sticker on the storage jar—I use large glass ones—to remind you when you actually purchased the contents. I've found that a year or even 18 months can slip by almost unnoticed in the larder.

Soaking

Most, though not all, dried vegetables have to be soaked to replace the moisture lost in the drying process. Overnight soaking may seem a long time: in fact I once mentioned it on a radio programme, and one listener wrote insisting that beans should never be soaked that long or they would be likely to ferment. (Just for the record—I checked with Queen Elizabeth College of Nutrition, who confirmed that they would have to soak under normal conditions for 36–48 hours before fermentation.)

So, if it's convenient, overnight soaking is perfectly all right. But (except for chick peas) there is an alternative, and that is to cover with cold water, bring to the boil, simmer for 5 minutes, then leave to soak for up to 2 hours depending on the type of bean. You usually need about 4 pints (2·25 l) of soaking water for every ½ lb (225 g) of beans.

Cooking

Most pulses except split peas and lentils need rather long cooking: 1½–3 hours according to variety. Perhaps the most important rule is *not* to add any salt until the end of the cooking, which is quite logical really: salt draws out moisture (to extract moisture from vegetables like courgettes you sprinkle salt on them), so even a small amount of salt in the soaking or cooking water will simply retard the process. Adding salt at the end doesn't make any difference, I find, but you should taste carefully to add just the right quantity. Pressure-cooking can cut down the cooking times for pulses drastically, especially for soups. However, since pressure-cooking requires a certain amount of unthickened liquid, it is not always suitable for all recipes. And pressure-cookers themselves vary, making it impossible to provide general guidelines: to cook pulses in them, therefore, consult the manufacturers' booklets, which should also provide information on soaking times.

Digesting pulses
Dried vegetables in the past have acquired a somewhat bad reputation, and are said to cause flatulence. This shouldn't be the case if the beans are properly soaked and carefully cooked. There is some evidence that throwing away the soaking water and using fresh for cooking helps to eliminate the problem. So if you suffer from bean side-effects I suggest you do just that.

Aduki bean and brown rice salad

(serves 6 people)

Aduki beans go very well with brown rice, especially in a salad.

1 mugful brown rice
2 mugs boiling water
4 oz aduki beans (110 g), soaked overnight
1 large green pepper, deseeded and chopped
2 stalks celery, finely chopped
½ cucumber, diced—leave the peel on
6 spring onions, finely chopped—including the green parts
Salt

For the dressing:
4 fl. oz olive oil (110 ml)
1 tablespoon wine vinegar
1 fat clove garlic, crushed
1 teaspoon mustard powder
1 teaspoon salt

2 tablespoons finely-chopped parsley

2 tablespoons finely-chopped celery leaves

Freshly-milled black pepper

First put the beans in a saucepan together with the water in which they were soaked (no need to add salt), bring to the boil and cook for 45 minutes to 1 hour or until the beans are tender.

Meantime, in another saucepan, place the rice with some salt and add the boiling water. Bring to the boil, cover and simmer very gently for about 40 minutes or until the rice is tender and all the water absorbed.

Next, put all the ingredients for the dressing in a salad bowl and whisk together. Then while the cooked rice and the beans (drained) are still warm, empty them into the salad bowl and mix everything together lightly with a fork. Leave the salad till cold, then add the chopped vegetables, mixing them in lightly. Taste and season again if it needs it and serve sprinkled with chopped parsley and celery leaves.

Thick pea soup
(serves 6 people)

This needs some crisp fried croutons of bread to sprinkle over just before serving.

3½ pints basic stock (2 litres)

¾ lb split peas (yellow or green) (350 g)

2 oz butter (50 g)

4 thick rashers bacon, diced

1 medium onion, roughly chopped

1 celery stalk, chopped

1 large carrot, sliced

A little extra stock, if needed

Salt and freshly-milled black pepper

First strain off 3½ pints (2 litres) basic stock into a large saucepan, then bring just up to simmering point, add the split peas, cover and simmer very gently for about 30 minutes (there is no need to soak the split peas first).

Meanwhile, heat 1 oz (25 g) butter in another saucepan and add the prepared vegetables and the bacon, and cook them over a medium heat until softened and nicely golden—this will take about

15 minutes. Add the softened vegetables to the stock and split peas, season lightly with salt and freshly-milled black pepper, then cover and simmer very gently for a further 40–50 minutes.

When the soup is ready, either press the whole lot through a sieve or liquidize in an electric blender. Now return it to the saucepan, taste to check the seasoning and add a little more stock if it seems to need thinning a bit.

Before serving, melt the remaining butter into it.

Chilli con carne
(serves 4 people)

This is very often made with minced beef, but I think it's far nicer made with chuck steak cut into very small pieces. It's medium hot as it is, so if you like things hotter or milder you can adjust the quantity of chilli.

1 lb chuck steak (450 g), cut into very small pieces
2 medium onions, chopped
1 fat clove garlic, crushed
1 pint hot stock (570 ml)
2 heaped tablespoons tomato purée
Salt
1 rounded tablespoon flour
½ lb red kidney beans (available from wholefood shops) (225 g)
1 large green pepper, deseeded and chopped
1 level teaspoon crushed dried chilli or chilli powder
Beef dripping or oil

Chilli con carne should be hot and spicy. In my opinion modifying it by cutting down the spiciness simply reduces it to an ordinary stew—so go carefully with the chilli by all means, but don't relegate it out of existence.

First of all start with the beans. Cover them with cold water, then bring them to simmering point, simmer for just 2 minutes, then turn the heat out and let them soak for an hour. Towards the end of the soaking time, pre-heat the oven to gas mark 2, 300°F (150°C).

Now in a flameproof casserole, melt about a tablespoon of beef dripping and gently cook the onion and garlic in it for about 6 minutes. Then turn the heat up, add the beef and brown it well, stirring it around a bit.

Next sprinkle in the flour, stir it in to soak up the juices, then combine the tomato purée with the hot stock and add it gradually to the meat and onion.

Now add the chilli, then after draining the red beans thoroughly, add them too, bring to simmering point, add salt, put a lid on, then transfer the casserole to the oven and cook for about 1½ hours; and when the time's up remove the lid, stir in the chopped pepper, cover again and cook for a further 30 minutes.

Italian bean and pasta soup

(serves 4–6 people)

This is a beautiful thick Tuscan peasant soup hardly needing anything more to follow it.

½ lb white haricot beans (225 g)
¼ lb small-cut macaroni (110 g)
2½ tablespoons tomato purée
1 teaspoon dried basil
1 large onion, chopped small
2 cloves garlic, crushed
2 oz grated Parmesan cheese (50 g)
2 tablespoons olive oil
Salt and freshly-milled black pepper

Place the beans in a saucepan, then add 3 pints (1·75 l) cold water to them, bring them to the boil, boil for 1 minute, then turn the heat out and let them soak for 2 hours.

Now gently fry the onion in olive oil together with the garlic for about 10 minutes. Then add the tomato purée and basil, stir for a minute, pour in the beans and the water they were soaking in. Now bring the soup up to simmering point, cover and simmer gently for about an hour. When the time's up season with salt and pepper, then put half the soup either through a sieve or blend in a liquidiser. Return the puréed half to the pan, bring to simmering point, then add the macaroni and simmer for a further 10–12 minutes, stirring from time to time. Serve the soup with lots of freshly-grated Parmesan cheese to sprinkle over.

Lentil, bean and anchovy salad

(serves 4 people)

This is a really delicious salad and substantial enough to serve as a main course for lunch.

8 oz whole lentils (brown) (225 g)
8 oz white haricot beans (225 g)
Salt and freshly-milled black pepper

For the dressing:
8 tablespoons oil
1 tablespoon wine vinegar
1 tablespoon lemon juice
1 small onion, peeled and finely chopped
1 clove garlic, crushed
1 heaped teaspoon mustard
4 tablespoons finely-chopped fresh parsley
A 2-oz (50-g) tin anchovy fillets

To garnish:
2 hard-boiled eggs, chopped
1 oz small black olives (25 g)
A few crisp lettuce leaves

Prepare the beans in advance by putting them in a saucepan and covering with cold water. Bring to boiling point and boil for 2–3 minutes, then remove from the heat and let the beans soak for about an hour. After that boil them again for about another hour until *just* soft.

About half an hour before the beans are ready pick over the lentils (there's no need to soak them); wash them and boil in plenty of water until *just* soft.

Meanwhile mix together in a bowl all the ingredients for the dressing and add the oil from the tin of anchovies. Chop the anchovies and put on one side.

When the beans and lentils are cooked, drain them, tip them into a bowl and, while they're still warm, pour on the dressing. Mix well so that they are well coated and leave to cool.

Before serving, taste and season the salad well with salt and freshly-milled black pepper, then place some crisp lettuce leaves on 4 plates and arrange the mixture on top. Finally garnish with the chopped hard-boiled eggs, chopped anchovies and olives.

Cassoulet

(serves 6 people)

Although this was originally a French peasant dish, I think it's particularly good for entertaining in winter because it's all done in advance and doesn't mind waiting in the oven if you want to eat a bit later than planned.

¾ **lb white haricot beans (350 g)**
½ **shoulder of lamb—the inside half, not the leg half, and ask the butcher to take out the bone for you**
1 lb belly of pork (450 g), boned and cut into strips
½ **lb streaky bacon in one piece (225 g)**
½ **lb garlic sausage in one piece (225 g)**
4 juniper berries
2 medium onions, chopped
A bayleaf
2 cloves garlic
A sprig of thyme
A small sprig of rosemary
A few parsley stalks
5 oz fresh white breadcrumbs (150 g)
Salt and freshly-milled black pepper

It's not necessary to soak the beans overnight, but wash them well in about two changes of water before placing them in a saucepan with about 3 pints (1·75 litres) of cold water. Bring to simmering point and after about 2 minutes put aside and leave for an hour for the beans to soak in the liquid.

Meanwhile prepare the other ingredients by first of all trimming any really excess fat off the lamb and cutting the meat into very large chunks. Then, using a sharp knife, pare the rind as thinly as possible from both the bacon and the pork, and chop the rinds into very small pieces.

Leave the pork slices whole, but chop the bacon into 6 chunks, also peel and chop the garlic sausage into largish pieces. Now tie in a little bunch of the thyme, rosemary, parsley stalks and bayleaf, then skin and crush the cloves of garlic, also crush the juniper berries using either a pestle and mortar or the back of a tablespoon.

When the beans have finished soaking drain them in a colander, throw away the water, then put them in a large saucepan together with the bacon, chopped bacon and pork rinds, garlic sausage, onions, garlic, juniper, bunch of herbs and some freshly-milled black pepper, but no salt as there will be some in the bacon. Cover with about $2\frac{1}{2}$ pints (1·5 litres) cold water, bring to simmering point and simmer gently for $1\frac{1}{2}$ hours.

Halfway through the cooking time pre-heat the oven to gas mark 3, 325°F (170°C), and roast the lamb and pork for 45 minutes.

When the meat is cooked the bean mixture will also be ready, so empty the contents of the saucepan into a sieve or colander placed over a bowl, let it drain, reserve this liquid and remove the herbs. Then in a buttered 5 pint (3 litre) earthenware casserole arrange half the bean mixture over the base, placing the pieces of lamb and pork on top. Season with salt and freshly-milled black pepper, then add the rest of the bean mixture. Now add to the casserole $\frac{3}{4}$ pint (425 ml) of the bean cooking liquid, cover the surface entirely with the breadcrumbs and cook in the oven—uncovered—for $1\frac{1}{2}$ hours.

Chilladas

(serves 8 people)

These lightly-spiced lentil cakes flavoured with green peppers really are just as good as having meat.

1 lb green or brown whole lentils (450 g)
$1\frac{1}{2}$ pints hot water (845 ml)
4 oz butter (or vegetable margarine) (110 g)
2 onions, peeled and finely chopped
2 small green peppers (or 1 large), deseeded and chopped small
2 carrots, scraped and finely chopped
1 teaspoon mixed herbs
$\frac{1}{2}$ teaspoon powdered mace
1 teaspoon cayenne pepper
4 teaspoons tomato purée
2 cloves garlic, crushed
Salt and freshly-milled black pepper
For the coating:
Dry fine breadcrumbs
1 egg, beaten
Groundnut oil for shallow frying

Wash the lentils and place them in a saucepan with 1½ pints (845 ml) of hot water. Let them come to the boil, then cover and simmer very gently for about an hour or until all the liquid has been absorbed and the lentils are mushy. Towards the end of their cooking time, heat the butter in a frying-pan and soften the onion, garlic and carrot in it for 5 minutes, then add the chopped peppers and cook for a further 5–10 minutes.

Next, season the lentils and tip them into a bowl to mash them to a pulp with a fork—though not too smooth. Now mix in the softened vegetables together with the cayenne, mace, herbs and tomato purée—then divide the mixture and shape it into 24 small rounds. To cook them, dip them first into beaten egg, then into the breadcrumbs, and shallow-fry them in about ¼ inch (½ cm) of groundnut oil till golden on both sides. Drain on kitchen paper, and serve with a home-made tomato sauce (see page 158).

Vegetarian shepherd's pie

(serves 4 people)

If you're not a vegetarian shepherd don't worry, I still think you'll find this recipe quite delicious and far better than many of the minced meat versions.

6 oz whole brown/green lentils (175 g)
4 oz split peas—green or yellow (110 g)
1 pint hot water (570 ml)
1 medium onion, peeled and chopped
½ green pepper, chopped
2 carrots, chopped
2 sticks celery, chopped
1 clove garlic, crushed
½ teaspoon dried mixed herbs
2 pinches ground mace
¼ teaspoon cayenne pepper
Butter or margarine

For the topping:
½ lb tomatoes (225 g), peeled and sliced
1½ lb cooked potatoes (700 g)
3 oz Cheddar cheese (75 g), grated
1 small onion, chopped

2 oz butter or margarine (50 g)
2 tablespoons top of the milk
Salt and freshly-milled black pepper

Begin by washing the lentils and split peas, then put them in a saucepan with the hot water and simmer gently, covered, for approximately 45–60 minutes or until the peas and lentils have absorbed the water and are soft.

Meantime, melt some butter in a frying-pan, add the celery, onion, carrots and chopped pepper, and cook gently until softened, then add these to the cooked lentil mixture after mashing it a little first. Add the seasonings and salt and pepper to taste, then spoon the mixture into a large pie-dish (3 pint or 1·75 litre) and arrange the sliced tomatoes on top.

Next, prepare the topping by softening the onion in butter in a small pan, then mash the potatoes, add the cooked onion, butter, top of the milk and grated cheese, and mix thoroughly. Season well, then spread on top of the ingredients in the pie dish.
Place in a pre-heated oven, gas mark 5, 375°F (190°C), and bake for about 20 minutes or until the topping is lightly browned. A home-made tomato sauce is a delicious accompaniment.

Thick bean and bacon soup

(serves 6 people)

8 oz dried butter beans (225 g)
2 pints water (1 litre)
1 bayleaf
4 oz streaky bacon (or offcuts) (110 g)
2 tablespoons oil
1 oz butter (25 g)
1 onion, finely chopped
1 leek, cleaned and finely chopped
1 large clove garlic, crushed
2 smallish stalks celery, finely chopped
About $\frac{1}{4}$ pint milk (150 ml)
2 tablespoons chopped parsley
Salt and freshly-milled black pepper

First put the butter beans and water in a saucepan and bring them to the boil, then boil for a minute, cover and leave on one side for about an hour. Now add the bayleaf and any bacon rinds you may have to the pan, bring to the boil again, cover and simmer for 45 minutes (removing the bayleaf and rinds at the end).

Meanwhile heat the butter and oil in a large saucepan, add the chopped vegetables, then chop up the bacon small and add that too. Stir to coat everything with butter and oil, and cook over a low heat for about 10 minutes.

Now tip the cooked beans and their cooking liquor into the pan containing the bacon and vegetables, add the garlic, cover and continue simmering for a further 20 minutes or until the beans and vegetables are soft. Then mash them against the sides of the pan with a large fork, and thin down the soup with milk. Re-heat, add the chopped parsley, taste to check the seasoning and serve.

Red bean salad
(serves 4 people)

A red bean salad always looks so good, as the beans are such a lovely colour, and it's always an attractive one to put in amongst other salads to provide a contrast.

12 oz dried red kidney beans (350 g)

For the vinaigrette dressing:
1 tablespoon wine vinegar
1 teaspoon mustard
1 teaspoon salt
2 cloves garlic, crushed
6 tablespoons olive oil
Freshly-milled black pepper

To finish off:
1 green pepper, deseeded and finely chopped
1 medium onion, finely chopped
2 drops tabasco sauce

First rinse the beans with cold water and then place them in a saucepan. Cover with plenty of water, bring up to the boil for 1 minute, then leave them for 2 hours.

Next pour off the water and cover with fresh cold water. Bring them up to the boil and boil gently for about $1\frac{1}{2}$–2 hours or until the beans are tender.

Meanwhile prepare the vinaigrette by combining all the

ingredients in a bowl. Then, as soon as the beans are tender, drain them and toss them in the vinaigrette while they are still warm. Then leave them to cool before adding the chopped onion, green pepper and tabasco.

If possible leave the salad to marinade for several hours before serving on crisp lettuce leaves.

Hummus bi tahina

(serves 6 people)

If you want to make the proper authentic version of this you'll need to hunt out some tahina paste, which is available at specialist food shops and health food shops.

4 oz chick peas (110 g)
Juice of 2 lemons
¼ pint tahina paste (150 ml)
2 fat cloves garlic
4 tablespoons olive oil
Cayenne pepper
Chopped parsley
Olive oil
Salt

To begin with put the chick peas in a saucepan and well cover them with boiling water, then put on one side to soak for 2 hours.

Next bring them to the boil, cover and simmer gently for approximately 1½–2 hours until the chick peas are tender. Then drain them—reserve the cooking liquid—and put the chick peas into a blender together with the lemon juice, garlic, olive oil and ¼ pint (150 ml) of the cooking liquid. Switch on and blend, adding the tahina paste to the mixture as the blades revolve. (It will probably be necessary to stop the blender every now and then to push the mixture down into the goblet.) The consistency should be something like a mayonnaise and, if you think it's too thick, add a little more of the cooking liquid. Taste and season with salt and cayenne pepper.

Place in a serving bowl and garnish with a thin layer of olive oil, some chopped parsley and a pinch or two of cayenne pepper. Have plenty of fresh, hot, crusty bread as an accompaniment.

Spiced lamb with chick peas

(serves 4–6 people)

If you can't get fresh chillies or root ginger for this recipe, you can use 1 level teaspoon of chilli powder and 2 level teaspoons of ground ginger instead.

6 oz chick peas (175 g)
2 lb boned shoulder of lamb (900 g)
4 tablespoons groundnut oil
1 aubergine (about ¾ lb, i.e. 350 g), unpeeled and cut into small chunks
1 teaspoon powdered turmeric
1 teaspoon garam masala
1 lb tomatoes, peeled and thickly sliced (450 g)
3 fresh chillies, halved, seeds discarded and finely sliced
2 cloves garlic, crushed
2 tablespoons finely-chopped mint
1 tablespoon finely-chopped root ginger
¼ pint natural yoghurt (150 ml)
1 Spanish onion, thinly sliced

First of all place the chick peas in a saucepan, cover with 2 pints (about 1 litre) boiling water, put a lid on and leave on one side for 3 hours. Then bring to the boil, and boil, covered, for approximately 1 hour or until the peas are really tender, put them on one side once again.

Next cut the meat into 1-in. cubes, trimming off any excess fat. Now heat the oil in a thick-based saucepan, add the cubes of meat (a small quantity at a time) and fry over a high heat, removing the meat to a plate, using a draining spoon, when nicely browned.

Then add the onion and aubergine to the pan, stirring them around in the fat and fry until coloured before adding the turmeric and garam masala. Cook for another minute then add the tomatoes, chillies, garlic, ginger and mint. Drain the chick peas, reserving the liquid, then return the meat to the pan together with the chick peas and about ¾ pint (425 ml) of their cooking liquor.

Bring up to simmering point, cover and cook very gently for 30 minutes, then take off the lid and continue cooking for approximately three-quarters of an hour or until the meat is really tender and the sauce thick. Lastly stir in the yoghurt and, when all is well heated through, serve with spiced pilau rice.

Pease pudding
(serves 6–8 people)

A real old-fashioned pease pudding is sometimes made in a cloth but more conveniently, I think, in a basin like this:

1 lb whole dried peas (soaked overnight) (450 g)
Generous pinch of thyme
1 bayleaf
1 small onion, quartered
2 oz butter (50 g)
1 large egg, beaten
Salt and freshly-milled black pepper

Put the peas, herbs and quartered onion together in a saucepan and cover with plenty of cold water. Bring to the boil, cover and boil gently for 2 hours or until the peas are tender (a sign that they are ready is that they start splitting their skins). Then drain the peas in a colander and discard the bayleaf—the onion can stay in.

Now mash the peas to a pulp. Beat in the butter and egg and, when the butter has melted, taste and season with salt and freshly-milled black pepper. Pack the pea purée into a well-buttered 2–2½ pint (1·25–1·5 litre) pudding basin. Put a sheet of greased foil over the top and secure with string. Then steam the pudding over boiling water for 1 hour. Uncover and turn it out onto a warmed plate. Cut in wedges like a steamed pudding to serve.

Pease pudding can be served with boiled bacon or boiled beef and any leftovers can be fried in butter the next day.

Puddings

Including recipes for:

If there is a gap in the repertoire of Haute Cuisine then it is surely in the area of what I'd call 'proper puddings'. You'd have thought it would have taken a really exotic dish to get a Frenchman beside himself with admiration for the cooking of any other country but his own: yet at the end of the 17th century M. de Valbourg, a French traveller in England, wrote this:

Ah! What an excellent thing is an English pudding! It is manna that hits the palate of all sorts of people, better than that of the wilderness.

But our puddings didn't stop there: throughout the 18th century and into Victorian times the British pudding was unsurpassed. George I (Pudding George—hence the nursery rhyme about Georgy-Porgy) was particularly partial to the boiled variety, and later Prince Albert became a champion of our puddings. Up at the Palace the royal chefs were very busy creating new temptations for the royal palate: Queen's pudding, Windsor pudding, Empress pudding, Albert pudding. If he had lived 150 years later how much more ecstatically would that nice Frenchman have written 'To come at pudding time is to come in the most lucky moment in the world!'

Nowadays of course he'd be hard pushed to find a traditional pudding on a restaurant menu. It has become a casualty of affluence and our national preoccupation with dieting and calorie-counting. However, our memories are not so easily dimmed as one might imagine, and people's eyes often light up at the mention of something steamy, curranty or syrupy. It would seem to me the height of irony if our figure-conscious generation should be the one that lets the traditional pudding die of neglect—even as it continues to push up the sales of confectionery, bars of chocolate, synthetic packaged desserts and artificial ice-creams.

Steaming

A steamed pudding is far easier to make and serve than most people seem to think. The mixing makes little demand on your time, needs no particular skill; and once the pudding is on the stove it requires very little attention. Extra steaming does no harm at all: so if you want to serve it an hour later than planned, say, it will be just as good.

Steamer Not a very costly piece of equipment but, I think, an essential one. Over the years it will earn its keep, even if it's only for making your own Christmas puddings. Modern steamers

are made to fit most sizes of saucepan. Because the pudding cooks only in the steam that rises from the water boiling in the saucepan underneath, there's no danger here of the water itself bubbling in to swamp the pudding. Filled three-quarters full, the water should not need topping up for most steaming recipes—but if it does look like getting a bit low, always top up with boiling water. I should add that one of the beauties of steaming is, if you possess more than one steamer (I find I need four at Christmas!), you can steam two puddings over one saucepanful of water—only remember to change the position of the steamers over at half-time.

An alternative form of steaming, if you don't have a steamer, is to sit the pudding basin on a small upturned plate or perhaps a wad of crumpled foil inside a saucepan (so it can sit above the water-line). The saucepan is then filled with boiling water but *only* up to a third of its capacity. There are snags: if the heat is too high, the water can boil up too fiercely and into the pudding—and it is liable to boil away rather quicker than with a steamer. The answer is to keep a vigilant eye on it.

Lids Whether you are using a steamer or a saucepan, it is essential to have a well-fitting lid, to prevent the steam escaping and the water drying up completely. Inevitably *some* steam will escape, but it won't be a problem if your lid fits properly.

Coverings Old-fashioned boiled puddings were sometimes made directly inside pudding-cloths. Nowadays china pudding-basins are much more convenient, and whereas once even these would be covered with greaseproof paper and linen cloth, today modern foil does the job on its own. The basin should be covered with double foil for extra strength, and this should be pleated in the centre (to allow room for expansion when the pudding is cooking). Before placing the foil over the basin, butter the side that will come into contact with the pudding—to prevent it sticking—then tie the foil all around the edge of the basin as tightly as you can with string.

And if you can make a little handle with the string at the same time, it will make it easier to lift the basin out of the saucepan at the end.

Pressure-cooking puddings

A pressure-cooker is ideal for steaming puddings, as it cuts the steaming time considerably. If you own one, the manufacturer's instruction booklet will explain the general principles. But first a couple of important points.

The preparation of the pudding is the same as for ordinary steaming, and the basins are covered and tied down in a similar way. Place the trivet inside the pressure-cooker, add 1½ pints (800 ml) of water and bring this up to simmering point. Then lower the pudding in, to stand on the trivet, and put the lid on but leave the vent open—so that the pudding gets 15 minutes' gentle steaming before the pressure is brought up (keep the heat very low for this, to prevent too much steam escaping, thus reducing the correct water level inside). Then after 15 minutes, start the pressure at Low (5 lb) and give the pudding 35 minutes if the ordinary steaming time was 1½–2 hours, or 60 minutes if the ordinary steaming time was 2–3 hours.

Some notes on pudding ingredients

Flour Self-raising flour must be used in all suet and sponge recipes. Plain flour plus baking-powder can be used, but self-raising is preferable because it already contains just the right balance of raising agent. Where an all-in-one sponge method is used an extra amount of raising agent is needed.

Fats I find packet shredded suet is actually better, as well as more convenient, for suet puddings than butcher's suet because it is shredded to exactly the right size and is completely free of skin and membrane.

Dried fruits One tip I can pass on when buying dried druit, and that is always buy it in cellophane packets or else loose. The important thing is to be able to *see* what you're buying. Those enclosed cardboard packets only too often carry last season's dried fruit with a very dry and musty look to them.

Pudding spices The mixed ground spices used in puddings can go stale and lose their strength if they're stored too long. So buy them in small quantities, and better discard any you have had for as long as a year. Nutmeg really should be *freshly grated* at all times: once ground its fragrance vanishes extremely quickly.

Candied peel The same tendency is to be found with this. Buy your candied peel whole and you'll find it has a great deal more flavour than the ready-cut peel (and only cut the peel as and when you need it). It will keep almost indefinitely in a screw-top jar, so it is worth buying in a stock of it when it's readily available at Christmas time. If at other times it is not to be found at your local shops or supermarket, you will probably be able to get some at a specialised food shop or health food store.

Chocolate can be tricky to work with if not handled carefully. Buy 'proper' chocolate rather than 'cooking' chocolate: it looks and tastes better. Never over-heat chocolate: this is what causes it to go grainy and lose its gloss. Break up the squares of chocolate into a bowl, and place the bowl over hot, but not boiling, water; then leave it for a few minutes to melt, and stir to a smooth cream.

Steamed raisin pudding
(serves 4 people)

This is a very special steamed pudding, suitable for a dinner party. Don't worry about the absence of sugar—the raisins provide enough sweetness.

2 oz breadcrumbs (brown) (50 g)
2 oz self-raising flour (50 g)
4 oz shredded suet (110 g)
$\frac{1}{2}$ lb prepared stoned raisins (225 g)
$\frac{1}{8}$ teaspoon salt
$\frac{1}{2}$ nutmeg, grated
$\frac{1}{2}$ teaspoon ground ginger
$\frac{1}{8}$ teaspoon ground mace
1 oz whole candied peel (25 g), (finely chopped)
The grated zest of an orange
3 eggs
3 tablespoons brandy

You will need a $1\frac{1}{2}$ pint (845 ml) pudding-basin well buttered.

In a large bowl mix together the breadcrumbs, flour and suet. Add the raisins, making sure there are none stuck together. When these ingredients are well mixed, add the salt, nutmeg, mace, ginger, candied peel and orange zest and again mix thoroughly.

Now in a small basin beat the eggs well and add them and the brandy to the mixture and stir for at least 5 minutes to amalgamate everything thoroughly and evenly. Pack the pudding basin with the mixture, cover with greaseproof paper and foil, and tie down with string. Steam for 4 hours, making sure that the saucepan doesn't boil dry. When ready to serve, loosen the pudding all round the sides with a palette knife and turn out onto a heated dish. Serve with *Port wine sauce* (below).

Port wine sauce

| 5 fl. oz ruby or tawny port (150 ml) |
| The grated zest of a Seville orange (or an ordinary one) |
| 2 oz caster sugar (50 g) |
| 5 fl. oz water (150 ml) |
| ½ nutmeg, *freshly* grated |
| 1 tablespoon Seville orange juice |
| 1 oz unsalted butter (25 g) |
| 1 teaspoon flour |

In a thick-bottomed saucepan put the orange zest, water and sugar and boil very gently for 15 minutes. Mix the flour with the butter, then divide it into about 6 pieces and add these to the syrup. Also add the port, nutmeg and orange juice, stirring all the time over a low flame. Let the sauce boil for 1 minute, then serve at once.

Christmas pudding

(for 2 puddings in 2 pint (1 litre) basins, or 4 in 1 pint (570 ml) basins).

This has proved to be one of the most popular recipes I've ever produced and, if you're making it for the first time, I hope you'll agree.

| 8 oz shredded suet (225 g) |
| 1 heaped teaspoon mixed spice |
| ½ teaspoon grated nutmeg |
| ¼ teaspoon ground cinnamon |
| 4 oz self-raising flour (110 g) |

1 lb soft brown sugar (450 g)
8 oz white breadcrumbs (225 g), grated from a stale loaf
8 oz sultanas (225 g)
8 oz raisins (225 g)
1¼ lb currants (560 g)
2 oz almonds (50 g), blanched, skinned and chopped
2 oz mixed peel (50 g), finely chopped whole candied and citron peel (if available)
The grated rind of 1 orange and 1 lemon
1 apple, peeled, cored and finely chopped
4 standard eggs
5 fl. oz barley wine (150 ml)
5 fl. oz stout (150 ml)
4 tablespoons rum

In a bowl put the suet, flour, breadcrumbs, spices and sugar, mixing in each ingredient throughly before adding the next. Then gradually mix in all the fruit, peel and nuts and follow these with the apple and the orange and lemon peel.

In a different bowl beat up the eggs, and mix the rum, barley wine and stout into them. Empty all this over the dry ingredients—and then stir very hard indeed (it's vital this mixing, so recruit some help if necessary). You may find you need a bit more stout—it's not possible to be exact with the liquid quantities, but the mixture should be of a good dropping consistency (that is, it should fall from the spoon when tapped sharply against the side of the bowl).

After the mixing, cover the bowl with a cloth and leave it overnight. The next day, grease 2 (or 4) pudding basins and pack the mixture into them right to the top. Cover each basin with a square of greaseproof paper, with a square pudding-cloth on top. Tie these round the rims of the bowls with string, then tie the corners of the cloth together on top.

Steam the puddings for 8 hours—keeping an eye now and then on the water to make sure it doesn't boil away. When cooked, remove the paper and pudding-cloths and replace with a fresh lot. Store in a cool dry place and, when ready to eat, steam for a further 2 hours.

St Stephen's pudding
(serves 4–6 people)

This pudding was sent to me by a television viewer in East Anglia and is a very good alternative pudding for those who prefer a less rich pudding for Christmas

4 oz breadcrumbs (110 g)
2 oz self-raising flour (50 g), sifted
2 oz soft brown sugar (50 g)
3 oz suet (75 g)
Pinch of salt
4 oz seedless raisins (110 g)
2 medium-sized cooking apples
Grated rind of 1 lemon
1 egg
3 tablespoons milk

A 2 pint (1 litre) pudding-basin, well greased.

In a large mixing bowl first combine all the dry ingredients, then add the raisins, the apples (peeled and then grated) and the grated lemon rind. Stir thoroughly to combine everything well. Now beat the egg into the milk, and stir the whole lot into the mixture.

Pack the mixture into the pudding-basin, cover the basin tightly with a sheet of greaseproof paper, then with a sheet of foil, and secure with string. Steam the pudding for 2 hours. Serve with custard or brandy butter.

Brandy butter

3 oz unsalted butter (75 g)
3 oz caster sugar (75 g)
2½ tablespoons brandy
1 teaspoon lemon juice

Make sure that the butter is at room temperature before you begin, then beat, using a wooden spoon, until white and creamy.

Add the sugar a little at a time and beat well after each addition. Continue until all the sugar is in, then gradually work in the brandy a few drops at a time, still beating. Lastly, beat in the lemon juice and, when everything is thoroughly amalgamated, transfer the butter to a suitable dish and chill for 2–3 hours before serving.

Apple and orange crunch

(serves 4 people)

I like this crunchy pudding served with proper custard (see below) or, failing that, a thick pouring cream.

Approximately 12 thinnish slices of bread from a small brown or white loaf
4 oz butter (110 g)
1 small orange (half the rind and all the juice)
3 oz demerara sugar (75 g)
3 medium cooking apples, peeled and sliced thinly

Pre-heat the oven to gas mark 4, 350°F (180°C)

A 1½ pint (845 ml) baking dish, well buttered.

Begin by melting the butter in a small saucepan over a very low heat, being careful that it doesn't brown.

Next cut the crusts off the slices of bread and, with a pastry brush, spread 6 or 7 of the pieces liberally—on both sides—with melted butter. As each slice is buttered place it in the baking dish to form a lining which covers the base and sides, and press the slices firmly down. Then sprinkle in a layer of sliced apple, a little grated orange peel and juice and a layer of sugar. Carry on like this until all the apples are used but keep back one tablespoon of sugar.

Now brush the rest of the slices of bread with melted butter and press these over the top of the pudding to form a lid. Sprinkle over the remaining tablespoon of sugar and add any melted butter left.

Bake the pudding for 45 minutes or until the top is crisp, golden and crunchy and the apples inside are soft.

Proper custard sauce

(for 4 people)

Packet custard is very popular, but if you want to serve a pudding for a special occasion a *real* custard with it is incomparably nicer. I'm afraid I do admit to cheating a little here, by using 1 teaspoon of cornflour. But in my experience, it saves an awful lot of anxiety by stabilising the sauce and preventing it from curdling.

½ **pint double (or single) cream (275 ml)**
3 egg yolks
1 level tablespoon caster sugar
1 level teaspoon cornflour
2 drops of pure vanilla essence

First heat the cream in a small saucepan up to boiling point; and while it's heating thoroughly blend the egg yolks, cornflour, sugar and vanilla together in a small basin. Then pour the hot cream in—stirring all the time—and return the mixture to the saucepan. Heat very gently (still stirring) until the sauce has thickened, which should only take a minute or two.

If it does overheat and start to look granular, don't worry. If you remove it from the heat and continue to beat it *will* become smooth again as it cools—because the small addition of cornflour does a very efficient stabilising job. Serve the custard warm or, with a hot pudding or pie, chilled.

Chocolate and walnut pudding

(serves 4 people)

This is a pudding popular with children, as when it's cooked it's surrounded with its own pool of chocolate sauce.

2 oz caster sugar (50 g)
1 oz cocoa powder (25 g)
½ **teaspoon ground cinnamon**
2 oz fine semolina (50 g)
1 teaspoon baking powder
1 oz butter (25 g) melted
¼ **teaspoon vanilla essence**
2 eggs, beaten
1 oz walnuts (25 g), finely chopped
½ **pint hand-hot water (275 ml)**
3 oz dark brown sugar (75 g)
½ **oz plus 2 teaspoons cocoa powder (10 g plus 2 teaspoons)**

Pre-heat the oven to gas mark 4, 350°F (180°C)

You'll need a 1¾ pint (1 litre) deep, oval baking dish, buttered.

Start by sifting the first 5 ingredients into a mixing bowl and, in a separate bowl, whisk together the melted butter, eggs and vanilla essence. Then stir this into the dry ingredients together with the chopped walnuts and pour this mixture into the buttered baking dish.

Now mix together the brown sugar and cocoa powder and, with a fork, gradually whisk in the hot water, then pour this all over the pudding (you may think this sounds unusual, but it's correct).

Place the pudding in the pre-heated oven and bake for 30 minutes or until the pudding has risen and is firm in the middle. Before serving sprinkle the top with some icing sugar.

Lemon surprise pudding

(serves 4 people)

In this pudding the 'surprise' is that after it is cooked you'll find that underneath the light sponge topping there's a delicious pool of lemony sauce.

2 eggs, separated
2 oz butter (50 g)
4 oz caster sugar (110 g)
2 large lemons (the rind and juice)
2 oz self-raising flour (50 g), sifted
¼ pint milk (150 ml)

1½ pint (845 ml) buttered deep baking dish.

Pre-heat the oven to gas mark 4, 350°F (180°C)

First beat the butter, sugar and lemon rind together until well softened (it won't go light and fluffy because there's more sugar than butter). Then beat in the egg yolks, a little at a time. Next fold in the flour, alternately with the milk and lemon juice. Finally whisk the egg whites and fold them in as well (the mixture will look a bit curdled at this stage, but that's normal). Pour the mixture into the baking dish and bake in the centre of the oven for 40–45 minutes or until golden-brown. It's usual to serve this pudding hot from the oven, but as a matter of fact it's just as nice served cold.

Wholewheat treacle sponge
(serves 4 people)

This is much lighter than it actually sounds and it's lovely served on a cold day with extra warmed syrup poured over.

4 oz wholewheat flour (110 g)
2 tablespoons golden syrup
2½ teaspoons baking powder
2 large eggs
4 oz soft brown sugar (110 g)
4 oz soft margarine (110 g)

You'll need a 1½ pint (845 ml) basin, well buttered.

Begin by putting the golden syrup in the base of the pudding basin.

Next place all the remaining ingredients in a bowl and beat well for 2 or 3 minutes until throughly mixed. Now spoon this mixture on top of the golden syrup and, using the back of the spoon, spread it out evenly. Cover this with a double piece of buttered foil, pleated in the middle (to allow for expansion) and press down over the rim of the basin and tie round with string. Cut off any extra foil about an inch from the string.

Place in a steamer over boiling water and steam for 1½ hours. Make sure that the saucepan does not boil dry or the water go off the boil and, when necessary, use *boiling water* to top it up. When cooked, turn it out onto a warmed serving plate and serve hot with custard or extra syrup.

Note: If using a pressure cooker the cooking time will be 20 minutes steaming and 45 minutes at 5 lb pressure.

Spiced fig pudding with rum butter
(serves 6 people)

8 oz dates (225 g), stoned and chopped
6 oz dried figs (175 g), chopped
3 oz rasins (75 g)
2 oz preserved ginger (50 g), chopped
6 oz fresh white breadcrumbs (175 g)
4 oz shredded suet (110 g)
2 oz self-raising flour (50 g)
2 tablespoons brandy
2 large eggs

Grated rind of an orange (also the juice)
½ teaspoon mixed spice
Generous quantity freshly-grated nutmeg

You'll need a generously buttered 1½ pint (845 ml) pudding basin

Place the measured flour, breadcrumbs and suet in a mixing bowl. Add the fruits, spices and the orange peel, and mix all together very thoroughly.

Next beat the eggs with the brandy and orange juice and add this to the mixture, stirring well to make sure all the ingredients are thoroughly mixed, then pack the mixture into the basin. Cover with a double piece of buttered foil, pleated in the middle, and tie it under the rim of the basin with string. Steam the pudding over boiling water for 4 hours.

This is delicious served with some ice-cold rum butter made as follows: Take 4 oz (110 g) unsalted butter and into it gradually beat 4 oz (110 g) dark brown sugar until you have a pale-cream mixture. Then beat in—a little at a time—2–3 tablespoons of rum and chill the butter for several hours.

Eliza Acton's rich rice pudding

(serves 4 people)

Tinned rice pudding might be convenient, but it bears no resemblance to the proper kind, which always has a dark caramelised skin on top, covering just the right amount of creaminess and stickiness inside.

4 oz short-grain rice (110 g)
1½ pints milk (845 ml)
2 oz butter (50 g)
3 oz caster sugar (75 g)
3 eggs
Grated rind of half a lemon
Whole nutmeg

Pre-heat the oven to gas mark 2, 300°F (150°C)

For this you'll need a 2 pint (1 litre) baking dish, well buttered.

First put the rice into a saucepan, add the milk and bring it slowly almost to simmering point, then let it cook very gently until the rice is practically tender, which should take about 10 minutes.

Next add the sugar and butter and stir until they have dissolved and melted. Now take the saucepan off the heat and let the mixture cool a little, then stir in the eggs—well beaten—together with the lemon peel.

Pour the mixture into the baking dish, sprinkle on some freshly-grated nutmeg and bake for 30–40 minutes—or longer if you prefer a thicker consistency. Serve with pouring cream.

Cider baked apples with toasted Muesli

(serves 4 people)

This is a very simple recipe but really delicious when the first Bramley apples come into season.

4 Bramley apples (medium sized)
$\frac{1}{2}$ pint dry cider (275 ml)
A little butter
4 tablespoons of any Muesli

Pre-heat the oven to gas mark 5, 375°F (190°C)

Begin by wiping and coring the apples—if you have an apple corer this is quite a simple job. Next, with a sharp knife, cut just through the skin around the centre of each apple.

Pour the cider into a shallow baking tin, then lightly grease each apple—wiping them with a buttered piece of kitchen paper is a good way of doing this. Now stand the apples upright in the cider.

Bake them for about 40 minutes or until they're tender when tested with a skewer and baste them occasionally with the cider during the cooking time.

After 15 minutes put the Muesli in the oven in an uncovered baking dish so that it will heat through and have a slightly toasted appearance.

When the apples are cooked, place them on top of the Muesli, pour the juices over and serve with some cold pouring cream.

Note: There is no need to add sugar to the apples if the Muesli is sweetened. Wholefood shops usually stock excellent Muesli.

Queen of puddings

(serves 4 people)

This, with a cloud of meringue on top, is probably one of the lightest of puddings.

1 pint milk (570 ml)
4 oz fresh white breadcrumbs (110 g)
½ oz butter (10 g)
2 oz caster sugar (50 g)
The grated rind of a small lemon
2 eggs
3 level tablespoons raspberry jam

Pre-heat the oven to gas mark 4, 350°F (180°C)

You'll need a generously buttered 1½ pint (845 ml) oval pie-dish.

First pour the milk into a saucepan and bring to the boil. Remove from the heat and stir in the butter, breadcrumbs, 1 oz (25 g) of the sugar and the lemon rind, and leave for 20 minutes to allow the breadcrumbs to swell.

Now separate the eggs, beat the yolks and add them to the cooled breadcrumb mixture and pour it all into the pie-dish and spread it out evenly. Bake in the centre of the oven for 30–35 minutes, or until set.

Meantime, in a small saucepan melt the jam over a low heat and, when the pudding is ready, remove it from the oven and spread the jam carefully and evenly all over the top.

Next beat the egg whites until stiff, then whisk in 1 oz (25 g) of caster sugar and spoon this meringue mixture over the pudding. Finally, sprinkle a teaspoon of caster sugar over it all and bake for a further 10–15 minutes until the topping is golden-brown.

Rich bread and butter pudding

(serves 4–6 people)

Never fear if you have some stale bread that needs using up. This is a light delicious pudding with a lovely dark toasted nutmeg crust.

½ pint milk (275 ml)
⅛ pint double cream (70 ml)
Grated rind of half a small lemon

2 oz caster sugar (50 g)
3 eggs
8 slices of bread (from a small loaf), buttered
½ oz candied lemon or orange peel (10 g), finely chopped
2 oz currants (50 g)
Freshly-grated nutmeg

Pre-heat the oven to gas mark 4, 350°F (180°C)

Begin by buttering well a 2 pint (1 litre) enamel baking dish (one of the oblong kind). Then slice the bread, not too thickly, butter it, then cut each slice in half—leaving the crusts on. Now arrange one layer of buttered bread over the base of the baking dish, sprinkle the candied peel and half the currants over, then cover with another layer of the bread slices and the remainder of the currants.

Next, in a glass measuring jug, measure out ½ pint of milk (275 ml) and add ⅛ pint (70 ml) of double cream. Stir in the caster sugar and lemon peel, then whisk the eggs, first on their own in a small basin and then into the milk mixture. Pour the whole lot over the bread, sprinkle over some freshly-grated nutmeg, and bake in the oven for 30–40 minutes. Serve warm.

Plum and cinnamon nut crumble

(serves 4–6 people)

The nuts in this can be any sort, but I think it's nicest with hazelnuts.

2 lb plums (900 g)
4 oz demerara sugar (110 g)
1 teaspoon powdered cinnamon

For the topping:
3 oz butter (75 g)
6 oz wholemeal flour (175 g)
3 oz demerara sugar (75 g)
3 oz finely-chopped nuts (75 g)
1 teaspoon powdered cinnamon

Pre-heat the oven to gas mark 4, 350°F (180°C)

You'll need a 1½ pint (845 ml) baking dish, buttered.

Rinse the plums and drain well, then place them in the baking dish, and sprinkle with the sugar and cinnamon.

To make the crumble topping, rub the butter into the flour, then add the sugar and mix to the breadcrumb stage. Then stir in the chopped nuts and cinnamon. Now sprinkle the crumble mixture evenly over the plums, then bake on a baking sheet in the centre of the oven for about 45 minutes to 1 hour, or until the plums are cooked and the crumble is golden and crunchy.

Serve with thick pouring cream to mingle with the plum juices.

Hot chocolate rum soufflé
(serves 4 people)

4 oz plain chocolate (110 g)
2 tablespoons rum
4 egg yolks
6 egg whites (large eggs)
½ pint double cream (275 ml)
Icing sugar

Pre-heat the oven and a baking sheet to gas mark 6, 400°F (200°C)

First of all well butter a 2 pint (1 litre) soufflé dish. Next break the chocolate into a mixing bowl, add the rum and place the bowl in the bottom of the oven for 5–10 minutes or until the chocolate is soft, then beat, using a wooden spoon, until it's smooth.

In a small basin whisk the egg yolks thoroughly and stir them into the chocolate. In another bowl—and making sure your beater is clean and dry—whisk the egg whites until stiff, then fold them gently and carefully into the chocolate mixture, using a metal spoon. Next pour it all into the prepared soufflé dish and bake, on the baking sheet, for approximately 20 minutes or until the soufflé is puffy and springy to touch.

Serve straight from the oven, dusting the top with some sieved icing sugar and with the double cream in a jug to pour over separately. (It's much better to serve pouring cream with this rather than whipped cream.)

Traditional apple charlotte

(serves 4 people)

This is a real apple charlotte, moulded in a basin, so that when it's turned out the outside is crisp and buttery with the apples cooked to a pulp inside.

1 lb apples (half Bramley and half Cox's if possible) (450 g)
1 tablespoon caster sugar
1 oz butter (25 g)
1 egg yolk
6 slices bread from a large loaf (about ¼ inch (½ cm) thick with crusts removed)
3 oz (extra) butter (75 g)

Peel, core and thinly slice the apples first of all: rinse them in cold water and put them in a saucepan with 1 tablespoon of sugar and 1 oz (25 g) butter. Cook them over a low heat until they are soft enough to beat into a purée. Beat them and leave on one side to cool. Meanwhile melt the 3 oz (75 g) of butter gently, and cut each slice of bread into 6 rectangles.

Next brush each piece of bread with melted butter (both sides), being careful not to leave any unbuttered patches, then line a 1 pint (570 ml) pudding basin with approximately three-quarters of the bread (or as much as you need). Don't leave any gaps between the pieces—overlap them and press firmly. When the apple purée has cooled, beat the egg yolk into it and fill the lined basin with the mixture. Finally seal the top with overlapping slices of the remaining bread.

Place a suitably-sized plate on top of the pudding and weigh it down with a 2 lb (900 g) weight.

Meanwhile pre-heat the oven to gas mark 6, 400°F (200°C). After half an hour place the basin (with the weight still on it) in the oven to bake for 35 minutes. Then, with an oven cloth, remove the plate and weight, and bake the pudding for another 10 minutes to brown on top. Leave the pudding to settle in the basin for a minute after removing from the oven, then carefully invert it onto a warmed plate to serve.

Index